Home Theater For Everyone

A Practical Guide to Today's Home Entertainment Systems

Second Edition

Robert Harley

$\mathcal{A}$capella Publishing
P. O. Box 80805
Albuquerque, New Mexico 87198-0805

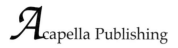capella Publishing

Post Office Box 80805
Albuquerque, New Mexico 87198-0805

First Edition—1997
Revised First Edition—2000
Second Edition—2002

International Standard Book Number:
Hardcover: 0-9640849-9-6
Paper: 0-9640849-8-8

Cover Concept and Design: *Robert Harley, Evalee Harley, Corrine Armijo-Vialpando, and Lorenzo Vialpando*
Cover Illustration: *Corrine Armijo-Vialpando*
Illustrations: *Rick Velasquez, Evalee Harley, and Nancy Josephson,* except where otherwise credited

6   7   8   9   10

Printed in the United States of America

Contents

3   Source Components: DVD, VHS Tape, D-VHS, PVR, HDTV Set-top Boxes, DSS, DVD Audio, and Super Audio CD   41

6   Home Theater Loudspeakers   121

7   Video Displays: Direct-View and Rear-Projection HDTV, Plasma Panels, Front Projectors, Screens, and Image Scalers   147

9   Putting It All Together: How to Connect and Configure Your Home Theater   205

Foreword

By Tomlinson Holman

Home theater is a rapidly expanding phenomenon for a reason: it is engaging and entertaining to large numbers of people. A whole group of family and friends can share something at home that, while taking each of them away from the cares of the day, nevertheless provides a link between individuals that comes about in few other ways. It is the shared experience of people with the storyteller that engages us, provokes us, and makes us laugh and cry together, that is so good for our souls. In this experience lies the roots of community, and the transmission of culture from one person to another and from one generation to another.

Home theater has two major ingredients, of course: picture and sound. Of the two, it is the sound that is the more obscure; everyone can tell apart a table and a chair in the picture, but few can tell ambience tracks from Foley ones. This very obscurity causes interesting phenomena. The best filmmakers realize that the soundtrack can produce emotional responses to a scene that are in the control of the filmmaker, but are subliminal to the audience. In this sense sound can be a direct path to the emotions. Take film scores, for instance. Those four low alternating notes that introduce the shark in *Jaws*, accompanying a scene of an otherwise calm ocean, mean a threat is just around the corner. In fact, this is one of the emotional equations—low frequencies equal threat—that is in commonplace use. Another example is to hear just crickets. We immediately place ourselves in a suburban or rural setting at night with no threats nearby, at least not yet. But add the far-off bark of a single dog and we are disturbed that something new has entered into our world.

There is one thing about the film-sound experience that is fundamentally different from the goals of reproducing other types of sound, particularly music. If it can be said that the audiophile seeks a musical experience like that delivered by a live performance of musicians, what must be clearly understood about film sound is that there is never such a thing as a live experience to compare to: the movie's soundtrack was originally made over loudspeakers under standardized conditions, and never existed as a "real" event. While a few films strive to "put you there" just as something was, practically all films manipulate both sound and picture. And the final manipulation occurs in a standardized setting and involves the director and sound personnel making the art. The fact that widely observed standards exist for the production of film sound helps to standardize the theater-going experience and, ultimately, the home-theater experience.

This is different, far different, from music production for CDs, where, for example, the monitor volume control is one of the largest knobs on most mixing consoles. On film consoles, the monitor volume is locked off at a standard setting. This emphasizes that the production of film sound for video release is much more standardized than music production. Do you adjust the volume control each time you put in a new CD? Most of the time you probably do. With properly transferred video, the level of the primary "clue" to loudness, the dialog, will be the same from picture to picture. This is because Hollywood turns out a consistent product with regards to volume and many other factors. So it is fair to say that the goal of a home-theater system is to reproduce the sound as it was heard reproduced when it was made.

I remember a major argument I had with a loudspeaker manufacturer over this issue many years ago. He was introducing a gigantic new home loudspeaker system and using the Hoth battle in *The Empire Strikes Back* to demonstrate it to the press. The footfalls of the snow walkers seemed to me to be very much "over the top." His point of view was "What do you know about what these things sounded like? It's all fiction and I can do what I like with it." While of course he could, that didn't make it "right," because there *was* an idea of how it should sound—the way it sounded in the dubbing stage where it was mixed. Here is the kernel of an ongoing argument: Who is to say what is "right"? Wouldn't you rather have the director make your movie than a loudspeaker manufacturer?

Of course, the picture is all-important in home theater, and has become increasingly good over the years. When I was Chief Engineer at Advent 20 years ago, developing projection television, we could only dream about sources as good as those available today. That was before even VHS was available. With only off-the-air television to work with, we wound up working some odd hours, determined by when the shows with the best video were on rather than when we wanted to work. Today there is a wide range of good sources available, and the sets or projectors on which they are shown have much better technology. Digital television broadcasting is now standardized after many years of work, and DVD is here today to provide the benefits of digitalization to the picture.

Although there are separate perceptual mechanisms for picture and sound, they can be integrated by the audience into a complete, seamless whole. In such a state, picture and sound together become greater than the sum of their parts.

Editor's note: Tomlinson Miles Holman is a recipient of the prestigious Cinema Audio Society's career achievement award. His initials are used to name the THX businesses. He is working hard on the next revolution in entertainment technology. His company, TMH Corporation, can be reached at www.tmhlabs.com.

Foreword Copyright © 1997 by Tomlinson M. Holman

Preface: The Home Theater Experience

Nearly everyone knows how enjoyable it can be to watch a movie on VHS tape, cable, or satellite in your own home. But a growing number of people are discovering that the experience can be much more than what's provided by a 19" TV set reproducing the soundtrack through a single 3" speaker built into your TV. The way we entertain ourselves at home is being transformed by a revolution in picture and sound quality unthinkable just a few years ago. You can now watch movies, concerts, sports, and some television shows with a sound quality that rivals or even exceeds that of movie theaters. It isn't just television anymore.

Imagine being at home on a Saturday night with your family. You pop a CD-sized disc into a component smaller than a VCR. Your big-screen television comes alive with a big, sharp, beautiful picture, and suddenly you're in the center of an enveloping, three-dimensional soundfield. When the starship *Enterprise* goes into warp drive, you hear it move across the room, then whoosh over your head. When the *T. rex* in *Jurassic Park* stomps his foot, the room shakes. A crack of thunder in the movie makes you wonder whether it's started raining outside. You can hear every word of dialog with a clarity you never thought possible. The film's score is big, rich, full, and powerful. You don't consciously think of all these elements, however, because you're totally captivated by the story unfolding before you. Instead of watching the action, you're suddenly *in* the action.

Welcome to the home theater experience.

This isn't some futuristic dream, but today's reality. Best of all, the technology that makes this powerful experience possible has never been more affordable. Television sets keep getting bigger, and their prices continue to drop. Audio/video receivers with Dolby Digital decoding are now manufactured in enough quantity to keep their prices within any budget. And although you may not know it, those VHS tapes you rent at the local video store contain the same Dolby Surround soundtrack that you often hear in the movie theater. It just takes the right home-theater components to hear in your home the same soundtrack encoded on nearly all VHS tapes (and some television shows).

What's more, there's an explosion in delivery systems for getting high-quality pictures and sound into your living room. The most dramatic example is the new DVD, a CD-sized disc that contains super-high-quality digital video and digital surround-sound audio. DVD's picture quality is light-years beyond that of broadcast television or VHS tape, and is even better than laserdisc. And DVD's Dolby Digital 6-channel surround format is a giant leap forward in sonic realism. In short, DVD is a revolution in video and audio quality, convenience, and features for home theater. In addition, high-definition television (HDTV) offers the consumer unprecedented picture quality.

The only problem with such technological sophistication is that it can leave many consumers confused about how to buy and assemble a home-theater system. Among the questions you may be asking are:

- How do I go about choosing and setting up a home-theater system?

- How much should I spend on a home theater?

- What do I look for when buying an HDTV set?

- How should I allocate my home-theater dollars to get the best possible performance for a given budget?

- What is THX, and do I need it?

- What do all those confusing initials and terms mean—DTS, AC-3, discrete surround, Dolby Pro Logic, and so on?

- What features are important, and which are purely marketing hype?

- How can I be sure I'm not buying yesterday's technology?

This book will guide you, in simple and direct language, through the maze of home-theater technology and components. Although written at a basic level, it includes enough detailed information for the serious home-theater hobbyist. I've put the emphasis on practical information that will help you choose the right components and get the best possible performance from those components—at any price level. Whether you simply want to turn your television set into a basic home theater, or build a system that rivals the sound quality of the best movie theaters, you'll find everything you need to know in this book.

This newly revised, updated, and expanded edition covers the latest developments in home-theater technology: HDTV, progressive-scan DVD players, digital video interfaces, HDTV set-top boxes, FireWire, plasma panels, 7.1-channel audio, digital copy protection, and the new family of LCoS video technologies, to name a few.

Home Theater for Everyone: A Practical Guide to Today's Home Entertainment Systems is your front-row ticket to enjoying the home-theater experience.

Robert Harley

About the Author

Robert Harley is the author of *The Complete Guide to High-End Audio*, and Editor-in-Chief of *The Perfect Vision* and *The Absolute Sound* magazines. His more than 500 published equipment reviews and articles on music and home-theater sound reproduction have helped thousands of enthusiasts improve their home-entertainment systems.

Robert Harley holds a degree in recording engineering and has taught a college degree program in that field. He has worked as a recording engineer and studio owner, compact disc mastering engineer, technical writer, and audio journalist.

Acknowledgments

Many individuals contributed to making this book a reality. I am grateful to my colleagues at *The Absolute Sound* and *The Perfect Vision* for their published articles and interesting discussions of audio and home-theater technology over the years. In addition, the late Peter W. Mitchell's writings on audio and home theater technology continue to stand as the benchmark of clarity. My friend and colleague Jonathan Valin at *The Perfect Vision* has contributed to my passion for film through his remarkable insights into movies. His film writing in *The Perfect Vision* and discussions with me are a continuing source of inspiration to pursue audio and video technical excellence in the service of art.

I thank Anthony Grimani of Lucasfilm's Home THX division for his expert technical editing of the first edition, and to Joel Silver of Imaging Science Foundation for his help with this new edition's video display chapter. Thanks also to Dolby Laboratories for reviewing the sections on Dolby technology.

Richard Lehnert deserves special credit for his masterful ability to polish my words without changing what I said. Every writer should be so fortunate as to have such an editor. Although he didn't copy edit this new edition, much of his contribution to this book's two earlier editions survived. Thanks to Mark Lehman for copy-editing the new sections of this edition, and to Ann Gendron for proofreading the entire manuscript.

I thank Corrine Armijo-Vialpando for the special cover art and title, and Lorenzo Vialpando for shepherding the cover art through the process from first sketch to finished cover. Rick Velasquez's technical illustrations contributed greatly to the book's clarity. To Nancy Josephson of Design Farm, thank you for your illustrations and help with the cover.

To Bryan, Jamie, and Stan at J.B. Stanton Communications, my gratitude for organizing many of the product photographs and illustrations.

Finally, I'd like to thank the visionaries, writers, artists, craftspeople, engineers, and technicians whose imagination, talent, and dedication make today's version of storytelling such a powerful and moving experience. They give meaning to what would otherwise be merely a pile of electronics.

1 The Big Picture: An Overview of Home Theater

Introduction

Home theater is the combination of high-quality video and sound presentation in your home. What distinguishes home theater from mere television is the size and quality of the video display, and the quality of the audio system. Although an ambitious home-theater system will include a high-quality video display such as a big-screen television, it's amazing how adding a good surround-sound system to a television transforms the experience of watching movies at home. Even a VHS tape player feeding a 25" television (a low-quality video presentation) can be part of a home theater if the system includes good sound reproduction. The importance of sound quality to films, concert videos, and even some television shows cannot be underestimated.

If you don't already own a home-theater system, try this experiment at a friend's house or dealer's showroom: Watch the same scene of a film twice, once with the home-theater system's sound turned up, then with the sound off. Without the soundtrack, the film loses much of its impact, drama, and ability to capture and hold your attention. It's a totally different experience without the sound.

A high-quality home-theater system more accurately delivers to you the filmmakers' artistic vision. Enormous amounts of thought, effort, and time go into creating a film's "look" and soundtrack. Filmmakers skillfully use the visual medium to tell their story, and use the soundtrack's music and effects to set a scene's overall mood or convey a specific feeling. Filmmakers carefully craft each aspect of a scene's lighting, composition, music and sound effects to better communicate the story. The greater the technical quality of a home-theater system, the more of the filmmakers' art reaches you. That's why the better the video and

Fig. 1-1 Adding an audio/video receiver and three loudspeakers to your existing stereo system converts your television into a home theater.

Courtesy PSB Speakers, photo by Anton Grassl

Fig. 1-2 A high-end home-theater system can provide film-like images and better sound quality than even the best movie theaters.

Courtesy Vidikron

audio quality of your home-theater system, the more intense and involving the experience. And with High-Definition Television (HDTV) becoming increasingly available, there's never been a better time to enjoy movies at home with stunning audio and video quality.

A scene in *Jurassic Park* perfectly illustrates how a soundtrack can convey a specific feeling. When the *T. rex* is threatening the Park-goers in a driving rainstorm, they take refuge in a 4-wheel-drive vehicle. Once they're inside, the rain takes on a slightly different character as it "pings" against the vehicle's roof. This minor change in the rain's sound suddenly makes us feel claustrophobic, trapped in the 4-wheel-drive along with the characters. We feel their peril more deeply—just by a change in the sound of raindrops. These subtleties aren't there by accident; the filmmakers know exactly what they're doing. You'd never hear that nuance—or feel exactly what the filmmakers intended—without a quality home-theater playback system.

The importance of *sound* quality has been underscored by recent research that attempted to understand and quantify the home-theater experience. Test subjects were shown an audio/video presentation and asked to rate separately the qualities of picture and sound. When the researchers improved the sound quality, the subjects thought the *picture* quality had improved as well. The quality of the sound turned out to be as important as the quality of the picture in creating the overall experience.

A home-theater audio system provides a more realistic portrayal of sounds in many dimensions, including their directionality, frequency range (low bass, for example), dynamic impact, and loudness. Let's face it—a train crash as reproduced by a television set's 3" speaker isn't very convincing. And accurately reproducing every nuance in the picture lets us absorb more deeply the thoughts, feeling, and expression the director intended.

Home Theater System Components

Let's take a brief tour of the components that comprise a home-theater system. We'll get into each component in much more detail later in this book. For now, let's look at the big picture so that the details, when presented later, can be understood in their proper contexts. Refer to fig.1-3, a block diagram of an entire home-theater system, throughout the rest of this chapter.

Surround Sound

Home theater is made possible by multichannel surround sound. Instead of two speakers in front of you as in a stereo system, home theater sur-

Fig. 1-3 A home-theater system includes source components, an audio/video receiver, a video monitor, and loudspeakers.

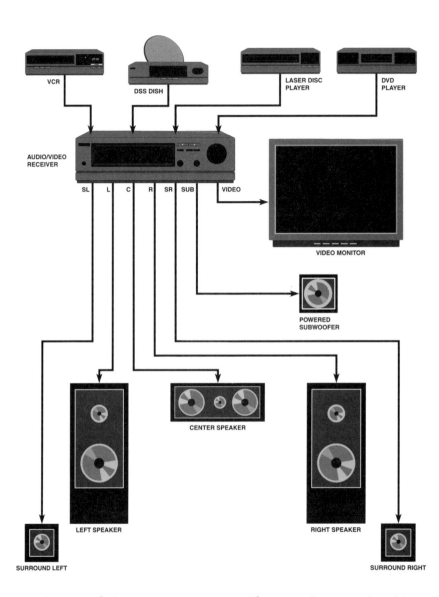

rounds you with five, six, or even seven. Three speakers are placed in the front of the room, with two, three, or four *surround* speakers located to the rear or sides of the listening/viewing position. Surround sound is what provides the sense of envelopment, of being in the action, that makes the home-theater experience so engrossing.

You may be wondering how home-theater systems can have more than two loudspeakers when VHS tapes, television broadcasts, and many satellite signals carry only two audio channels.

The solution to delivering multichannel sound through a two-channel medium is provided by the *Dolby Surround* format. First developed for movie theaters and now available in home-theater systems, Dolby

Surround electronically "folds" the surround and center channels into the front left and right signals. When the soundtrack is mixed from its original multichannel state into a 2-channel mix for consumer release, the center and surround channels are encoded into the left and right channels. When played back through a *Dolby Pro Logic decoder* (a circuit found in all audio/video receivers), the surround channel is separated from the front signals and sent to the rear surround loudspeakers. Nearly all VHS tapes, laserdiscs, and some television broadcasts are encoded with Dolby Surround. Although you'll see the Dolby logo on home-theater products, Dolby Laboratories doesn't manufacture equipment. Instead, they license their Dolby Pro Logic technology to electronics manufacturers.

A variation on Dolby Surround, called *Dolby Pro Logic Surround,* is merely a higher-quality implementation of the Dolby Surround decoder. Dolby Pro Logic provides a center-channel output and greater separation between the channels. Dolby Surround decoding has been replaced by the superior Pro Logic decoding.

Note that Dolby Surround and Pro Logic each provide only a single surround channel. Although we use two surround loudspeakers, they are fed the same monophonic signal. (Dolby Surround has other limitations we'll hear about later.)

Dolby Laboratories introduced in 1997 a new surround format called *Dolby Digital*. Dolby Digital has many advantages over Dolby Surround. First, as its name implies, Dolby Digital is a digital format, meaning that it carries its sound information in the form of ones and zeros. Second, Dolby Digital is a 6-channel format rather than Surround's four channels (left, center, right, surround). Third, the six channels in a Dolby Digital soundtrack are completely discrete (separate), in contrast to Surround's matrix system, which "folds" the center and surround channels into the 2-channel signal stored on VHS tape or laserdisc. Dolby Digital is also called a "5.1-channel" format because it provides five channels (left, center, right, surround left, surround right), plus an optional channel (the ".1" channel) for carrying low bass.

Another discrete digital format, called *DTS* (Digital Theater Systems), is widely available for home-theater playback. Both Dolby Digital and DTS have variations (EX and ES) that provide even more than 5.1 channels. We'll talk more about Dolby Digital and DTS, along with their latest variations, in Chapter 2.

Source Components

Source components are any products that retrieve information from a storage medium or pick up a broadcast signal. A VHS tape machine is a source component because it reads the audio and video signals on a tape and presents them to the rest of the home-theater system. Other audio/video source components include DVD players, HDTV set-top boxes, or a Digital Satellite System (DSS) dish. Audio-only source components include CD players, FM tuners, and LP turntables.

From about 1980 to 1997, laserdisc was the format of choice for home-theater enthusiasts. These 12″ discs provide much better picture quality than VHS tape, all the advantages of an optical format (instant search to any point on the disc, for example), and have kept up with the latest advancements in surround-sound technology.

Laserdisc's dominance has ended, however, with the introduction of the vastly better DVD format. A DVD is a CD-sized disc that can hold an entire movie with stunning digital picture quality, and six completely separate channels of digital surround sound.

Similarly, the Digital Satellite System can deliver excellent picture and sound quality to your home-theater system—without you ever leaving your house. You simply select what movie you want to watch and the movie is beamed digitally into your home. All you need are a dish about the size of a large pizza, and a VCR-sized receiver.

Newer source components include the *Personal Video Recorder* (PVR) that records audio and video on a hard-disk drive, and *DVD recorders* that let you make your own DVDs.

All these products can be housed in an equipment rack near your video monitor, or tucked out of sight in a custom installation. You'll also need cables to connect all the components together, and some accessories to get the best performance from the system.

Home Theater Controllers, Power Amplifiers, and Receivers

The job of separating (decoding) the 2-channel Dolby Surround or discrete Dolby Digital signal into multichannel surround sound is the job of the *audio/video controller,* also called an *audio/video preamplifier* or *surround-sound decoder*. In addition to performing surround-sound decoding, the controller is also the Grand Central Station of your home-theater system. It receives audio and video signals from the source components (VHS, DSS, set-top boxes, DVD) and selects which one is decoded and amplified by your home-theater audio system and sent to your video monitor for display. The controller also performs digital signal processing, adjusts the overall volume, and fine-tunes the levels for individual channels. The controller's output is six low-level signals (called *line-level* signals): the left, center, right, left surround, right surround, and subwoofer channels. As mentioned earlier, newer surround-sound formats deliver more than 5.1 channels of audio information. These formats, called *THX Surround EX* and *DTS-ES* have an additional channel (called "back-surround") that drives additional surround speaker or speakers located directly behind the listening position. Controllers that support THX Surround EX and DTS-ES have eight line-level outputs rather than six.

Fig. 1-4 An audio/video receiver is the simplest and least expensive route to turning your television into a home theater.

Courtesy NAD

These six or eight separate outputs are fed to a 5- or 7-channel power amplifier (plus an optional subwoofer), where they are amplified to a level sufficient to drive the home theater's loudspeaker system. A home-theater power amplifier can have five, six, or seven amplifier channels in a single chassis. Alternately, some power amplifiers have three channels, others have two, and some are available as *monoblocks*: one amplifier channel per chassis. A 3-channel power amplifier allows you to use your existing 2-channel stereo power amplifier on the surround channels and the 3-channel amplifier on the front three loudspeakers, for example. Many subwoofers have built-in power amplifiers to drive their woofer cones.

An *audio/video receiver* includes in one chassis a controller, AM/FM tuner, and five, six, or seven power-amplifier channels. A/V receivers are the simplest and least expensive route to home theater (fig.1-4).

Home Theater Loudspeakers

A conventional stereo system provides two audio channels, left and right, which are reproduced by the left and right loudspeakers. When correctly set up, two channels of information driving two loudspeakers produce a soundfield in front of the listener that seems to exist between and around the two loudspeakers.

A home-theater system provides multiple channels, each channel feeding a loudspeaker located in front of, alongside, and/or behind the listening/viewing position. Specifically, a home-theater system has three *front* loudspeakers located across the front of the room, and two, three,

Fig. 1-5 The layout of a home-theater system's five loudspeakers and optional subwoofer.

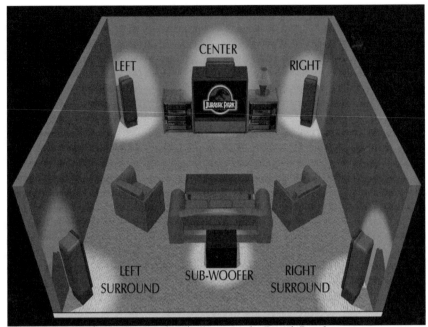

Courtesy Digital Theater Systems (DTS), illustration by Patrick Beard

or four *surround loudspeakers* behind or to the side of the listening position. Two of the front three loudspeakers flank the video monitor; the third is positioned above or below the video monitor. The front loudspeakers are called *left, center,* and *right.* A complete home-theater loudspeaker array is shown in fig.1-5.

The left and right loudspeakers reproduce mostly music and sound effects. The center loudspeaker's main job is reproducing dialog, and anchoring onscreen sound effects on the television screen. By having three loudspeakers across the front of the room, the sound's location can more closely match the location of the sound source in the picture. For example, in a properly set-up home-theater system, if a car crosses from the left side of the picture to the right, you hear the sound of the car move from the left loudspeaker, through the center loudspeaker, and then to the right loudspeaker. The sound source appears to follow the image on the screen.

The surround loudspeakers have a different job. They're generally smaller than the front loudspeakers, and handle much less energy. Consequently, they can be mounted unobtrusively on or inside a wall. Surround speakers mostly reproduce "atmospheric" or ambient sounds, creating a diffuse aural atmosphere around the listener. In a jungle scene, for example, the surround loudspeakers would re-create sounds such as chirping birds, falling raindrops, and blowing wind; in a city scene, the viewer would be surrounded by traffic sounds. The surround loudspeakers' contribution is subtle, but vitally important to the overall experience. Correctly set-up surround loudspeakers should not be able to be heard directly, but should instead envelop the viewer/listener in a diffuse soundfield.

There's one other loudspeaker you should know about. The *subwoofer* is dedicated to reproducing low bass frequencies, and is typically housed in a cubical box that can be placed almost anywhere in the room. When the *T. rex* stomps his foot in *Jurassic Park*, the room-shaking thump is reproduced by the subwoofer. Not every home-theater system uses a subwoofer; it is an option rather than a requirement. If your system uses very small speakers for the left and right channels that cannot reproduce low bass, a subwoofer becomes a requirement.

Video Displays

Every home-theater system needs a *video display*, also called a *video monitor*. Many home theaters use a direct-view television, another name for the conventional TV set with which all of us are familiar. A TV is described by the size of its picture tube, measured diagonally. Although you can build a home-theater system around a 25" set, 32" is generally considered the minimum size for serious home theater. Today's 35" set costs about what a 25" TV did just a few years ago. A 40" TV will give you a larger screen, but at a cost disproportionately high compared to a 35". The largest direct-view television available measures a whopping 40", but is extremely expensive.

For picture sizes larger than 35", the *rear-projection television* is ideal. Rather than project the video image directly onto a picture tube as in a direct-view TV, the rear-projection set uses lenses and mirrors to project an image onto a screen mounted in the front of the projector's cabinet from behind that screen (see fig.1-6). When people talk about a "big-screen" TV, they're usually referring to a rear-projection television.

Rear-projection sets start in size at about 40"and go up to 70". Their picture quality can be less bright, sharp, and clear than that of a direct-view set, but a rear-projector makes up for those shortcomings with the sheer size of its presentation. The rear-projector is the most popular choice for home-theater enthusiasts.

The older analog direct-view and rear-projection sets with which we're familiar are quickly becoming a thing of the past as HDTV sets continue to drop dramatically in price.

For the serious videophile, the front-projector offers the ultimate in quality. Like the rear-projector, the Cathode Ray Tube (CRT) front-projector uses three lenses, but projects its image from a distance across the room onto a separate screen. Unlike those of the other sets discussed so far, a front-projector's image size isn't fixed. By changing the screen size, and the distance between projector and screen, you can make the picture

Fig. 1-6 A rear-projection television provides picture sizes from 40" to 70".

Courtesy Mitsubishi Digital Inc.

almost any size you want. Screen sizes up to 10′ wide are possible with good-quality front-projectors.

Recent advances in Liquid Crystal Display (LCD) and Digital Light Processing (DLP) techniques have made front projectors using these technologies vastly better than they were just a few years ago. LCD and DLP projectors, described in Chapter 7, are affordable, lightweight, and easy to set up, yet offer some of the qualities of CRT projectors.

In addition to providing stunning video quality, a front-projector also offers the opportunity to further improve the picture with an add-on device called a line doubler, line quadrupler, or image scaler. These devices increase the number of scanning lines projected so we don't see the line structure inherent in the video format.

Finally, the plasma display is rapidly becoming a realistic alternative to all the technologies just described. A plasma display panel (PDP) is the proverbial "TV that hangs on the wall," with a depth of about 3" and screen sizes up to 61".

Review of Home Theater Components

To review, a home-theater system comprises:

• source components such as DVD, VHS, hard-disk recorder, HDTV set-top box, or DSS satellite dish to supply the signal to the rest of the system;

• a Dolby Pro Logic, Dolby Digital, or DTS decoder to separate the encoded soundtracks into separate front and surround channels;

• a multichannel power amplifier to drive the five loudspeakers (an audio/video receiver includes a Dolby decoder, FM tuner, and five (or more) power-amplifier channels in one chassis);

• five, six, or seven loudspeakers (plus an optional subwoofer) to reproduce the soundtrack's multiple channels;

• a video display device such as a television set, big-screen TV (preferably an HDTV set), front projector, or plasma display panel; and

• cables to connect all of these components to each other, and a storage rack to hold them.

Armed with this background in how a home-theater system goes together, in the next six chapters we'll look at each of these component categories in depth. Chapter 8 discusses how to choose the right home-theater components for you, and Chapter 9 contains detailed information about how to put all these components together in your home to achieve the best performance.

2 Surround Sound and Home THX

Introduction:
Why Surround Sound is So Important to Home Theater

Home theater is made possible by the delivery of multichannel surround-sound audio into the home. Whereas normal 2-channel stereo provides a soundfield in front of the listener, surround sound ideally produces a soundfield both in front and around the listener. With surround sound, we feel as though we are in the middle of the action on the screen, not just watching it on the video monitor.

Without multichannel surround-sound audio, we could never hope to emulate the experience of sitting in a theater, enveloped in a film's soundtrack—the line between the reality of sitting in your living room watching a 2-dimensional moving picture inside a box, and the illusion of actually being in that runaway mine car with Indiana Jones, is perfectly defined by the edges of the video monitor's display. What occurs outside the screen is your reality; what occurs inside the screen is illusion.

This is where surround sound plays such an important role in the home-theater experience. When we hear sounds all around us that are related to onscreen actions, the line between reality and illusion is no longer defined by the edges of the video monitor—the illusion of what's happening inside the edges of the video display isn't confined to a visual image in front of us. Instead, we feel enveloped in a soundfield that gives reality to what we're seeing on the screen. Surround sound expands the illusion inside the video monitor to the entire living room. The result is an experience much more powerful, involving, and intense.

The job of delivering the multichannel surround-sound experience to a home-theater system is performed by the surround-sound format. Several different formats are in use today, but the primary surround-sound formats for home theater are Dolby Surround, Dolby Digital (formerly called "AC-3"), and DTS Digital Surround. Each of these formats works a little differently, but their goal is the same. We'll look at each of these formats in detail in the next section.

Although some of the following information is theoretical, a little background in how the surround formats work goes a long way toward understanding the entire home-theater playback system. The more you know about surround decoding, the more you'll know about how to set up and fine-tune your home-theater system for the best performance. Many of the setup adjustments you'll make to your home-theater system are related to the surround format. If you know *why* you're making a certain adjustment, you're more likely to get that adjustment just right. In addition, you'll need to choose which surround-sound format (or formats) you want in your home-theater system—a factor that will influence your purchasing decisions.

Dolby Surround and Pro Logic

Dolby Surround is the original surround format, developed in the early 1970s for movie theaters (where it was called "Dolby Stereo"). Installed in more than 30,000 movie theaters and 35 million home-theater products, Dolby Surround is the granddaddy of home-theater surround formats.

The Dolby Surround process is a *matrix* system that encodes four audio channels onto stereo soundtracks for storage on video tape or laserdisc (or for television broadcast). When played back over two loudspeakers in conventional stereo, these two surround-encoded channels sound like any conventional stereo program. But if your home-theater system includes a Dolby decoder, the original four channels can be separated for playback in your home. The multichannel surround sound signal then drivers the loudspeakers in your home-theater system. Nearly all VHS tapes, laserdiscs, and many television programs are encoded with Dolby Surround. Dolby Surround–encoded software carries the logo shown in fig.2-1. Fig.2-2 is a block diagram of the Dolby Surround encode/decode process.

Fig. 2-1
Software encoded with Dolby Surround bears this familiar logo.

Courtesy Dolby Laboratories

Fig. 2-2 Dolby Surround encoding matrixes four audio channels into two channels for storage or transmission; Dolby Pro Logic decoding recovers the four audio channels for home playback.

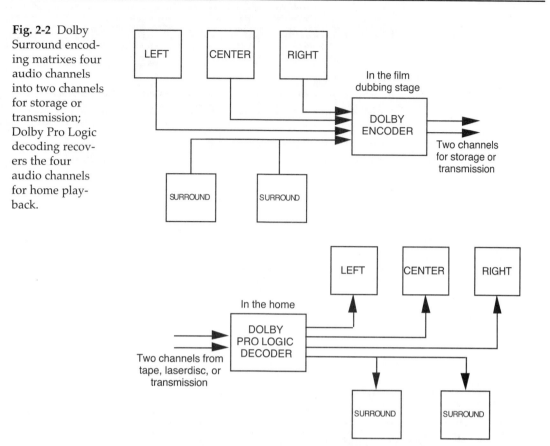

You're probably more familiar with the term *Dolby Pro Logic,* which is simply an enhanced version of Dolby Surround decoding. Pro Logic differs from Dolby Surround in that Pro Logic provides a center-channel output, greater separation of sounds in one channel from sounds in other channels, and better localization of onscreen sounds. Note that the term "Dolby Surround" encompasses both Dolby Surround and Dolby Pro Logic decoding. Although there are two types of Dolby Surround *de*coders, there is only one form of Dolby Surround *en*coding. Dolby-encoded software works with both Dolby Surround and Pro Logic decoders. Because Dolby Surround decoders have largely been superseded by Pro Logic decoders, the rest of this book will consider Pro Logic only. (Home-theater products equipped with Pro Logic decoding carry the logo shown in fig.2-3.)

Fig. 2-3 Home-theater products equipped with Dolby Pro Logic decoding are identified by this logo.

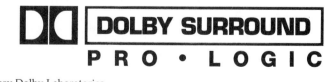

Courtesy Dolby Laboratories

In addition to decoding the 2-channel audio output of a VCR or television broadcast into left, center, right, and surround channels, Pro Logic decoders usually have an additional output for driving a subwoofer. Note that Pro Logic is strictly a four-channel decoding process. While many A/V receivers and controllers have a subwoofer output that can be used with Pro Logic playback, the subwoofer output is not part of Pro Logic decoding. This subwoofer output is a monophonic mix of the front-channel information below 100Hz (a midbass frequency). Using this subwoofer signal is optional; many home-theater systems simply use full-range left and right loudspeakers to reproduce the entire frequency spectrum, including bass.

Note that the subwoofer signal isn't a separate channel in the way the surround channel is. Rather, it is created simply by mixing the bass from the front channels together. That way, your main left and right loudspeakers won't have to reproduce low bass, and can thus be small and unobtrusive.

It is important to understand that while Pro Logic provides *four* playback channels (left, center, right, and a monophonic (or mono) surround channel), five speakers are used for playback, including two surround loudspeakers to reproduce the same mono surround signal.

Limitations of Dolby Surround

Although Dolby Surround is an amazing technology that has served us well for two decades, the format has several inherent limitations that limit the quality of the reproduced sound. First, because it is a matrix system, the separation between channels is limited. This means that sounds in one channel can "leak" into other channels. The result is less precise localization of sounds. If distinct, loud effects appear in the front and rear channels simultaneously, the soundstage collapses into one big "mono" presentation.

The more serious problem associated with limited channel separation is the possibility of the surround loudspeakers reproducing sounds intended to accompany an image in front of us—particularly dialog. This can be extremely distracting if heard to originate from the surround loudspeakers behind or alongside the viewer/listener.

Dolby Pro Logic uses two tricks to overcome the format's limited channel separation. First, the signal driving the surround loudspeakers is delayed slightly in relation to the front loudspeakers. This delay improves the apparent front-to-rear separation by a psychoacoustic phenomenon called the *Haas Effect*, which works like this: When exposed to two equal sounds coming from different directions, the ear tends to localize the sound source in the direction of the sound that arrives first, and ignore the sound that arrives later. By delaying the surround channel, unwanted leakage into the surround loudspeakers arrives at the listener's ears slightly later in time than sound from the front loudspeakers. This delay causes the ear/brain combination to hear only the sound coming from the front loudspeakers. Every Dolby Pro Logic receiver or controller incorporates a variable rear-channel delay. (How to set the rear-channel delay is described in Chapter 9.)

Another technique for increasing the apparent separation between the front and rear channels is to limit the frequency range of the surround channels. Specifically, the Pro Logic decoder cuts off treble frequencies above 7kHz (seven kilo-Hertz, or seven thousand cycles per second) and bass frequencies below 100Hz. The treble cutoff prevents dialog sibilants (*s* and *ch* sounds) from appearing in the surround channel.

Another problem with Dolby Surround is that the surround channel is mono. This means the same signal feeds both the left and right surround loudspeakers. Consequently, there's no way to "steer" sounds to only the left or only the right surround loudspeaker. A good example of how this limits a home-theater system's performance is when an airplane takes off toward the viewer. The sound may begin at the left front loudspeaker, move toward the center, and then to the rear as the plane apparently flies overhead. With Dolby Surround's monophonic surround channel, the sound can't move toward the left rear or right rear of the room, only to the center rear. In addition, sitting between two loudspeakers reproducing the same signal can cause that sound to be localized inside the listener's head—like the "phantom" center image formed between two stereo loud-speakers. Unfortunately, this phantom image is projected right where the listener is sitting. This phenomenon distracts from the goal of surround loudspeakers, which is to create a diffuse, enveloping "atmosphere" of sound. Consequently, several techniques are used to minimize this possi-bility, including the use of dipolar surround loudspeakers (described in Chapter 6) and THX *surround decorrelation* (described later in this chapter).

Finally, Dolby Surround uses a modified version of Dolby B noise reduction on the surround channels. This is similar to the Dolby NR noise-reduction system widely used in cassette decks.

Dolby Pro Logic II

In mid-2001, Dolby Laboratories made available a more sophisticated ver-sion of Pro Logic decoding, called *Pro Logic II*. The idea behind Pro Logic II was to create from 2-channel sources a listening experience similar to that of a discrete 5.1-channel digital format. And with more consumers having 5.1-channel playback available to them for reproducing music sources, Pro Logic II attempts to deliver multichannel sound from 2-chan-nel recordings, even those that have not been surround-encoded.

Found on most A/V receivers made after early 2002, Pro Logic II offers improved performance over its predecessor in several areas. First, Pro Logic II delivers full-bandwidth stereo surround channels rather than the bandwidth-limited monophonic surround channel of conventional Pro Logic decoding. This attribute provides a more enveloping soundfield, greater precision in the placement and pans (movements) of sounds behind the listener, and more natural timbre of sounds reproduced by the surround channels. In this respect, Pro Logic II emulates the experience of listening to a 5.1-channel discrete digital source.

Pro Logic II uses more sophisticated "steering" circuits that monitor the level in each channel and selectively applies attenuation (reduction in level) to prevent sounds in one channel from leaking into another channel.

In Pro Logic II's MOVIE mode, you can fine-tune the soundfield with three controls. *Center Width* spreads out the center-channel signal into the left and right channels, allowing you to achieve a better blend between the front three channels. The *Panorama* control moves some of the signal from the front left and right channels to the surround left and surround right channels, respectively. This technique produces a "wrap-around" effect. Finally, the *Dimension* control adjusts the overall front-to-rear balance. Some A/V receivers and controllers with Pro Logic II include a MATRIX mode that produces surround sound from monophonic sources.

Dolby Digital

A more sophisticated format for delivering multichannel surround sound, called *Dolby Digital*, made its debut in 1997. Technically known as *AC-3*, Dolby Digital overcomes the limitations of Dolby Surround to take the home-theater experience to the next level.

As its name implies, Dolby Digital is a digital format; that is, it stores the film soundtrack as a stream of ones and zeros. Consequently, Dolby Digital is available only via formats that can deliver digital information, such as DVD, digital television broadcasts, laserdisc, and the digital satellite system (DSS). Dolby Digital cannot be recorded on normal VHS tape (but has been recorded experimentally on S-VHS). Dolby Digital has, however, been mandated as the worldwide standard for the DVD format, as well as for digital television (DTV). Dolby Digital can also be transmitted by DSS systems, although you need a Dolby Digital-equipped receiver. As of early 2002, more than 3800 films had been encoded in the Dolby Digital format, and more than 150 million Dolby Digital decoders were in use worldwide. Products that incorporate Dolby Digital decoding carry the logo shown in fig.2-4.

Fig. 2-4 Products and software equipped with Dolby Digital are identified by this logo.

Courtesy Dolby Laboratories

In addition to being digital, Dolby Digital provides six discrete (separate) audio channels. Because the six channels are discrete, there's no chance of unwanted sounds from one channel leaking into another. Remember that the older Dolby Surround was a matrix system that "folded" the surround- and center-channel information into the left and right channels for separation on playback. With no need to mix the signals, Dolby Digital can maintain nearly infinite separation between channels. The result is an unprecedented ability to precisely steer sounds to any part of your living room.

Moreover, Dolby Digital provides "split" surround channels rather than a mono surround channel. This means the left and right surround loudspeakers can be fed completely independent signals. Instead of just hearing sound vaguely around us, we can now hear surround sounds more distinctly to the left or right. A great example of how split surround channels enhance the home-theater experience is found on the laserdisc of *Star Trek Generations*. This laserdisc has both Dolby Surround and Dolby Digital soundtracks; you can select which one you want to hear by pushing a button on the receiver's remote control. Early in the film, the *Enterprise* goes into warp drive, moving toward the viewer from the left side of the screen to the right, then over the viewer's head. When listening in Dolby Pro Logic, the *Enterprise* appears to fly overhead, but the sound doesn't match the picture very well because the starship is moving to the right rear. But in Dolby Digital, the *Enterprise* can be clearly heard to whoosh to the right rear. This apparently small difference is quite large when you experience it for yourself. The sound better matches the visual image, further blurring that line between reality and illusion I talked about at the beginning of this chapter. There are hundreds of other examples of how Dolby Digital's high channel separation and split surrounds better convey the filmmakers' intent.

Another important benefit of split surround channels is that ambient information, which the surround channels predominantly carry, can be stereo rather than mono. This makes ambient sounds such as rain or traffic sound more realistic, and also prevents the "inside the head" localization of ambience.

As mentioned in the discussion of Dolby Pro Logic, the older format's surround channel doesn't carry bass information below 100Hz or treble above 7kHz. But with Dolby Digital, all five channels carry the entire audio bandwidth, from very low bass (20Hz) to the highest frequencies humans can hear (20kHz).

Because Dolby Digital can carry up to 5.1 discrete audio channels, it doesn't necessarily imply that all Dolby Digital sources deliver 5.1-channel sound. Older movies mixed in mono will still be reproduced in mono through the Dolby Digital format. Some DVDs carry a graphic that indicates the number of channels encoded in the Dolby Digital bitstream (fig.2-5), and some A/V receivers and controllers indicate the number of channels in a front-panel display. You may also see the designation "Dolby Digital 2.0" on the back of some DVD cases, indicating that the soundtrack is 2-channel stereo carried via a Dolby Digital bitstream.

Fig. 2-5 Some
DVD covers
carry a graphic
representation
of the number
of channels
encoded in the
Dolby Digital
bitstream.

Mono

Stereo

Dolby Surround

5.1-ch. Dolby Digital

Courtesy Dolby Laboratories

Setting up a DVD Player for Dolby Digital Playback

To hear the Dolby Digital track on DVD, you must verify that your DVD player is set to output a Dolby Digital signal. Some older DVD players (and the DVDs themselves) default to delivering a Surround-encoded two-channel signal at the DVD player's analog and digital output jacks. You must enter the DVD player's set-up menu and turn on the Dolby Digital output (and also the DTS output, if you have a DTS-equipped A/V receiver or controller).

Similarly, some DVDs give you the choice of hearing the Dolby Digital 5.1-channel mix or the Dolby Surround–encoded mix. Before starting the movie, go to the DVD's set-up menu, select LANGUAGES or AUDIO SETUP, and choose the output format. Note that if you choose the surround-encoded mix, the DVD player converts the 5.1-channel Dolby Digital mix to a 2-channel surround-encoded mix on the fly by a process called *downmixing*. Including this feature in DVD players is essential because not all consumers have Dolby Digital 5.1-channel decoders.

This surround-encoded signal appears on both the DVD player's analog output jacks and digital output jacks (fig.2-6). If you have an older A/V receiver without a digital input, connect two (left and right) cables from the DVD player's analog outputs to the receiver's analog audio inputs. If your receiver has a digital input, connect a single digital cable between the DVD player and receiver. This single digital cable can carry the full 5.1-channel signal, or the surround-encoded downmix, as a Dolby Digital bitstream. If you have a choice between analog and digital connection, opt for the digital connection. And if your DVD player and A/V receiver offer both coaxial and optical digital outputs (fig.2-6), choose the coaxial connection. (Note that only the digital output can carry a discrete 5.1-channel Dolby Digital signal; the analog output carries a Dolby Surround downmix.)

Fig. 2-6 A DVD
player's digital-
audio output
appears on both
digital coaxial and
optical jacks, as
well as an analog
signal on RCA
jacks.

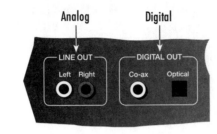

Courtesy Dolby Laboratories

Dolby Digital's Dynamic Range Control and Dialog Normalization

Dolby Digital also offers the opportunity to use sophisticated digital-signal processing to enhance the home-theater experience. One of these enhancements is a *Dynamic Range Control* that reduces the volume of loud sounds for late-night listening or for watching a movie without disturbing other family members. Specifically, Dolby Digital's Dynamic Range Control turns down the volume on loud sounds, turns up the volume of quiet sounds, and leaves the all-important dialog at the same level. Dynamic range is the difference between the soundtrack's loudest and quietest sounds; the Dynamic Range Control compresses the dynamic range.

Some A/V receivers and controllers allow you to adjust the amount of this compression (25%, 50%, 75%, and 100%, for example), while others simply let you turn the Dynamic Range Control on or off. You may see this control called by the more descriptive names "Late Night" or "Midnight" modes, for examples. Note that the compression of the dynamic range isn't arbitrary, but is instead controlled by the film-sound mixers through digital codes inserted in the Dolby Digital bitstream.

Another refinement made possible by Dolby Digital is *Dialog Normalization*, a feature that automatically adjusts the volume when switching between Dolby Digital sources to keep the dialog volume constant. Dialog Normalization doesn't affect the dynamic range as does the Dynamic Range Control; rather, the overall volume is increased or decreased, based on data about the dialog volume encoded in the program signal. Dialog Normalization lets you switch from DVD to HDTV, channel surf, and switch back to DVD without adjusting the volume control.

Dolby Digital's Low-Frequency Effects (LFE) Channel

Another advantage of Dolby Digital is the completely separate channel it provides for carrying additional low-bass information to maximize the impact of such sounds as explosions and crashes. Dolby Digital provides a separate channel for low bass called *Low-Frequency Effects* (LFE). The output from the LFE channel is connected to a subwoofer to reproduce the low bass, while the bass from the main channels can be reproduced by the front loudspeakers, or fed to the subwoofer along with the LFE channel. In movie theaters, the Dolby Digital LFE channel is reproduced by a dedicated subwoofer. In a home-theater system, the subwoofer reproduces the LFE channel and, selectively, bass from any of the five other channels. Note that the LFE channel is not a "subwoofer" channel. Rather, it carries low-bass information that, through the A/V receiver's bass management, is directed to whatever speakers can handle low bass. In a system with large, full-range left and right speakers, the LFE channel would be reproduced by those speakers, and no subwoofer is needed.

The LFE channel offers the opportunity to deliver more low bass to your home-theater system. Using the LFE channel is an option for both the filmmaker and consumer. Not all Dolby Digital–encoded programs use the LFE channel—it's hard to imagine *Driving Miss Daisy* needing an additional bass-impact channel. Soundtracks without information in the LFE channel are sometimes labeled "5.0." (About half the DVD titles available offer either a 5.0-channel or 5.1-channel soundtrack.) Similarly, film soundtracks that put bass in the LFE channel do so only occasionally. Many controllers equipped with Dolby Digital include a display to tell you when the LFE channel has been used by the filmmakers.

Without a subwoofer connected to the LFE channel, you'll still hear low bass from your left and right loudspeakers, but you won't get the ultimate floor-shaking impact that only a subwoofer can provide.

With five discrete, full-bandwidth channels plus the separate LFE channel, Dolby Digital is called a "5.1-channel" format. The ".1" channel refers to the bandwidth-limited LFE channel. The 5.1 format was universally adopted several years ago for film-sound recording.

Dolby Digital is a far better method of delivering multichannel sound to your home-theater system than Dolby Surround. But it doesn't make Dolby Surround obsolete; more than 12,000 films are encoded with Surround, and tens of millions of Surround and Pro Logic decoders are in use worldwide. The two formats will no doubt comfortably co-exist for many years. I still greatly enjoy watching films encoded with Dolby Surround in my home-theater system.

Dolby Digital on Laserdisc

I've removed from this edition the sections on laserdisc because the format is essentially dead, except to those of us who bought laserdisc players before DVD was available. There is, however, one important piece of information you need if you plan to play laserdiscs: the Dolby Digital output on laserdisc players cannot be connected to a conventional Dolby Digital input on an A/V receiver or controller. That's because Dolby Digital is stored on laserdisc as an RF (radio frequency) signal, not as a digital bitstream as on DVD. To play Dolby Digital tracks from laserdisc, you need an *RF demodulator* to convert the RF signal into a bitstream your A/V receiver will recognize. Some top-end A/V receivers have a built-in RF demodulator.

Dolby Digital Surround EX

Dolby Laboratories and Lucasfilm THX teamed up in 1999 to create an extension of 5.1-channel surround sound called *Dolby Digital Surround EX*. First used for the film *Star Wars: Episode I—The Phantom Menace*, Dolby Digital Surround EX adds an additional surround channel to 5.1-channel sources. This third surround speaker, called the *back-surround* speaker, is mounted directly behind the listener to augment the sound from the left and right surrounds. The first home-theater products with Dolby Digital EX decoding were licensed by THX, so the format is also referred to as *THX Surround EX*.

Adding a back-surround speaker behind the listener allows the film-sound mixers to more precisely position sounds, and to create more realistic pans (apparent movements of sounds). For example, the sound of a spaceship that is made to appear to fly over the viewer's head tends to move along the side walls when reproduced through just two surround loudspeakers; adding a third surround speaker behind the listener allows the ship to seem to move directly overhead. EX's development was spurred by the sound designers for *Phantom Menace*, who wanted greater realism in panning sounds, particularly such "flyovers."

Fig. 2-7 Products with THX certification and Dolby Digital EX decoding are identified by this logo.

THX SURROUND EX™

Courtesy Lucasfilm

Although you can achieve full EX playback with one back-surround speaker, Dolby Labs and THX recommend two back-surround speakers, and two back-surround amplifier channels to drive them. Two back-surround speakers produces greater envelopment than one, and smoother pans of sounds behind you. According to Dolby Labs and THX, the optimum configuration is two surround speakers located on either side of the listening position, and two back-surround speakers behind the listener. Chapter 9 includes a complete guide to loudspeaker placement.

Surround EX can be carried in the conventional Dolby Digital soundtrack by existing 5.1-channel media such as DVD. That's because EX's third surround channel is matrix-encoded into the left and right surround channels. Earlier in this chapter we saw how the center channel of Dolby Surround is "folded into" the left- and right-channel signals, then "unfolded" on playback to create the signal driving your center-channel speaker. Surround EX works exactly the same way—the third surround channel in EX is encoded into the left and right surround signals, then extracted on playback in the movie theater or your home theater. In fact, the two encoding and decoding techniques—the center channel in Dolby Surround and the back-surround channel in Surround EX—are identical.

More specifically, back-surround information is a signal common to the left and right surround channels. The EX decoder simply extracts any sounds that appear simultaneously in the left and right surround channels, and presents them to the back-surround speaker or speakers. When using two back-surround speakers, they are fed the identical monophonic signal. THX recommends one amplifier channel for each back-surround speaker not because the two speakers reproduce different signals, but to ensure that the dynamic range and impact of the back-surround channel isn't compromised.

Because extracting the center channel in Pro Logic decoding and extracting the back-surround channel in EX decoding are identical, you can add Surround EX decoding to your existing 5.1-channel system by using a Dolby Pro Logic decoder to extract the back-surround channel. If you have an old Pro Logic receiver lying around, now is the time to put it to good use.

Here's how it works. Run the left and right surround signals from your controller into the main inputs on the Pro Logic receiver. Take the left and right preamp outputs from the receiver and feed them to your surround power-amplifier inputs. Connect a back-surround speaker located behind the listening area to the receiver's center-channel speaker output. When calibrating individual channel levels, use the receiver's volume control to match the volume of the center surround speaker to that of the other speakers. Once the receiver's volume is set, you don't need to adjust it again. Your home theater is now equipped with Surround EX.

Here are some details you should be aware of. First, put the Pro Logic receiver in "3 Stereo" mode. Second, calibrate the three surround speakers relative to each other by turning on the Pro Logic receiver's internal noise signal and adjusting the center-channel volume level so that it matches the left and right surround levels. Turn off the noise signal. Third, be sure that the Dolby Digital receiver's left- and right-channel level controls are set identically (this ensures that the Pro Logic receiver is fed a balanced signal). Fourth, turn on the Dolby Digital receiver's internal noise signal and adjust the Pro Logic receiver's master volume until the left and right surrounds are the same level as the front left, center, and right channels.

If you are buying an A/V receiver for the first time, or upgrading your existing unit, you'll find EX decoding on most receivers, along with the additional amplifier channels required to drive the back-surround speakers. Receivers bearing the THX Surround EX logo have been certified by Lucasfilm/THX for the performance criteria described later in this chapter, and also include seven channels of amplification (left, center, right, surround left, surround right, and two back-surround channels). Dolby Labs is now licensing Dolby Digital EX decoding, and the first products carrying the Dolby EX logo (rather than the THX Surround

EX logo) appeared in mid-2002. (THX was the exclusive licensor of the technology to the home-theater market until November 1, 2001.)

Note, however, that some receivers and controllers on the market are billed as "6.1-channel" and employ a generic matrix decoder to extract the back-surround channel from EX-encoded sources. These products are not certified by Lucasfilm/THX or Dolby, and generally have a single amplifier channel to power a single back-surround loudspeaker. There's nothing magical about THX or Dolby EX certification; these "6.1" or "7.1" products can extract the back-surround signal properly and often provide superb performance. Keep in mind that EX soundtracks are monitored and mixed on true EX equipment using encoders built by Dolby. There is, however, one feature mandated in EX-certified products: the noise generator found on all home-theater receivers and controllers used to adjust individual channel levels is specially modified to ensure correct calibration of the back-surround channels. This isn't necessarily true of non-THX EX products. More information on this subject is included in Chapter 9.

Note that very few films have been mixed in Surround EX—about 80 as of early 2002, compared with 3800 films mixed in Dolby Digital—but mixer interest is growing and EX usage is increasing. Incidentally, the format is officially called Dolby Digital Surround EX in movie theaters and on soundtracks, including the DVDs of EX films; the home playback decoder is called THX Surround EX on THX-licensed home-theater products, and Dolby Digital EX on Dolby-licensed home-theater products. They two names describe the same format. As of early 2002, about 500,000 home-theater products with EX decoding are in use.

Although not many DVDs are EX-encoded, it's easy to see how applying EX decoding to a conventional 5.1-channel source can enhance the experience. If the EX decoder extracts any information common to the left and right surround signals and presents that information to loudspeakers behind you, you will hear a more solid soundfield behind you than if those back-surround speakers weren't present. In my experience, leaving EX decoding on all the time benefits many conventional 5.1-channel sources as well as those encoded with Surround EX. Note, however, that THX recommends turning off EX decoding for non-EX-encoded sources. DTS, on the other hand, recommends leaving its competing DTS-ES decoding on with non-ES–encoded sources. Dolby Labs says EX decoding works well on some non-EX soundtracks, and not so well on others, and recommends using EX decoding on non-EX soundtracks on a case-by-case basis.

There are a couple of miscellaneous pieces of information you should know about Dolby Digital EX. First, EX-equipped A/V receivers and controllers have an automatic decoding mode that recognizes an EX-identifying flag in the Dolby Digital datastream. This flag, once incorporated into the data stream on DVDs, will automatically engage EX decoding. For now, however, you must look to see if the DVD is EX encoded, and manually engage EX decoding. EX DVDS are expected to incorporate this flag later in 2002.

Second, you can add back-surround decoding to your existing 5.1-channel system with an add-on decoder, such as the Parasound CSE-6.1. This small device takes the existing surround left and right signals, and extracts a back-surround signal for presentation to a power amplifier. The unit includes a noise generator and remote control for accurately adjusting the volume of the back-surround speakers.

Finally, the competing DTS surround-sound format has its own system for delivering sounds from behind the listener, and is described later in this chapter.

How Dolby Digital Works

For the technically minded, I've included a brief description of the fundamental technology behind Dolby Digital. But the following information is of practical as well as theoretical significance; the differences between Dolby Digital and DTS may influence your purchasing decisions.

Dolby Digital is a digital, multichannel sound-storage and transmission format with what Dolby Laboratories claims is "near-CD-quality" sound. But unlike conventional digital audio stored on a CD, Dolby Digital reduces the number of bits of data that represent the audio signal. Reducing the number of bits allows six channels of digital audio to be "squeezed" into consumer media.

In the film dubbing stage where the film soundtrack is mixed, the six separate analog channels of the film soundtrack (left, center, right, surround left, surround right, LFE) are fed into a Dolby Digital encoder. After converting the signals to digital form, the encoder analyzes the signal to determine which sounds are less likely to be heard. For example, it's unlikely that we could hear birds chirping during an explosion. The Dolby Digital encoder therefore ignores the chirping birds and encodes the explosion. This technique, called "perceptual coding," reduces the number of bits that must be stored on the DVD or transmitted as part of an HDTV signal. In practice, perceptual coding is vastly more complex. The MP3 format that allows music to be downloaded from the Internet is an example of perceptual coding.

Specifically, Dolby Digital produces a single datastream in which the signals for each of the six channels are lined up behind one another, like a train with six cars. The data rate is typically 384,000 bits per second (384 kilobits per second, or 384kbs) for all six channels. (A data rate of 448kbs is also widely used on DVD.) For comparison, just two channels of digital audio on a compact disc produce a datastream with a rate of 1,411,200 bits per second. In other words, Dolby Digital encodes each audio channel with less than a tenth as many bits as are used on a CD.

Digital Theater Systems (DTS)

Digital Theater Systems (DTS) has invented a format for delivering multichannel surround sound that competes with Dolby Digital. Officially called "DTS Digital Surround" but generally known simply as the DTS format, the method has the potential to deliver higher audio quality than Dolby Digital. Like Dolby Digital, DTS delivers 5.1 channels of surround-sound audio to the home. The DTS logo (fig.2-8) identifies DTS-encoded software and products that incorporate DTS decoding.

Fig. 2-8 Software encoded in the DTS surround format, and home-theater hardware with DTS decoding, are identified by this logo.

Courtesy Digital Theater Systems

As mentioned earlier, Dolby Digital encodes six audio channels with 384,000 or 448,000 bits per second. By contrast, the DTS format in "master quality" mode uses 1,536,000 bits per second to produce a higher-quality 5.1-channel audio signal. The drawback of DTS is that it requires more bits of information to be stored on the DVD or digital satellite broadcast. On DVD, this increased data rate reduces the number of bits available for encoding the picture, limits the amount of supplemental material on the DVD (director commentary, "making of" feature, for examples), or both. Note that Dolby Digital can be run at a higher data rate for better sound quality (640kbs, for example), and DTS can run at a lower data rate for higher storage efficiency.

Dolby Digital is the market leader because it was available for consumer use before DTS, and because it uses fewer bits. Both Dolby Digital and DTS decoding are available on high-end controllers and most A/V receivers. The integrated circuit that performs Dolby Digital decoding is easily programmed to decode DTS sources as well. Consequently, it costs manufacturers virtually nothing to include both formats on their products. All controllers and A/V receivers sold today offer decoding of both formats.

All DVDs are required by the DVD governing body to carry a Dolby Digital soundtrack. DTS is an option to the movie studio. Thus, you'll find DVDs with Dolby Digital and no DTS, Dolby Digital plus DTS, but never just DTS. I mentioned earlier that about 3800 DVDs have been released, all of which contain a Dolby Digital soundtrack. For comparison, about 125 DTS-encoded DVDs are available.

When you first start a DVD that includes a DTS soundtrack, you can specify through the DVD's menu whether you want to hear the Dolby

Digital or DTS soundtrack. If you have a DTS-equipped A/V receiver or controller, you can audition both and decide which you prefer. When comparing the two formats, however, keep in mind that the Dolby Digital and DTS soundtracks can come from completely different mixes. The DTS mix usually has more bass and louder surround channels, factors that can lead one to erroneously conclude that the DTS format is inherently better than Dolby Digital. When given a choice, I opt to listen to the DTS track.

You've probably heard both Dolby Digital and DTS at your local movie theaters. For theatrical release, some films are encoded with Dolby Digital, others with DTS. Look for the Dolby Digital and DTS logos at the beginning of the film to see which format you're about to experience. Incidentally, the first film to use DTS was *Jurassic Park*.

DTS-ES Matrix, DTS-ES Discrete, DTS Neo:6 Music, and DTS Neo:6 Cinema

Digital Theater Systems has developed a suite of surround-decoding technologies that either enhance the DTS experience or provide decoding of non-DTS sources such as conventional stereo.

Looking first at extensions of the DTS format, *DTS-ES Matrix* is identical in conception to Dolby Digital Surround EX described earlier in this chapter. DTS-ES Matrix matrix encodes a back-surround channel within the existing left and right surround channels in the 5.1-channel soundtrack. The DTS-ES Matrix decoder in your A/V receiver or controller extracts this back-surround signal and presents it to one or two loudspeakers located directly behind the listening position. A flag in the DTS datastream alerts your receiver or controller than the soundtrack is ES encoded, and the ES decoder engages automatically.

DTS took the concept a step further with the *DTS-ES Discrete* format. As its name implies, DTS-ES Discrete delivers a completely separate (discrete) back-surround signal rather than a matrix-encoded back-surround signal. Consequently, ES Discrete has none of the drawbacks of a matrix system, particularly poor separation between channels. The discrete back-surround channel allows film-sound mixers to more precisely position and pan sounds behind you. Although Dolby Digital Surround EX and DTS-ES Matrix are sometimes called "6.1-channel" formats, only DTS-ES Discrete can truly be called 6.1-channel.

Although DTS-ES Discrete is the best of the surround formats, very few DVDs have been encoded with a true discrete 6.1-channel soundtrack.

DTS Neo:6 Music and *Neo:6 Cinema* are decoding algorithms that convert stereo or Dolby Surround–encoded two-channel sources into multichannel surround sound. Neo:6 Music leaves the front left and right channel signals unprocessed for the purest reproduction, and extracts center and surround-channel signals from the two-channel source. DTS recommends this mode for all two-channel sources, such as CD and FM broadcasts.

Neo:6 Cinema is similar to Dolby Pro Logic II decoding, and can be used with Dolby Surround–encoded sources. Neo:6 Cinema has a much larger effect on the signal, rearranging the signal distribution among the front three channels. Both Neo:6 Music and Neo:6 Cinema create a 7.1-channel signal from two-channel sources.

Not to be outdone, Lucasfilm has developed a similar decoding technique called THX Ultra2, described later in this chapter.

Surround Sound for Music

Surround-sound formats developed for film soundtracks can also be used to encode music with more than two channels. The same techniques that surround you in the ambience of a movie's rainstorm can be used to immerse you in the acoustic of a concert hall or jazz club.

Surround sound for music has been offered to the public once before, and was a resounding artistic and commercial failure. It was called Quadraphonic. Quad failed for two reasons: the technology was vastly inferior compared to what's possible today; and artists and producers used the rear channels in totally inappropriate ways. For example, it was common in the Quad era to hear trumpets or electric guitars emanate from behind you, a situation you'd never experience listening to live music. Such techniques were prevalent with Quadraphonic because the system's promoters wanted to hit listeners over the head with how different it was from 2-channel stereo.

There's a fundamental problem with putting loud or percussive sounds behind the listener; human beings react to a loud sound behind them by reflexively turning around to see the sound source. This reaction distracts the listener from the expression of the musical performance—the worst possible result. The movie industry has known for decades not to position percussive sounds behind the audience—they even have a name for the problem it creates: the "exit sign syndrome." This name comes from the fact that when the audience turns around to look at the source of the sound, they see the theater's illuminated exit sign. Nonetheless, the vast majority of musical surround-sound demonstrations I've heard use the rear channels for gimmicky effects, not to more accurately recreate the experience of listening to live music in an acoustical space.

Having said that, however, I believe that when executed with artistic sensitivity, multichannel music reproduction should be fundamentally superior to 2-channel reproduction. Live music reaches our ears from many directions, not just from two sources in front of us. In a concert hall, the reverberation and room ambience largely reach listeners' ears from behind. If this reverberation were reproduced with rear loudspeakers, we could more accurately re-create in our homes the soundfield that existed in the concert hall.

Storing surround-sound music on a CD or DVD-Video disc involves compromises that degrade audio fidelity. Specifically, a CD or DVD-Video disc doesn't provide enough storage for the massive number of bits consumed by five or six channels of high-quality digital audio. Consequently, compression systems such as Dolby Digital or DTS have been used to reduce the bit-rate to make music surround-sound possible. These compression systems inevitably reduce sound quality.

With the introduction of two new formats—DVD-Audio and Super Audio CD—created specifically for delivering high-quality multichannel music, that compromise is no longer necessary. These formats are covered in the next chapter, but you should know that they can provide 6-channel surround sound with far greater fidelity than CD.

Dolby Digital and PCM Tracks on Music DVDs

Some music DVDs give you the choice of listening to a 5.1-channel Dolby Digital–encoded mix, or to a 2-channel Dolby Surround–encoded mix. This choice is made in the DVD's set-up menu. You can then choose to listen to this mix in straight stereo through the left and right speakers, or decoded into multichannel surround sound with Pro Logic, Pro Logic II, or DTS Neo:6 Music decoding, depending on the surround formats supported in your A/V receiver or controller.

The 2-channel mix is called the *PCM* (Pulse-Code Modulation) mix. PCM is the near-universal method of encoding sounds in digital form, and is familiar to everyone because it's used in the compact disc. PCM does not employ data compression to "squeeze" the music into a signal with fewer bits. Consequently, the 2-channel PCM mix delivers digital audio with a sampling rate of 48kHz (slightly higher than CD's 44.1kHz) and resolution of 16 bits (same as CD). If we multiply the number of samples per second (48,000) by the number of bits in each sample (16), we see that the PCM tracks have a data rate of 1,536,000 bits per second (for *two* channels). Compare this with the 384,000 bits per second for *5.1 channels* of Dolby Digital.

Obviously, the PCM tracks contain more information and have greater fidelity to the source. The tradeoff is that when listening to the PCM tracks with Pro Logic decoding, all the limitations of Pro Logic are apparent, primarily reduced channel separation and a monophonic, limited-bandwidth surround channel. The spatial precision of sounds delivered by the PCM tracks not as great as that of the Dolby Digital tracks.

In my experience, however, some loss of spatial dimension is well worth the increase in musical realism, transparency, smoothness in the treble, natural rendering of timbre, sense of ease, and more solid and extended bass response heard from the PCM tracks. Try this comparison for yourself; two good music DVDs with both Dolby Digital and PCM tracks are James Taylor's *Live at the Beacon Theatre* and *G3 Live in Concert* with virtuoso guitarists Joe Satriani, Eric Johnson, and Steve Vai. I always chose to listen to the Surround-encoded tracks. The introduction of Pro Logic II, with full-bandwidth stereo surround channels, further widens the sonic divide between Dolby Digital and PCM surround on music DVDs.

THX Processing and Certification

From the 1940s to the 1970s, film-sound quality stayed pretty much the same. It was monophonic, had a narrow frequency response and limited dynamic range, and couldn't steer the directions of sounds to match movements on the screen. The creation of Dolby Stereo in the early 1970s provided an opportunity to greatly improve the sound quality possible in theaters. Unfortunately, most theaters remained equipped with the abysmal audio systems that had been installed in the 1940s and 1950s, and which didn't begin to exploit the potential of Dolby Stereo.

But the release of *Star Wars* in 1977 made theater owners pay attention to the commercial and artistic benefits of better sound quality. In early 1977, only 46 theaters were equipped to play back Dolby Stereo soundtracks. Just one year later, more than 2000 had installed Dolby Stereo decoding.

Star Wars creator George Lucas used the huge success of the film to pursue his goal of vastly improving film-sound quality. Hearing his creation in a typical theater made Lucas realize just how much of his vision was being lost because of poor sound quality. He wanted everyone to hear the soundtrack exactly as he had intended it to be heard.

In addition to building state-of-the-art film post-production studios at Skywalker Ranch, Lucas hired an engineer named Tomlinson Holman to re-think the entire film-sound recording process. Part of Holman's mission was to find ways to improve the playback quality in theaters. The result of "Tom Holman's eXperiment" was THX, a set of patents and technical criteria for film-sound playback equipment and theater acoustics. Implementation of these criteria would ensure that what an audience heard in a movie theater was pretty close to what the engineers heard on the dubbing stage. A theater that met these technical criteria could then bill itself as "THX Certified."

After the commercial and artistic success of THX theaters, the program was expanded to include home-theater products. Manufacturers of A/V products who choose to participate in the Home THX program work with THX engineers to develop home-theater products. In the final stages of development, manufacturers send a sample of the product to the THX division of Lucasfilm, where it is subjected to a battery of tests. If the product correctly implements Home THX processing and meets the criteria established by Lucasfilm, the product can then claim to be "THX Certified." The manufacturer pays a royalty to Lucasfilm on every unit sold. (THX-certified products carry the logo shown in fig.2-9.)

Fig. 2-9 THX-certified products carry the THX logo.

Courtesy Lucasfilm

Just as a THX-certified movie theater delivers a closer representation of the filmmaker's intentions, a THX-certified home-theater system theoretically lets you hear the film soundtrack as it was intended to be heard. The goal of Home THX is to re-create as closely as possible in a home-theater system the sound that the mixing engineers heard on the film dubbing stage.

THX-certified A/V receivers and controllers incorporate certain signal-processing circuits as well as meet a set of technical performance criteria. THX processing also helps overcome the more common distortions that plague film soundtracks when played in the home. Note that THX isn't a competing surround-sound format; it is instead based on such existing surround-sound formats as Dolby Pro Logic, Dolby Digital, and DTS. THX and Dolby aren't mutually exclusive; THX builds on Dolby's strengths to provide the highest possible sound-reproduction quality.

THX-certified controllers and A/V receivers include four processes that Lucasfilm has found to improve the home-theater experience: *re-equalization, surround decorrelation, timbre matching*, and the *subwoofer crossover*. Let's look at each of these processes in detail.

THX Re-equalization

When film mixers set a film soundtrack's tonal balance (how much bass and treble, for example), they are listening in a large dubbing stage nearly the size of a movie theater. Moreover, they mix to achieve good tonal balance in a movie theater full of seats and people. In a typical movie theater, high frequencies (treble) are attenuated (reduced in volume) compared with lower frequencies. This is due to several factors. First, high frequencies are absorbed more readily by air than low frequencies over a movie theater's long speaker-to-listener distances. Second, movie-theater sound-system calibration standards call for attenuated high frequencies. Third, a theater's reverberation time is shorter at high frequencies because of the sound-absorption characteristics of seats and draperies. The mixing engineers therefore make the soundtrack bright (too much treble) to compensate for the treble attenuation in a large theater. The end result is a natural sound when the soundtrack is reproduced in a movie theater. When you play that same soundtrack in your living room, however, the sound is too bright. THX processing therefore includes a *re-equalization* circuit that reduces the amount of treble on playback so you hear a more natural balance in your home theater. Re-equalization is, in my view, the most important of the THX technologies.

Determining the re-equalization circuit's characteristics (how much to reduce the treble, and at what frequency) was solved in an ingenious way. Tomlinson Holman played film soundtracks on a home-theater system for the engineers who originally mixed them. The engineers were asked to adjust an equalizer in front of them until the sound they heard over the home-theater system sounded like what they remembered hearing on the dubbing stage. Holman took note of the equalizer's settings. This process was repeated with many mixers, who made nearly identical changes to the equalizer. Holman used this information to create and patent the THX "re-equalization curve," which removes just the right amount of brightness from film soundtracks for natural-sounding home-theater reproduction.

Re-equalization is an integral part of THX processing. The re-equalization circuit can, however, be defeated in some products when watching sports or concerts that weren't mixed with excessive treble for movie theaters. In addition, the re-equalization part of THX is now available on products that don't incorporate the full suite of THX processing.

THX Surround Decorrelation

The next THX signal-processing technology attempts to make Dolby Surround's monophonic surround channel sound less monophonic. Called *surround decorrelation*, the process slightly changes the sound (specifically, the time and/or phase between the signals in the midrange and treble frequencies) in the left and right surround loudspeakers. This difference between left and right surrounds prevents the "inside-the-head" localization of surround signals that can occur when you sit between two loudspeakers reproducing the same signal. Surround decorrelation produces greater ambience, spaciousness, diffusion, and envelopment from the surround loudspeakers, and widens the area over which listeners hear these characteristics.

You may have noticed the rows of surround speakers mounted on the sidewalls in your local movie theater. This large surround-speaker array naturally delivers a diffuse surround field to the listeners because the audience sits at different distances from each surround speaker. But in a home-theater system with only two surround speakers, there's the danger of hearing the surround speakers directly. THX's surround decorrelation attempts to mimic the impression of a movie theater's surround-speaker array with only two surround speakers.

Surround decorrelation works great with Dolby Surround's monophonic surround channel. But what about when listening to the separate surround channels provided by Dolby Digital and DTS? The answer is that decorrelation is unnecessary when the source contains different left and right surround signals. Note, however, that just because a source may be encoded with a discrete surround format such as Dolby Digital or DTS doesn't necessarily mean that the surround channels aren't monophonic. If the original source had a monophonic surround channel, the DTS- or Dolby Digital–encoded surround channel will also be monophonic. In this case, the "inside-the-head" localization problems mentioned earlier will continue.

THX-certified controllers and A/V receivers with Dolby Digital and/or DTS have a new function called *adaptive decorrelation*. These controllers and receivers turn on the surround decorrelation circuit only when a monophonic surround channel is detected. This automatic switching also occurs during a movie; parts of the soundtrack that contain monophonic surround information are decorrelated. When the surround channel temporarily contains separate signals, surround decorrelation is turned off.

THX Timbre Matching

THX processing includes *timbre matching* to compensate for the different timbres heard from front-arriving and rear-arriving sounds. The term "timbre" (pronounced "tamber") means "the quality given to a sound by its overtones" (*Merriam-Webster's Collegiate Dictionary, Tenth Edition*). The ear perceives the timbres of sounds differently depending on the direction from which they arrive. You can demonstrate this for yourself with a quick experiment. Snap your fingers in front of your face, then at the side of your head. The finger-snap's timbre is "sharper" when it arrives from the side of your head. THX timbre-matching ensures that, as sounds move from in front of to behind the listener (or vice versa), their timbres remain constant.

These processes cannot be invoked individually via most home-theater products. When you select the THX mode on your controller or receiver, all three circuits are activated simultaneously. Some products, however, let you turn off the re-equalization. THX's re-equalization, timbre matching, and adaptive decorrelation are beneficial with discrete digital sources such as DTS and Dolby Digital.

You can easily evaluate the effects of THX processing by simply selecting between straight Pro Logic or Dolby Digital decoding and the THX CINEMA mode on your A/V receiver's remote control. I find that THX processing improves the sound quality by reducing the brightness of the front channels, particularly dialog sibilance (s and ch sounds). The smoother treble results in lower listening fatigue and greater involvement in the film. In addition, the sense of surround envelopment and diffusion is heightened by THX's more seamless surround field along the sides of the room.

THX Subwoofer Crossover

Finally, THX processing includes a *crossover network* that separates bass frequencies from the midrange and treble frequencies. The bass from the main channels (left, center, right) is sent to the SUBWOOFER OUT jack on the back of the controller or receiver, and the rest of the audio spectrum is reproduced by the left and right loudspeakers. This keeps midrange and treble out of the subwoofer, and bass out of the left and right speakers. For the technically minded, the THX crossover frequency is 80Hz, with a fourth-order (24dB/octave) low-pass rolloff and a second-order (12dB/octave) high-pass rolloff.

Note that the SUBWOOFER OUT jack on all THX-certified A/V receivers or controllers carries a carefully specified signal: a monophonic sum of the front three channels filtered above 80Hz. In THX-certified products with Dolby Digital decoding, the subwoofer output is a mix of the LFE channel plus bass from any number of the other five channels. The subwoofer output level, crossover frequency, and crossover slope (how sharply the crossover splits the frequency spectrum) are all precisely defined in THX-certified products.

Products without THX certification don't adhere to any standard for what's contained in the subwoofer out signal—it could contain only the left- and right-channel bass, for example, rather than a mix of all three channels. The subwoofer output level also isn't standardized, and can vary from product to product—as can the crossover frequency and slope. Consequently, mating a subwoofer to a non-THX receiver or controller may be more difficult than with a THX product. There's a greater compatibility among products that share THX certification.

THX Power-Amplifier Performance in A/V Receivers

In addition to the processes just described, THX certification of A/V receivers, controllers, and power amplifiers also includes a high standard of technical performance. Lucasfilm doesn't publicize these performance criteria outside its pool of licensees, but some of the specifications have leaked out. The THX test conditions are designed to emulate how the product is used in the real world when reproducing film soundtracks.

First, a THX-certified A/V receiver has five amplifier channels, not four. Some receiver manufacturers try to get away with providing only a single amplifier channel for the left and right surround loudspeakers; but because THX processing includes surround decorrelation (making the left and right surround signals slightly different), it follows that two separate amplifier channels must be used.

Second, a THX-certified receiver must produce a minimum of 80W across the front three channels and 50W to the two surround channels.

This measurement is made with the amplifier driving an 8 ohm impedance (the ohm is the unit of resistance to electrical current; impedance is the electrical resistance provided by a loudspeaker) and with all five amplifier channels driven simultaneously.

Many loudspeakers have impedances of less than 8 ohms, which puts more demands on the receiver's power amplifiers. A low-impedance speaker draws more electrical current than a high-impedance speaker, which makes the receiver work harder. When driving loudspeakers with an impedance of 3.2 ohms, a THX-certified receiver must provide 211Wpc (that is, 211 watts per channel) to each of the three front channels and 125Wpc to each of the two surround channels.

Buying a THX-certified receiver guarantees this level of technical performance from the receiver's power amplifiers. THX certification also means that the product incorporates the four technologies just described (re-equalization, surround decorrelation, timbre matching, and the subwoofer crossover). Finally, the THX logo on the front of a home theater product assures you that the product meets other criteria that have been judged important by Lucasfilm engineers in the reproduction of film soundtracks.

THX Power-Amplifier Performance

The power requirements for THX certification in separate power amplifiers are more stringent than for the power-amplifier sections of A/V receivers. Otherwise, the certification criteria are the same. A separate power amplifier must simultaneously deliver a minimum of 100Wpc to each of five channels when driving an 8 ohm load. When driving a low-impedance load (3.2 ohms), a test condition that simulates driving low-impedance loudspeakers, the amplifier must deliver 250Wpc across all five channels. In other words, a THX-certified power amplifier must deliver a total continuous output power of a whopping 1250W. This figure is contrasted with the 883W of total output power required of the THX-certified A/V receiver. ("Continuous" in this context doesn't mean that the amplifier can deliver this high power indefinitely, but over a period of minutes.)

A THX-certified power amplifier will therefore be large and heavy. The criteria for THX certification ensure that the listener/viewer will never hear the amplifier run out of power or change its sound quality during loud peaks. When driving THX-certified loudspeakers (described in Chapter 6), a THX-certified power amplifier will also reproduce the full impact and dynamic range of film soundtracks.

THX Certification of Loudspeakers

Loudspeakers that meet the THX standard are designed to deliver a sonic presentation similar to what you would hear in a THX-certified movie theater or a film dubbing stage. The specific criteria for THX loudspeaker performance are:

Frequency response. The loudspeaker must reproduce all frequencies without emphasizing one range of frequencies over another. A loudspeaker that reproduces all frequencies accurately is called "flat," which describes the shape of its frequency-response curve. For example, a loudspeaker that had too much treble or not enough bass wouldn't pass THX certification. The loudspeaker must also reproduce the frequency extremes (low bass and high treble) at the same level as other frequencies. Subwoofers can also be THX-certified.

Dynamic range. Dynamic range is the difference in volume between loud and quiet sounds. The loudspeaker system must be capable of resolving low-level subtleties such as leaves rustling or wind blowing, but also the liftoff of *Apollo 13*. Dynamic range is measured in decibels (dB), a unit that expresses the volume of sounds.

An issue related to dynamic range is a loudspeaker's sensitivity—the measure of how much sound (in dB) a loudspeaker produces for a given amount of amplifier power (one watt). A THX-certified loudspeaker must have a certain sensitivity in order to reproduce loud parts of a film soundtrack without the amplifier running out of power. (See Chapters 4 and 6 for a complete description of loudspeaker sensitivity.)

Precise localization of onscreen sounds. Actions on the screen should be accompanied by sounds that appear to come from the direction of the screen. This is the job of the three front loudspeakers.

A continuous soundstage. As a sound travels from one loudspeaker to the next, it should do so smoothly rather than jump from one loudspeaker to another.

Dialog intelligibility. There's nothing worse than watching a movie and straining to hear the dialog. THX improves dialog intelligibility, even when the dialog must compete with music and loud special effects. A loudspeaker's dispersion pattern (the way it spreads sound in various directions) must be carefully controlled to reduce unwanted acoustic reflections from the room's walls and ceiling. This provides good dialog intelligibility, a continuous soundstage, and precise localization of onscreen sounds.

Surround diffusion. The surround loudspeakers must produce a sense of diffuse ambience, with no apparent source of direction. The surround loudspeakers are of special design to provide this impression, and THX's electronic processing (surround decorrelation) further enhances the sense of envelopment in the film's "atmosphere."

You should know that THX-certified loudspeakers are designed to create in your home an experience similar to that of the movie theater. While that's a laudable goal, it is achieved at the expense of musical fidelity, in my experience. Simply put, THX-certified loudspeakers don't sound as good on music as loudspeakers designed first and foremost for accurate musical reproduction. Because most of us use our home-theater systems for music listening, you may want to think carefully before buying a THX-certified loudspeaker system.

THX Reference Level

THX also specifies a recommended playback volume, called the *THX Reference Level.* Controllers and receivers have digital volume readouts (or markings around the volume knob) that show you a number either above or below THX reference level. For example, if the volume display reads "-5," the volume is set 5dB below THX reference level. THX reference level reproduces dialog at an average level of 75dB. (Setting up a system for THX reference level is described in Chapter 9.)

THX Select, THX Ultra, and THX Ultra2

To make THX processing available in lower-priced products, Lucasfilm has split the Home THX certification into two quality levels: THX Select and THX Ultra. THX Ultra is identical to plain old THX; products that would once have been certified "THX" are now labeled "THX Ultra." The "Select" designation has lower performance criteria, and applies to products that will be used in smaller rooms that are less demanding of power amplifiers and loudspeakers. Only A/V receivers and loudspeakers are candidates for Select certification: separate controllers and power amplifiers must conform to the original THX requirements, and will be labeled "THX Ultra."

THX Select-certified receivers can have lower output power than THX Ultra products, and THX Select loudspeakers don't need to meet the stringent directivity and power-handling requirements of the original THX program. THX Select A/V receivers will still incorporate the four Lucasfilm technologies that better translate a film soundtrack to the home: re-equalization to remove excessive treble, surround decorrelation to increase the sense of surround envelopment, timbre matching to provide smooth movements of sound, and the THX subwoofer crossover to blend the subwoofer with the main loudspeakers.

THX Ultra2 is a combination of new performance criteria for switching video signals in A/V receivers and controllers, as well as a new signal-processing algorithm for creating 7.1-channel playback from 5.1-channel sources. As described in Chapter 7 (Video Displays), progressive-scan DVD players and HDTV sources output a wider-bandwidth video signal than conventional interlaced DVD players and non-HD sources (VHS, laserdisc, NTSC tuners). Some A/V receivers and controllers lack sufficient bandwidth in their video-switching circuits to pass these signals without alteration. The result can be a reduction in high-frequency video information, and a loss of fine picture details. Products bearing the Ultra2 certification meet Lucasfilm's criteria for video bandwidth.

THX Ultra2 uses seven channels of amplification to play back any multichannel-encoded program through a fixed seven-speaker/one subwoofer layout. In the THX Ultra2 Cinema mode or THX MusicMode, all program material with 5.1 channels or more is auto-detected and proprietary processing is applied that blends the directional and ambient surround information for reproduction through four surround speakers—two side surround speakers and two back-surround speakers. Ultra2 receivers and controllers also feature switchable Boundary Gain Compensation (BGC) to reduce boomy bass caused by positioning loudspeakers near a wall.

Loudspeakers that meet the new THX Ultra2 requirements have different directional characteristics that reportedly produces a smoother tonal balance over a wider listening area. THX Ultra2-certified subwoofers have bass extension to 20Hz or below. Products meeting the Ultra2 specification carry the logo shown in fig.2-10.

Fig. 2-10 Products meeting the new THX Ultra2 certification bear this logo.

LUCASFILM

THX.

U L T R A2

Courtesy Lucasfilm

Should You Choose a THX-Certified System?

Despite the tight specifications for THX-certified electronics and loudspeaker systems, each product or system from each manufacturer has its own sonic signature. Just because a product is THX-certified, don't assume that you'll like its sound or that it will fit your system. Similarly, many worthy products are *not* THX-certified; their manufacturers simply choose not to participate in the THX licensing program. Whether or not a product is THX-certified is only one variable in making a purchasing decision. (More information about THX certification of specific products, and whether you should consider them, can be found in Chapters 4, 5, 6, and 8.)

Overall, the THX program has contributed substantially to the quality of home-theater sound. By adding signal processing, and standardizing home-theater playback electronics and loudspeaker systems, Home THX provides a greater assurance that what you hear at home is closer to what the filmmakers intended you to hear.

3 Source Components: DVD, VHS Tape, D-VHS, PVR, HDTV Set-top Boxes, DSS, DVD-Audio, and Super Audio CD

As discussed in Chapter 1, a source component reads audio and video information from a recording medium and presents that information to the rest of the home-theater system. The video signal is sent to the video monitor, and the audio signal drives your home-theater receiver or controller, power amplifiers, and loudspeakers. Audio/video source components include DVD players, VHS videocassette decks, HDTV set-top boxes, and DSS satellite dishes. You can see in fig.3-1 that the source components are at the very beginning of the playback chain, supplying signals to the rest of your home theater. In this chapter we'll look more closely at each of these formats, as well as at home-theater software. Knowing the strengths and limitations of each format will help you decide which components are right for your home-theater system.

VHS Tape

The most popular source for watching movies at home is undoubtedly the VHS cassette. In fact, the VHS video cassette recorder, or VCR, is one of the most successful consumer products of all time. VHS is unique among the audio/video source components in that nearly all VHS machines also record audio and video programs. This feature lets you record programs when you're away from home or otherwise occupied, then watch the recorded programs at your leisure, a feature known as *time shifting*.

VHS's popularity has been fueled by the widespread availability of rental tapes at reasonable prices—nearly everyone in America lives within a few miles of a video rental store. Moreover, the cost of renting tapes

Fig. 3-1 Source components supply audio and video signals to the rest of your home-theater system.

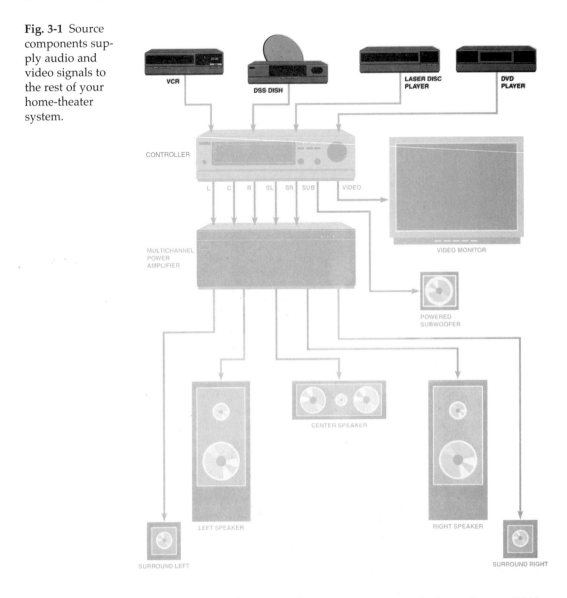

is negligible, and you can buy most pre-recorded movies on VHS for less than $15 each. VHS recording and viewing are thus convenient, ubiquitous, and inexpensive. The drawback of VHS tape is its picture—of all the source components, VHS has the lowest quality of image.

Video quality can be measured in several ways, one of which is by *horizontal lines of resolution*. The greater the number of lines of resolution, the better the picture—specifically, the finer the detail that can be resolved. While VHS can deliver about 240 lines of resolution, laserdisc provides 450 lines, DVD 720 lines, and HDTV up to 1920 lines. Other technical factors make these sources superior to VHS in additional ways, but the result is that DVD and DSS provide greater clarity and sharpness, more freedom from horizontal lines across your picture, and less color bleeding (colors in one object spilling over into surrounding areas). VHS provides poor color resolution, less-well-defined edges, and a general blurring of fine detail.

Here are a couple of quick tests for evaluating and comparing the quality of video sources. Look at a scene with a bright patch of red, such as a car or a sweater. The lower-quality source will render the red object as a blob whose bright hue bleeds past its edges. A higher-quality source will show detail within and a sharp edge around the red object. To evaluate resolution of fine detail, look in actors' eyes: With a low-resolution source you can't distinguish detail in the eyes, which become coarse dark-and-light patches on an actor's face. A high-resolution source will show subtle variations in shadow, the whites of the eyes, and the pupil.

Fortunately, VHS tape is capable of delivering high-quality sound. Every prerecorded VHS tape made in the past 15 years or so has been recorded in a sound format called *VHS HiFi*, short for VHS High Fidelity. VHS HiFi records two audio channels on the tape in the same space occupied by the video signal, but at a different frequency and a different depth in the tape's magnetic coating. The HiFi audio tracks are read by the spinning video head, and consequently provide superb audio quality. VHS's HiFi audio channels are nearly always encoded with Dolby Surround. When played back through a home-theater system equipped with a Dolby Pro Logic decoder, the sound quality of VHS can be excellent.

Before the invention of HiFi audio channels in 1984, VHS tape's sound quality was dismal—noisy, dull, deficient in treble, and unable to reproduce the dynamic impact of movie soundtracks or concert videos. All VHS tapes still contain the old audio tracks, called the *linear* tracks because they're recorded in two thin strips at the edge of the tape, rather than along with the video information as a frequency-modulated signal over the tape's full width. Some VHS machines made today still lack the ability to read HiFi tracks. Needless to say, a VHS machine that can read HiFi tracks is essential if you're going to feed the audio signal through your home-theater system.

The VHS format has enjoyed a long and successful life. Its days are numbered, however, as DVD takes over as the standard format for playing movies in the home. As we'll see later in this chapter, DVD offers vastly better picture and sound quality, special features not possible on VHS tape, no wear from repeated playings, instant random access to any point in the movie, and a host of other advantages. With an average of more than two VCRs in every American household, however, and VHS rental outlets in nearly every grocery store, the VHS format will be around for some time.

How to Choose a VHS VCR

There are several things you should know when shopping for a VHS machine. First, the unit should have HiFi playback capability. Without this feature, you'll never get even mediocre home-theater sound. Every VCR also has a tuner to receive television broadcasts. To record in stereo, the VHS machine must have a tuner capable of receiving stereo broadcasts. The letters MTS (for Multichannel Television Sound) on the machine indicate that the tuner can receive stereo broadcasts.

VHS machines also vary in their picture quality. Home-theater magazines test and report on a variety of machines for sound and picture quality and ease of use. You can rely on some magazine reviews, or simply record on several machines yourself in a store and compare their picture qualities. All of the VHS machines under evaluation must be connected to the same video monitor for the comparisons.

Most VHS machines today are loaded with such features as slow motion and still frame, also known as special effects. Convenience features found only on upper-end machines include a "jog wheel," which can be turned to move the tape quickly forward or back while the image remains visible. Some units will read the time of day encoded in some television broadcasts and set the machine's clock display at the correct time, even after a power failure—no more blinking "12:00" on the time display. Many VHS machines are touted as "four-head," a feature that improves picture quality. One pair of heads are optimized for the two-hour recording speed, the other pair for the slower tape speed that provides six hours of recording time on the same tape.

The VHS format calls for three tape speeds: Standard Play (SP), Super Long Play (SLP), and Extended Play (EP). With a video tape of T-120 (120 minutes) length, these speeds correlate with record/play times of two hours (SP), four hours (SLP), or six hours (EP). Most VHS machines can't record in SLP speed, but will play in all three. As the tape speed slows, the picture quality degrades dramatically. The EP mode should be used only under extreme circumstances, as when programming the machine to record many television shows while you're away for an extended period.

A feature called a *flying erase head* allows you to record from one machine onto a machine equipped with a flying erase head without glitches at the edit points. For example, let's say you recorded an event with a camcorder and want to transfer only the interesting parts to VHS. The camcorder is put in PLAY mode, the VHS machine in RECORD. At the end of every section of the camcorder tape you want to keep, you'd put the VHS machine in PAUSE while you found the next scene on the camcorder tape you wanted to copy to VHS. Without a flying erase head, the VHS tape would preserve an annoyingly visible glitch at the point where the tape was put in PAUSE. With a flying erase head, the edit point is seamless—just like the edits you see on television. A flying erase head adds $50 to $75 to the cost of a VHS machine.

A variation on the VHS format, called *S-VHS*, provides excellent video quality but has never caught on the way conventional VHS has. In S-VHS, the video signal's brightness and color information (called Y and C, respectively) are recorded separately and with a wider bandwidth, a technique that greatly improves picture quality. S-VHS machines and tapes (both blank and pre-recorded) are expensive and not widely available. If you find VHS picture quality unacceptable for your recordings, you'll have to live with the expense and inconvenience of S-VHS.

Some videophiles still use the Beta-format VCR, the original home-video recording system, invented by Sony. Beta provides a better picture quality than VHS, but lost out in the marketplace largely because of VHS's longer playing time. If you want superior picture quality and don't care about compatibility with VHS tapes, the Beta format provides an alternative. Astonishingly, Sony still offers new Beta-format VCRs and blank tapes.

Connecting a VHS machine to your television and home-theater system is described in Chapter 9.

D-VHS

A new type of VHS recorders, called *D-VHS* VCRs, can capture digitally broadcast programs on D-VHS tape. The machines connect to a digital television set-top box (or to an HDTV set that has an integral ATSC tuner) and can record both standard-definition and high-definition digital television signals. D-VHS machines will also record and play back standard VHS tapes. Because the D-VHS machine stores a digital video bitstream as digital ones and zeros, rather than as an analog signal, the video quality is indistinguishable from that of digital television broadcasts. D-VHS machines record in the "native resolution" of the source signal; that is, if the high-definition broadcast is in the 1080i format (1080 lines, interlaced scanning), the D-VHS machine records and plays back 1080i. You must have a high-definition television or HD set-top box to record HD signals on a D-VHS recorder.

The connection between the D-VHS machine, signal source, and video display is through a FireWire (IEEE1394) cable, or Digital Visual Interface (DVI). (Both these interfaces are described in Chapter 7.) D-VHS machines can be easier to operate than analog VCRs because of this FireWire or DVI connection; the machine can be controlled by on-screen icons rather than via a conventional remote control with lots of tiny buttons. FireWire also allows D-VHS machines to be HAVi-enabled. As described in Chapter 7, the Home Audio/Video interoperability standard allows your home-theater system to operate as a single "smart" system rather than as a collection of "dumb" boxes. The first D-VHS machines were introduced in Japan in late 1999, and started becoming popular in mid-2002.

The D-VHS format provides for three bit-rates, resulting in three possible recording durations using the same tape. The HS mode records four hours of full HD quality at a bit-rate of 28.2 million bits per second (Mbs); STD mode provides eight hours at a bit-rate of 14.1Mbs; and LS3 records at 4.7Mbs for up to 24 hours of recording time. All times are based on a DF-480 cassette, the longest tape available. The DF-420 cassette provides seven hours in STD mode, and the DF-300 tape can hold five hours in STD mode. Obviously, the higher the bit-rate, the better the picture quality. For comparison, DVDs have a variable bit-rate that averages about 3.5Mbs. The highest-resolution HDTV format (1920 x 1080 pixels) has a data-rate of 19.2Mbs. Thus, the HS mode can record full 1080i high-definition signals with no loss of picture quality. Medium-quality STD can record either 480i or 480p signals. The lowest quality LS3 mode records analog NTSC broadcasts by converting them to an MPEG-2 bitstream. Note that a DF-480 tape can store a whopping 44 gigabytes of data.

D-VHS also presents the possibility of making movies in the HD format commercially available. Several studios, including Fox, Universal, DreamWorks, and Artisan have announced that they will release films on D-VHS on a trial basis. Although D-VHS offers significantly better picture quality than DVD (and even has the potential of better picture quality than broadcast HD), consumers may not want to return to a tape-based format after becoming so enamored of DVD with its wealth of features that only an optical-disc format can provide. In addition, the copy-protection system developed by JVC, called *D-Theater*, hasn't been adopted by other manufacturers. Consequently, tapes made on one brand of machine may not play on those made by another company.

Personal Video Recorder (PVR)

The *Personal Video Recorder* (fig.3-2) is an entirely new product category that threatens to displace VHS tape as the dominant method of home-video recording. Like a VHS recorder, a PVR records television shows for later viewing. But the similarities end there. In fact, the PVR is much more than a replacement for the VCR.

First, a PVR records the audio and video signals digitally on an integral large-capacity hard-disk drive. Second, the PVR can record and play at the same time, allowing you to "rewind," "fast-forward," pause, or advance the program in slow motion while it's being recorded. Let's say you're watching a TV program in real time as it's being recorded on the PVR. If you want to take a break, you can pause the PVR playback, then resume watching at the spot where you left off, even while the rest of the show continues being recorded. Similarly, if you had set a PVR to record an hour-long program starting at 8pm, you could start watching the show from the beginning at 8:30.

Fig. 3-2 Personal Video Recorders store audio and video programs on a hard-disk drive.

Courtesy TiVo Inc.

In addition to these startling new features, the PVR can be programmed to automatically record programs you're likely to be interested in. The PVR is connected by modem to the host company's computer and program guide that recognizes, based on your previous recording activity, which programs you like. And it can be instructed to record those shows, and even similar shows you haven't specifically told it to record. Some PVRs let you enter key words relating to programs of interest; the central computer to which your PVR is connected will then search the database of available programs and tell your PVR to record that show. For example, the PVR could automatically record all movies featuring Robert De Niro. The latest programming information is downloaded into your PVR every night through the modem. The central computer can even update your PVR's operating software while you sleep.

The PVR organizes recorded shows into "channels," then lists them in an onscreen menu. For example, all news shows would be categorized together; comedies would occupy another "channel," and sports a third. Because the video and audio are recorded digitally on a hard-disk drive, access to any program is nearly instantaneous. Similarly, skipping commercials is extremely fast and easy.

These features transform the way television is watched. While the VCR allowed time-shifting, the PVR goes much further in eliminating broadcast times as a constraint in television viewing. You simply turn on the PVR and your TV, select which shows you want to watch from the PVR's menu, and watch them whenever you want. Moreover, the storage capacities of PVRs have greatly increased to the point where devices that can store 300 hours' worth of programming are commonplace. This amount of storage lets you record virtually everything of even remote interest to you; when you sit down to watch, you select only the programs of most interest. The PVR makes possible the closest thing to "video on demand."

One manufacturer of PVRs charges a monthly fee for the subscription service that performs these automated recording functions. Another charges more for their PVR, but no monthly fee.

The PVR's video and audio quality ranges from poor to excellent, depending on the quality mode selected. You can increase the PVR's recording time by selecting a lower video quality, which produces a lower bit-rate for storage on the machine's internal hard-disk drive. In high-quality mode, video and audio consume about 1 gigabyte per hour, and most PVRs have expansion jacks that allow you to add to your unit's storage capacity. Prices of PVRs have dropped dramatically in recent months, and storage capacities have increased. With PVRs now costing less than $100, they have become a serious challenge to the dominance of VHS tape. Still, the VHS/VCR format combines two functions that neither PVR nor DVD alone can provide: removable media (you can remove the tape from a VHS recorder and play it on another machine) and the ability to record.

PVR manufacturers have devised a novel trick to overcome this limitation: building in the ability to send a video program over the Internet as an e-mail attachment. You can thus record home movies and send them to a relative, or share a favorite program with a friend. Needless to say, movie studios and television networks (the so-called "content providers") are opposed to such a scheme, and have filed lawsuits to prevent the sale of these Internet-enabled PVRs.

Laserdisc

From its commercial launch in 1980 to the arrival of DVD in 1997, laserdisc was the source format of choice for quality home theater. Invented by Philips in the late 1970s, laserdisc for years offered the highest video and audio quality of any consumer format. Moreover, LD has evolved to accommodate new technology while remaining "back-compatible" with the earlier players. Back-compatibility means that newer laserdiscs made with today's technology will still play on even the first laserdisc players.

A laserdisc is a 12"-diameter disc made from two thinner discs of plastic bonded together. It is a two-sided medium—program material is recorded on both sides of the disc. The video and audio signals are encoded on the LD in a spiral track of microscopic "pits" impressed in the plastic, as on a CD. When a low-power laser beam is reflected from the disc surface, the pit edges reduce the reflected beam's intensity and the flat areas reflect the beam at full strength. This varying-intensity laser beam is converted into a varying-intensity electrical signal, then decoded into audio and video signals that can feed the rest of your home-theater system.

A laserdisc carries high-quality video, two analog audio tracks, and two digital audio tracks. The digital audio tracks, called *PCM* (Pulse Code Modulation) tracks, were added to the format in 1987. Although all players made since about 1989 can read the digital audio tracks, nearly all LDs still include the analog tracks as well, to ensure that the discs are compatible with older machines. You can select which tracks you want to hear with the laserdisc player's remote control. Both the analog and digital audio tracks on nearly all laserdiscs are Dolby Surround–encoded.

A laserdisc player is similar to a CD player, only bigger. In both machines, a drawer opens to accept a disc, which is then loaded horizontally. In fact, many LD players are so-called "combi" (for "combination") players that play both LDs and CDs. Some models even include DVD playback. A laserdisc player's rear panel will have a video output and a left-and-right-channel audio output. You simply run a video cable from the player's video output to the video input on your audio/video (A/V) receiver or controller. A 2-channel audio cable carries the laserdisc's Dolby Surround–encoded signal to your home-theater receiver or controller for Dolby decoding.

Many home-theater systems still include laserdisc machines to play existing libraries, but the format is essentially dead. DVD is vastly superior in every way, less expensive, and a mass-market item rather than the niche market occupied by laserdisc.

Digital Satellite System (DSS)

The Digital Satellite System, or *DSS*, is an enormously popular method of receiving programming for your home-theater system. DSS's overwhelming success in the marketplace can be attributed to its high video and audio quality, moderate cost, and vast range of programming. As of this writing, DSS dishes are available for less than $150 (after manufacturer's rebate). Programming ranges in price from about $20 per month to more than $100, depending on your selection of premium channels and the number of PPV (pay-per-view) programs watched.

DSS is a satellite-based system for delivering high-quality digital video and audio programming to your home. Unlike old satellite television technology—which required dishes several feet in diameter, large motor drives, costly installation, and multiple decoder boxes—DSS works with an easy-to-install, fixed-mount dish only 18" in diameter. The new dishes can be so small because the DSS satellites in earth orbit relaying the signals are much more powerful than the so-called "C-band" satellites that deliver signals to the large dishes common in rural areas and sports bars. Moreover, because DSS is a digital system, it is largely immune from the noise, screen snow, and interference of the older satellite technology. (A DSS dish and receiver are shown in fig.3-3.)

DSS is also becoming the primary medium for getting high-definition (HD) video signals into your home. DSS systems introduced after late 1999 can receive standard-definition and high-definition signals from a single oval dish slightly larger than the 18" round dish of non-HD systems. Many pay-per-view films are now transmitted in the HD format. To receive HD signals by satellite, you need an HD-capable dish and HD-capable receiver box.

Fig. 3-3 A DSS dish is about the size of a large pizza; a DSS receiver is about the size of a VCR.

Courtesy Sony Electronics Inc.

A DSS dish sits on your roof facing south toward the three satellites in geostationary orbit (the satellites remain in the same position above the earth). The dish receives a combined digital video and audio signal transmitted from the DirecTV Castle Rock Broadcast Center in Castle Rock, Colorado, or from the competing EchoStar facility, also in Colorado. The audio/video signal is sent from Colorado to one of three satellites, from which it is relayed back to earth and your dish. A DSS receiver (a box about the size of a VCR player) unscrambles the combined digital video and audio signal and converts them into the analog form required by your video monitor and home-theater audio system.

DSS Programming

A variety of service providers deliver programming to your DSS dish. The two largest are DirecTV and EchoStar, which are attempting to merge into a single company with more than twenty million subscribers. You must become a subscriber to one of the services to access DSS programming. Some of the programming packages are linked to certain DSS hardware; not every program package is available in every area of the country, or for every brand of DSS dish.

Entry-level programming packages start at about $10 per month, with mid-level packages costing about $20 and full access about $45. On top of these basic services are pay-per-view programs such as recent movies and sporting events. Additional services include Prime Time 24 ($5 per month), which provides the network broadcast signals of ABC, NBC, CBS, Fox, and PBS.

Selecting programs from the DSS menu is simple and direct. The system works much like a computer, with the DSS receiver's remote control functioning as the mouse. A menu appears on the screen listing all the available programs. You can select the program you want to watch by moving a cursor over the desired program and clicking a button on the remote control. The system features a "blockout" function to keep children from viewing certain programming. If you find scanning the TV screen for programming inconvenient, *Satellite Direct* magazine (800-285-5454) offers the same information in easier-to-read paper form.

A good question is, "How does the service provider know how many—and which—pay-per-view programs I've watched?" The answer is that every DSS receiver contains a memory that stores information about which programs have been viewed during the month. The DSS receiver is continuously connected to your phone line, and is polled once a month by a master billing computer.

The phone connection is also used to turn on and off the DSS receiver's descrambling function. After installing a DSS dish and receiver, you call an 800 number to begin service. The computer at the other end of the line reads the receiver's serial number, which is unique to your unit and identifies you to the service provider, and activates the receiver in your home. (This is also how the service provider shuts *off* your service if you don't pay your bill.)

Watching a movie via DSS is considerably different from owning a disc or tape of that movie. A pay-per-view DSS movie costs about $5—much less than buying the movie on laserdisc or DVD. With DSS, you don't need to shop at the video store (or over the Internet) for the movie you want. Instead, you scan the available movies from your couch and select what you want to see. Moreover, you don't need to physically store the disc or tape in your home.

The advantages of having the physical movie in your home are, however, compelling. First, you can start the movie any time you want, not just when it's transmitted by your DSS program provider. Second, you can pause the movie for breaks or if you're interrupted. Third, having the disc in your home lets you repeat certain segments, scan forward or back, and watch the movie as many times as you like. Moreover, many DVDs contain "supplemental material" such as director commentary, theatrical trailers, and other extras not available on DSS. Finally, some films shown on DSS are modified from their original theatrical aspect ratio, a condition unacceptable to many film enthusiasts. With DVD, you virtually always see the film in the aspect ratio the director intended.

Although DSS has the potential of delivering high-definition programming to a wide range of viewers who live outside HD reception areas, it has largely failed in that role. The satellite providers have deemed it in their commercial interests to offer more programs rather than programs in HD. Programs in HD require more of the satellite's bandwidth, which is a fixed commodity. That's unfortunate, because it's still impossible to receive a wide variety of over-the-air HD programming in many parts of the country.

Choosing and Installing a DSS system

Installing a DSS system is fairly simple: The dish is mounted on hardware attached to your roof and a cable is run to the DSS receiver. An installation kit costs about $75 for do-it-yourselfers, with full professional installation costing about $200 (including the kit). Before buying a DSS dish, you must determine if you will want to watch different DSS-sourced programs on different televisions in the house at the same time. If so, the dish must be equipped with a dual Low-Noise Blocking Converter (LNB), and you'll need two DSS receivers. Single-LNB dishes generally can't be upgraded to dual-LNB capability. Note that a single-LNB dish and receiver will send signals to multiple televisions, but without independent channel selection between the sets. Adding this independent channel-selection option increases considerably the up-front costs of installing DSS.

DSS picture and sound quality are determined largely by the quality of the transmitted signal rather than by the quality of the receiver. Consequently, all DSS packages offer comparable video and audio performance. Some DSS receivers have an S-video output, which carries the brightness and color information (called "discrete Y/C") separately. This connection will provide better picture quality than a DSS receiver connected to a video monitor with a standard "composite" video signal. The DSS signal received at the dish is inherently separate, which is why you'll see a benefit from S-video connection. Note that using the S-video output on VHS machines (except S-VHS recorders) and laserdisc players doesn't always confer an advantage, because the signal is stored in those formats without the separation of brightness and color information. HD-compatible DSS receivers provide digital output and component-video connection, the highest quality connection method. (Component video is described in Chapter 7.)

Some DSS units can receive the Dolby Digital signal included in some DSS transmissions. To take advantage of this feature, you need a controller or receiver with a Dolby Digital input. Expect to pay about $100 more for a DSS receiver with Dolby Digital output.

When installing a DSS dish, it's a good idea to run RG-6 coaxial cable to the dish and to remote televisions. RG-6 is a higher-quality cable, with denser shielding and a thicker center conductor compared with conventional RG-59 coaxial cable. RG-6 provides better picture quality, and costs about 25¢ per foot compared with 16¢ per foot for RG-59.

The differences between competing brands of DSS packages are largely in their user interfaces—some models are much easier to use than others. Unfortunately, no method of graphic display or program selection has yet been standardized. Try several systems before you buy; each DSS package has specific advantages and disadvantages.

MPEG-2 Video Compression on DSS

A digital video signal consumes enormous quantities of data—far more than could be practically transmitted over a DSS-type distribution system without drastically limiting the number of program choices. To give you an idea of how many data digital video consumes, a 1-gigabyte hard-disk drive in a computer can store less than a minute of uncompressed digital video—and would take much *longer* than a minute just to read out the data. For comparison, the same 1-gigabyte drive could store 100 minutes of 2-channel, CD-quality digital audio. (This book, with all its text and graphics, consumes about 100 megabytes of data storage.) The wide bandwidth required by a digital video signal must be reduced for DSS to work.

This quandary is solved by reducing the number of bits required to represent the video signal in a process called *video compression*. The compression scheme used for DSS is called MPEG-2. MPEG stands for Moving Pictures Experts Group, the committee formed to establish international standards for video compression. Video-compression schemes such as MPEG-2 reduce the number of bits by more efficient coding of the video image. The scheme exploits similarities in the image from one frame to the next, as well as similarities in the same scene. For example, a scene may include a blue sky that doesn't change much from frame to frame. Rather than encode each *pixel* (picture element, the smallest component of a video signal) of each frame, the compression algorithm exploits this redundancy by using a small number of data to indicate that large areas of the frame are identical to those of the previous frame. This is a simplified explanation; in practice, video compression systems are enormously sophisticated and complex. (Before 1995, DSS used an older, lower-quality video compression scheme called MPEG-1.) MPEG-2 encoding reduces the number of data in a digital video signal from about 168 million bits per second to an average rate of about 3.5 million bits per second. This data rate varies with the amount of action in the video. Moving objects in the picture require more bits than stationary scenes.

DSS picture quality is far superior to those of VHS tape, cable, and broadcast television. The difference is less when DSS is considered against LD, but most viewers agree that DSS offers a sharper picture, with truer color rendering, less "chroma noise" (moving horizontal streaks), and better resolution. Laserdisc offers a slightly softer picture that resolves less fine detail, but has a more "film-like" quality. Of course, the transmitted picture quality is largely dependent on the quality of the source. A poor-quality original will produce a poor-quality DSS signal, no matter how good the transmission format. Recent pay-per-view movies on DSS often use what's called a "D1" digital master as the source—the highest possible quality.

One problem of MPEG-2 compression is a tendency for fast-moving objects to become "pixelated," or converted into small blocks. This phenomenon is similar to the way someone's identity is concealed on a TV news program. Pixelation is particularly apparent if the background is complex rather than a solid color. Fortunately, such artifacts are rare, and will become even rarer as improvements are made to the MPEG-2 compression algorithm. MPEG-2 picture quality can only get better as the technology improves. Note that MPEG-2 *encoding* technology can be updated without making the MPEG-2 *decoder* in your DSS receiver obsolete.

DSS Audio Quality: Dolby Digital and Dolby Surround

A DSS signal contains a Dolby Surround–encoded audio signal along with the MPEG-2 digital video, and, on certain programs, a Dolby Digital signal as well. Some listeners report that the Dolby Surround performance of DSS is inferior to those of VHS tape and laserdisc. Part of the problem is undoubtedly the low-quality digital-to-analog converters built into DSS receivers. Because DSS is a mass-market item, these converters were likely designed for low cost, not high performance. I expect to see aftermarket DSS receivers that incorporate good-sounding DACs from specialty audio companies. Some DSS receivers offer a digital out jack that lets you connect a separate DAC to the receiver. Such outboard converters are usually far superior to those found in DSS receivers. Expect to pay at least $300 for a high-quality outboard DAC. If your controller or A/V receiver has a digital input, you can connect the DSS receiver's digital output directly to your controller and realize improved sound quality. The DSS receiver's converters are replaced by the higher-quality converters built into your controller or A/V receiver.

Set-top Boxes

The *set-top box* (*STB*) is a new breed of source component that connects to a high-definition-ready television set. The STB usually incorporates an HDTV tuner, NTSC (conventional television) tuner, and satellite receiver in one small chassis. The first set-top boxes cost more than $2000; the price has since dropped to less than $700, with further price reductions expected.

The trend has been toward packing more and more functions into the STB, including hard-disk based video recorders and satellite receivers. As its name suggests, the STB often sits on top of your HD-ready TV (fig.3-4).

Fig. 3-4 A set-top box often combines an ATSC tuner, NTSC tuner, DirecTV receiver, and even a PVR in one chassis.

Courtesy Sony Electronics Inc.

The STB as a product category arose because early HDTV sets didn't incorporate an HDTV tuner. These so-called "HD-Ready" sets could display high-definition video signals, but couldn't receive them. Manufacturers split these reception and display functions in these early HD sets because the transmission standard was still changing, and putting integrated HD tuners in HD televisions could have eventually made the sets obsolete. In addition, separating the HD tuner from the set allowed the sets to be priced lower than if the tuner were built in.

You'll see the term *ATSC tuner* associated with set-top boxes. ATSC stands for Advanced Television System Committee, the organization that standardized the technical aspects of HDTV. An ATSC tuner receives over-the-air HD broadcasts from an antenna, and converts the signal to a form your HD-ready television can use. Within the ATSC standard are 18 possible signal formats, all of which can be received and decoded by an ATSC set-top box.

The STB also has an *NTSC tuner* for receiving conventional analog broadcasts. NTSC stands for the National Television System Committee, the body that standardized color television in 1953. NTSC is plain old TV that everyone has been watching for decades.

Most STBs include a satellite receiver for connection to a DSS dish. The STB thus receives signals from satellite, HD terrestrial broadcasts, and analog terrestrial broadcasts, then outputs a signal to your television set. The STB also includes a video upconverter that takes in 480i video (480-line interlaced video, or conventional standard-definition television) from conventional analog television broadcasts and turns it into 1080i for display on an HD-ready television.

All STBs include analog video outputs, such as component video and S-video. Newer models also offer a digital output for direct connection to a digital television. These digital outputs are either FireWire (more technically called IEEE1394, but also called "i.LINK" by Sony) or DVI (Digital Visual Interface). Both connection methods bypass the digital-to-analog converter in the STB, and the analog-to-digital converter in the digital television. Removing these unnecessary conversions from the signal path significantly improves the picture quality. Note that all digital-video connections are encrypted and copy protected to prevent copying of high-resolution digital video. Digital interfaces and copy protection are described in Chapter 7.

Interestingly, most HD-ready televisions aren't connected to a STB. According to recent figures, only one HD-ready television in 17 is fed from a STB. The other sixteen HD-ready televisions display non-HD content, such as DVD and analog broadcasts. This situation is the result of high prices for STBs, along with the dearth of HD programming. As more HD content becomes available, and STB prices drop, a greater number of HD televisions will be paired with a STB.

The recent trend has been to include the ATSC tuner as an integral part of the television rather than having the ATSC tuner in a separate STB. These sets function more like conventional televisions.

When shopping for a STB, the important points to be aware of are the user interface, quality of the upconversion from 480i to 1080i, sensitivity (ability to pick up HD broadcasts), and number and type of video outputs. Some STBs are easy to use; others are frustrating. Try the unit in the store before you buy. Watch 480i sources (analog television broadcast, for example) and look for artifacts in the picture, particularly a jagged stair-step appearance on angled lines.

Just because your set-top box receives digital rather than analog signals doesn't mean you can enjoy worry-free reception. You'll still need an antenna, either on the roof or in the home. Rooftop antennae provide more reliable reception; the motorized variety, which rotates to better lock in on the signal for the best picture quality, might be required in fringe reception areas. Digital television signals are prone to *multipath distortion*, which occurs when the antenna receives a signal directly from the broadcast tower, and an "echo" of the same signal reflected from a building or hillside. Multipath distortion can prevent a set-top box from receiving signals altogether.

Some set-top boxes receive DTV signals more reliably than others. I've heard of cases where two different brands of set-top box were connected to the same antenna, but only one would receive a signal. Unlike analog signals, whose quality is nearly infinitely variable, a DTV set-top box either receives the signal or it doesn't. You'll know if it isn't receiving by seeing a "NO PROGRAM" message on your video monitor.

DVD

The DVD format is nothing short of a revolution in picture and sound quality for home theater. A DVD looks identical to the familiar CD, but contains high-quality *video* as well as sound. When connected to your home-theater system, a DVD player brings you bright, sharp, clear video along with a 5.1-channel, Dolby Digital–encoded soundtrack. In addition to providing superb picture and sound, the DVD format's astonishing array of features sounds like some futuristic dream.

DVD has been a massive commercial success, with more than twenty million players sold between the format's introduction in May 1997 and mid 2002. Players are available for less than $100, and you can rent a wide selection of DVD titles at many locations for $1 or $2 each. In just a few years, DVD has become a mass-market item (generally defined as an installed base of more than ten million players) and is rapidly replacing VHS tape for movie playback in the home. (DVD once stood for Digital Video Disc, then Digital Versatile Disc. According to the official DVD body, the letters DVD are no longer an initialism.)

A DVD player's appearance is similar to that of a CD player, with the familiar-looking disc-loading drawer, remote control, and front-panel display. A DVD player feeds your television through one of several video-connection methods, and sends the Dolby Digital soundtrack to your home-theater receiver or controller. Installing a DVD player in your system couldn't be easier; it requires just two sets of cables (one video, one audio) and a few minutes of time.

DVD's popularity has made the stand-alone CD player nearly a thing of the past. Because all DVD players also play CDs, there's no need to buy a separate CD player. Some DVD machines also play MP3-encoded discs for even greater versatility.

A DVD can hold as much as 135 minutes of picture and sound on a single disc side. The format has the capacity for dual layers of information on each of two disc sides, which brings the potential playing time up to a whopping four-and-a-half hours. More than 90% of all movies can be accommodated by only a single layer of data on a single-sided DVD.

DVD Picture and Sound Quality

Although it's easy to think of a DVD as just a miniature laserdisc, the two formats couldn't be more different. First, DVD is a purely digital format: the video and audio data are encoded with digital ones and zeros. By contrast, the laserdisc carries its information as analog signals, which are much more prone to degradation when stored or transmitted. DVD uses the same video compression system, MPEG-2, as the DSS satellite format described earlier in this chapter. Every DVD player is outfitted with an MPEG-2 decoder chip to "decompress" the video information.

DVD provides an advantage over VHS and even laserdisc in resolution of fine detail, sharpness, color rendering, and freedom from video "noise." VHS and laserdiscs suffer from an artifact called "chroma noise," a phenomenon that adds grainy lines over saturated colors. DVD's lack of chroma noise gives it an even cleaner-looking picture than LD.

Another reason DVD provides a sharper picture than VHS and laserdisc is that a spinning laserdisc or moving tape has slight variations in speed. These irregularities show up as a "roughness" on the edges of vertical objects, as each scanning line doesn't precisely line up with the scanning lines above and below it. Conversely, all DVD players have a digital circuit called a "frame buffer" that stores one entire video frame in a computer memory chip, then releases that frame with perfect time precision. The result is a sharper, more detailed picture. This difference is grossly obvious on small text, such as in film credits.

So far I've described DVD's video quality as a step above laserdisc, itself a format of very high quality. But in relation to VHS tape, there's simply no comparison. The difference in picture quality between VHS and DVD is like the difference between a faxed copy of a photograph and the original.

If you don't have a Dolby Digital decoder in your A/V receiver or controller, you can tell the DVD player to output a 2-channel Dolby Surround–encoded signal that your receiver can decode. Every DVD player includes a "downmix" converter that converts the Dolby Digital audio channels into a Dolby Surround–encoded signal. You won't get all the benefits of Dolby Digital (described in Chapter 2), but the sound quality will still be excellent.

DVD Features

In addition to offering the highest quality of picture and sound, DVD also provides unprecedented features. A single DVD's audio tracks can contain up to three languages and 32 sets of subtitles. Although this feature lets film studios release a film in a single edition that will serve many different markets around the world, it also lets you watch a foreign film in different ways. For example, if you had a DVD of Akira Kurosawa's *Ran*, you could watch it in Japanese with English subtitles, or in English with no subtitles.

DVD technology also opens the possibility of choosing the camera angle at which you see the scene. One DVD demonstration disc is of a countryside as seen from a moving train. By pressing buttons on the DVD player's remote control, you can see the scene from the front of the engine, the left or right side of the train, or from the caboose, looking back.

Unlike a VHS tape or laserdisc that is formatted with a single aspect ratio, some DVDs let you choose: A menu comes up before the film, offering choices of language, subtitle, and aspect ratio. Other DVDs with dual aspect ratio record the widescreen version on one disc side and the pan&scan version on the other. Not all DVDs, however, offer selectable aspect ratios. Those marked "4:3" provide only the inferior pan&scan version.

Nearly all DVDs made today are marked "16:9 Enhanced," "Widescreen Enhanced," or "Enhanced for 16:9 Displays." All of these terms mean the same thing: that the video is presented in the *anamorphic* format. This technique, described later in this chapter, provides vastly better video quality when the DVD is displayed on a widescreen TV or front-projector system.

Because DVD is an optically read format, skipping to certain scenes is nearly instantaneous. A DVD has index marks at key scenes in a film, or at the beginnings of songs in a concert or music-video presentation. In addition, some DVDs have screens that display the chapter numbers, along with a still-frame or short moving clip that identifies a key scene. To access that chapter, you simply choose its still-frame or chapter number from the screen; in less than a second you're viewing the chosen scene.

This instant search capability, along with the DVD's digital nature, confers some unique features. For example, let's say a film was originally rated R in its theatrical release, but you want to watch it with your children. You can tell the DVD player to play the PG-13, PG, or G version of the film—the player will automatically and seamlessly skip the offending scenes. Your children will never know the scenes were omitted.

Just because the DVD format can provide 5.1 audio channels in the Dolby Digital format doesn't mean that all DVDs actually contain 5.1 audio channels. Older films originally released in mono will be presented in mono on the Dolby Digital soundtrack. Films first presented in Dolby Surround will be presented on the DVD with four audio channels (left, center, right, and one surround channel). Some DVD packages indicate the number of channels, such as 2.0 (stereo), 4.0 (Dolby Surround), 5.0 (Dolby Digital or DTS with no LFE channel), or 5.1 (Dolby Digital or DTS with the LFE channel). The presence of the ".1" indicates that the soundtrack carries a Low-Frequency Effects channel for additional bass impact.

A limited number of DVDs contain a DTS soundtrack. To play these discs, your DVD player must recognize the DTS bitstream, and your controller or receiver must be equipped with a DTS decoder. DTS-compatible DVD players are identified by the DTS logo on the front panel.

How to Choose a DVD Player

Just as CD players vary in sound quality, some DVD players provide higher-quality video and audio than other machines. Budget machines start at about $100, with many players falling in the $200–$400 range. Higher-quality players from the major electronics companies cost between $800 and $1200. High-end units from specialty companies can run as much as $5000.

One distinguishing feature of DVD machines is the type of video output provided. While all DVD players offer conventional *composite video* (RCA jacks), and nearly all include *S-video* output, the better players will also have *component-video* output. Component video, described in Chapter 7, offers a dramatic improvement in picture quality over composite video and even S-video. You need a video monitor with component-video input to take advantage of this feature; TV sets with component-video input are becoming increasingly common. Even some $200 DVD players now offer component-video output.

DVD players convert the digital video on the DVD into analog video for display on a television or video projector. But with more and more video displays operating digitally, it makes sense to keep the video signal in the digital domain rather than subject the signal to multiple digital-to-analog and analog-to-digital conversions. To that end, the industry has adopted the SDI/DVI interface for DVD players. This interface, described in detail in Chapter 7, provides a direct digital connection between a DVD player (or any other digital source) and a video display capable of accepting a digital DVI input.

Large differences among DVD players can be seen in their user interfaces, which determine how easy or difficult the player is to operate. Some are so poorly designed that even professionals in the field of consumer electronics (including me) have a hard time figuring them out. Pick up the remote controls of the players you're considering buying and go through their setup menus. You'll quickly find out which player has the best user interface.

Many DVD players (and probably all DVD players in the future) have the capability to play back high-resolution multichannel digital audio in the DVD-Audio or Super Audio CD (SACD) formats. Described later in this chapter, DVD-Audio or SACD adds to the player's price.

Not all DVD players will play every disc format. For example, some DVD players won't play discs made on CD recorders (CD-R, CD-RW), and most won't play discs in the MP3 format. When shopping for a DVD player, be sure it is compatible with the types of discs you intend to play. One day, all DVD players will be "universal" machines that play all formats.

A final but important consideration when choosing a DVD player is the unit's sound quality when playing music. If you use the DVD player's analog outputs, the quality of the machine's digital-to-analog converters and analog-output stage will affect the sound. If you connect the DVD player to your receiver or controller through a digital cable, the sound will be determined by the quality of the digital-to-analog converters and analog-output stage in your receiver or controller. Better-quality DVD players have better-sounding digital-to-analog converters inside them than the converters in an A/V receiver. If that's the case, use the DVD player's analog outputs for music listening, and the digital output for transmitting the Dolby Digital or DTS soundtrack from DVD movies to a receiver. Virtually all DVD players sold today feature "24-bit, 96kHz" digital-to-analog converters. This means the player will convert digital signals in this higher-resolution format to analog. The compact disc format uses a 16-bit, 44.1kHz format. Keep in mind, however, that the "24-bit, 96kHz" designation doesn't guarantee good sound quality.

Progressive-Scan DVD Players

Many DVD players offer what's called *progressive-scan output*, which sometimes provides better picture quality when used with High-

Definition TV (HDTV) sets that can accept progressive-scan input. To understand how this works, you need to know that all conventional television sets (those that are not high-definition) work on the principle of *interlaced scanning,* in which the picture is formed by an electron beam tracing a total of 480 visible horizontal scanning lines of video information quickly from left to right. The electron beam starts at the top of the picture and works its way down to the bottom of the screen.

On the first pass, the electron beam traces every other line of video information—the odd-numbered scanning lines. On the second pass, the beam traces the even-numbered lines. Although interlaced scanning presents half the picture in one pass and the other half of the picture in the second pass, we perceive the image as being continuous because the process happens so quickly. In the NTSC television system used in North America, thirty "frames" (a complete picture composed of one "field" of odd-numbered lines and one field of even-numbered lines) are presented every second. Interlaced scanning was chosen for television broadcast because it is a more efficient method of transmitting video information.

In progressive scan, by contrast, the electron beam traces each line in order, from the top of the screen to the bottom. The progressive-scan display presents 60 complete frames per second, rather than the 30 frames per second of interlaced scanning. With nearly double the number of lines, progressive scanning offers higher picture resolution and reduces bothersome motion artifacts—those jagged edges on moving objects that are typical of a converted interlaced signal. (Progressive scan has other advantages over interlaced scan, as we'll see in the discussion of HDTV in Chapter 7.)

The video output of earlier DVD players was interlaced for two reasons: most conventional TV sets require interlaced scanning signals, and progressive-scan video is easier to copy and duplicate with high quality than is interlaced video, so DVD-player manufacturers—sensitive to the movie industry's concerns about copyright protection—were hesitant to make it available to consumers.

But now that digital television (DTV) sets with progressive-scan inputs are widely available, it makes sense to drive them with a progressive-scan signal DVD and avoid the compromises of interlaced-scan. Many inexpensive DVD players (less than $200) now offer a progressive output, which can produce a considerably better picture when viewed on an HDTV set with 480p (480-line progressive scan) input. Virtually all HDTV sets accept 480p signals. All progressive-scan DVD players can be set to output either interlaced (480i) or progressive (480p) signals.

Note that HDTV sets incorporate an integral image scaler to convert various input formats to the television's native scanning frequencies. For example, an HD-ready television may operate internally at 480p (480 lines progressive) or 1080i (1080 lines interlaced). The set's internal image scaler would convert the 480i output from an interlaced-output DVD player to 480p progressive. So what's the difference between letting the TV's image scaler convert the signal to 480p progressive for display, or bypassing the TV's scaler by using a 480p progressive-output DVD player? Although in both cases the image is displayed in 480p, you'll often get a better picture by bypassing the TV's internal scaler and using a progressive-scan DVD player. That's because the scalers built into most HDTV sets are sometimes of poor quality. You can perform a quick experiment to evaluate the quality of an HDTV set's scaler: drive the set with a 480p progressive signal from a high-quality progressive-scan DVD player, then switch the DVD player to interlaced output. In most cases, driving the TV with a 480p progressive signal will result in better picture quality. If, however, the set's "native" scanning frequency is 540p, the set's image scaler will still process the signal.

3/2 Pulldown

The quality of the circuits that create the progressive-scan output have a large effect on picture quality. Some progressive-scan players look no better than interlaced machines; others produce breathtaking pictures. A large part of this difference is attributable to a circuit that performs a process called *3/2 pulldown*, also known as *inverse telecine*. Technically, it is more correct to call the process 3/2 pulldown *removal*, although it's generally called simply 3/2 pulldown.

I mentioned earlier that video runs at a rate of 30 frames (pictures) per second, with each frame composed of two interlaced fields. Some of you will know that film runs at a rate of 24 frames per second (fps). When 24 fps film is transferred to 60 interlaced fields per second, each film frame is repeated either twice, or three times in an alternating sequence. This 3/2 cadence is shown in fig.3-5. Note that two film frames result in five video fields, with one film frame converted to two fields, and the other converted to three fields. In one second, 24 film frames are converted to 60 video frames (120 interlaced fields). This results in a slight jerkiness of motion (called "judder") because every other film frame occupies a slightly longer period of time.

In a progressive-scan DVD player with 3/2 pulldown removal, circuits remove these extra fields, restoring the original film-frame pairs. The same integrated circuit generates a progressive-output signal by converting interlaced video to progressive video, a process called *deinterlacing*. The quality of this deinterlacing varies greatly with the sophistication of the deinterlacing algorithm. Specifically, deinterlacing circuits vary in how they process moving images. Poor deinterlacers produce *motion artifacts*, which are manifested as jagged lines on moving objects. Faroudja Laboratories, who owns the patents on 3/2 pulldown, pioneered an advanced deinterlacing technology it calls Directional Correlational Deinterlacing (DCDi), which greatly reduces motion artifacts. Faroudja has incorporated DCDi technology into an affordable integrated circuit that is found in some DVD players and HDTV sets.

Fig. 3-5
3/2 pulldown
removal restores
the 24fps film
pairs.

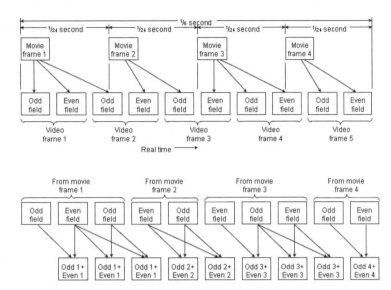

Courtesy Faroudja/Sage Inc.

Classic tests for motion artifacts are the deck railings on the DVD of *Titanic*, and guitar strings in music programs. Fig.3-6 shows poor deinterlacing and its attendant motion artifacts (left) and excellent deinterlacing with better reconstruction of the interlaced fields (right). Motion artifacts occur because images move between one interlaced field and the next and are displayed as slightly staggered. The larger the video display, the more apparent the motion artifacts.

Fig. 3-6 Poor deinterlacing (left) results in incorrect assembly of individual fields. Faroudja's motion-adaptive deinterlacing (right) produces fewer motion artifacts.

Courtesy Faroudja/Sage Inc.

The deinterlacer must detect whether the original source material was 30 fps video or 24fps film, and engage the the 3/2 pulldown removal only for 24fps sources. Some deinterlacers switch between "film" and "video" modes automatically (a feature called "auto detect"), while others must be manually set by the user.

DVD Recorders: DVD-R, DVD-RW, DVD+R, DVD+RW

The DVD format has been expanded to include machines that can record digital video and audio on a blank disc. Generally called "DVD recorders," this product category encompasses several different—and incompatible—formats. The first DVD recorders, introduced in 1997, cost nearly $20,000. Today, machines are available for less than $700, with prices continuing to drop rapidly.

First, the DVD-RAM format was developed as a high-density removable storage medium for computers. It uses a recordable optical disc housed in a caddy. The other two recordable DVD formats are designed for home recording, but are incompatible with each other. These two incompatible formats, which compete with each other, each encompass two versions within the format family.

The first of these format families is DVD-R and DVD-RW. The DVD-R format is a write-once format, similar to the familiar CD-R. DVD-RW can be erased and re-recorded virtually indefinitely. Some machines can write to both types of discs. DVD-R discs will play in about 95% of existing DVD players; DVD-RW discs play in only 75% of DVD machines. Disc capacity is 4.7GB, the same as read-only DVD discs, which corresponds to a user-selectable recording time of one to six hours, depending on the picture quality required. Pioneer Electronics is the leading force behind DVD-R/DVD-RW.

The second recordable DVD family is DVD+R and DVD+RW, developed primarily by Philips and Sony, and supported by several computer and consumer-electronics companies. DVD+R is a write-once format; DVD+RW is re-recordable. DVD+RW machines can also record on CD-R and CD-RW media. DVD+R and DVD+RW discs have greater compatibility with existing DVD players compared with DVD-R and DVD-RW. As mentioned earlier, the DVD-R/RW and DVD+R/RW formats are incompatible with each other.

How DVD Works

DVD expands on the CD format by packing more data on a CD-sized disc. A conventional CD can hold about 680 megabytes of data. Although this is a huge amount, it's still not enough to store much digital video. A single-sided, single-layer DVD can store 4.7 gigabytes (4700 megabytes), or seven times the information capacity of a CD. This high density of data storage is accomplished by making the "pits"—small indentations in the plastic disc that encode the digital ones and zeros—smaller and closer together. Fig.3-7 is a comparison of CD and DVD surfaces.

Two aspects of the DVD standard increase this capacity even further. First, the DVD format calls for dual-sided discs: Two thin discs, each carrying 4.7 gigabytes of information, are bonded together to form a single disc the thickness of a CD. Second, a DVD can have two layers of information on each side, one layer embedded below the other; the laser beam simply focuses on one or the other. This means that a double-sided, dual-layer DVD (the so-called "DVD-18" format) can store nearly 18 gigabytes of data, or 25 times the capacity of a CD.

Fig. 3-7 The information-carrying pits on a DVD are about half the size of those on a CD.

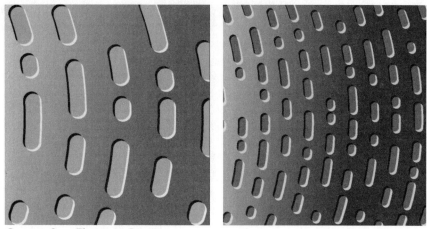

Courtesy Sony Electronics Inc.

While this is a huge amount of storage capacity, digital video eats it up quickly. Specifically, digital video as found in professional digital videotape recorders consumes about 168 million bits per second. This is too many data to store even on a DVD, so this rate is reduced with the MPEG-2 video-compression scheme—the same compression system used in DSS transmission. MPEG-2 compression results in a variable bit-rate that averages between 3 and 8 megabits (Mbs) per second. Ten megabits per second is the fastest bit-rate possible in the DVD format. With a maximum video rate of 8Mbs, 2Mbs are left for the Dolby Digital soundtrack in several languages, plus subtitles.

This variable bit-rate has implications for picture quality: The higher the bit-rate, the better the picture. The shorter the movie, the higher the bit-rate that can be used while still making the movie fit on a single-sided DVD. Most commercial releases are encoded using a bit-rate of 3Mbs to 5Mbs for films with running times shorter than 120 minutes.

Films with extended scenes of fast-moving images and complex backgrounds (both of which require a higher data rate) may look better when encoded at higher bit-rates. The average bit-rate is set by the "compressionist," the person responsible for converting the high-bit-rate video into the MPEG-2-compressed video that ends up on the DVD. The compressionist monitors the image for any sign that the bit-rate is too low for a particular scene, and adjusts accordingly. Some DVD players let you display the instantaneous bit-rate right on your video monitor; it's interesting to watch the bit-rate soar when the scene includes a detailed background, such as a crowded baseball stadium, and drop when the background is a cloudless sky.

DVD's video quality can vary from the quality of the MPEG-2 encoding and decoding. The better the MPEG-2 encoder is set up, the better the picture quality. And the MPEG-2 decoders found in all DVD players also vary in quality.

DVD can provide much greater picture detail because, in technical terms, the video signal stored on a DVD has a wider bandwidth. The downside of this greater detail is that a DVD player feeding a television set with its sharpness control turned up too high will produce a very poor picture, with an unpleasant over-emphasis on the edges of objects and actors. In fact, it's possible to make a DVD picture look worse than VHS. DVD manufacturers have countered this potential problem by filtering some of the detail out of the picture. (Specifically, the filter begins at 0.5MHz and gradually rolls off to –6dB at 5.5MHz.) For those of us with properly set sharpness controls on our video monitors (setting a monitor's sharpness control is described in Chapter 7), the filters in the first DVD machines result in a less detailed picture than the DVD format can ultimately provide. High-end DVD machines don't have this filter because their manufacturers assume that anyone buying a high-end machine will be using a calibrated monitor. Mass-market DVD players are now appearing without this filter because the general public is becoming increasingly aware of the need for correctly setting the TV's sharpness control. When your neighbor calls you over to see his new DVD player, do him a favor and turn down his TV set's sharpness control. In fact, the best position for the sharpness control is usually all the way down.

DVD-Audio

The DVD format was expanded in late 1999 to provide super-high-quality audio playback. Called DVD-Audio or DVD-A, this format uses the entire disc capacity to store music with greater fidelity than is possible on the compact disc. A DVD-Audio disc can contain 2-channel stereo along with a 6-channel surround-sound mix of the music. You select which version you prefer.

The compact disc uses a sampling frequency of 44.1kHz, meaning that the analog-to-digital converter takes a "snapshot" of the music signal's waveform 44,100 times per second. This sampling frequency isn't high enough to accurately encode all the musical information. Just as important, the low sampling frequency forces designers to make compromises in the circuitry processing the digital audio signals. Consequently, CD-quality audio is inferior to the performance of such high-end analog formats as analog master tape and, on a good turntable, the LP record. DVD-Audio, by contrast, can support sampling rates from 44.1kHz up to 192kHz. The higher sampling rate produces better sound quality.

Another factor that determines digital audio sound quality is called the *word length*. This is the number of digital bits created at each sample point that encode the audio signal's amplitude information. The louder the signal, the higher the number represented by the "word." CD uses 16-bit words, which were as many as the technology of the day could support. (In fact, the CD was nearly a 14-bit format; no 16-bit converters existed in the late 1970s, when CD was developed.) The greater the number of bits in each word, the wider the dynamic range (the difference in level between the softest and loudest sounds), the lower the noise and distortion, and the greater the resolution of low-level musical detail. DVD-Audio can store digital audio with word lengths of up to 24 bits—a huge advance over the CD's 16-bit maximum.

The result is that music on DVD-Audio can sound vastly better than even the best CDs. The difference doesn't require a "golden ear" to appreciate; it's dramatic and obvious. DVD-A provides much more realistic rendering of instrumental timbres, creating a greater impression of hearing an actual musical instrument, not a facsimile of it. The sound-stage is larger, wider, deeper, and has a feeling of air and space between the performers, just as we hear in real life. The music has more dynamic impact, punch, and rhythmic flow. In addition, the treble sounds more smooth, more natural, and less metallic or artificial. Once you hear a good DVD-A disc, it's hard to go back to CD.

DVD-A discs can contain a wide range of sampling frequencies and word lengths. For example, the record producer can specify that the front channels be encoded at the highest resolution possible (192kHz, 24-bit), with the surround channels encoded at 48kHz and 20-bit. Because six channels at the highest resolution would exceed the DVD format's maximum data transfer rate, a "lossless" compression system called *Meridian Lossless Packing* (*MLP*) is employed. MLP encoding compresses the digital audio data for storage on the DVD; an MLP decoder in the DVD-A play uncompresses the data on playback. It's vital to note that this lossless compression process results in exact bit-for-bit accuracy with the original audio data. Consequently, there's absolutely no loss in sound quality. MLP is contrasted with "lossy" compression systems such as MP3, Dolby Digital, and DTS, which reduced fidelity to the original source.

The twenty million DVD players sold between the format's introduction and early 2002 cannot realize the advantages of the DVD-A format, however. The DVD-A specification wasn't finalized until mid-1999, and the first players weren't available until November 1999, when a few machines capable of playing CD, DVD-Video, and DVD-Audio hit the market. A DVD-Audio player has six analog outputs, which will drive a 6-channel analog input on your receiver or controller. Unfortunately, the digital information on the DVD-A is converted to analog inside the player, then converted back to digital in the receiver or controller, then back to analog by the receiver or controller's DACs. These conversions degrade sound quality. Future DVD-A players will have an encrypted digital output that provides a direct connection to a receiver or controller, subjecting the signal to only one D/A conversion. But before this direct digital connection becomes a reality, the world's electronics companies and music labels must agree on a system of copyright protection to prevent illegal copying of the high-resolution digital bitstream.

In 2002, manufacturers introduced DVD players and controllers with high-resolution multichannel digital interfaces that can carry DVD-A's six channels. These interfaces are, however, proprietary to their respective manufacturers. This means that a DVD-A player from one manufacturer won't work with the A/V receiver or controller made by another manufacturer, at least through the high-resolution digital connection. You can, of course, still connect these components through their analog interfaces.

DVD-Audio discs can be played back on older DVD-Video machines, but the sound quality isn't nearly as good as the performance I've described. Record companies have the option of including a 5.1-channel Dolby Digital mix of the music on the DVD-A disc. This track will deliver surround-sound on any DVD player, but with compromised fidelity. That's because Dolby Digital uses a data-compression scheme to reduce the number of bits representing the music. It's ironic that the format designed to deliver better sound quality by providing more bits than CD will be listened to with far fewer bits than on CD.

Super Audio CD

A second high-resolution digital audio format made its debut a few months ahead of DVD-Audio. Developed by Sony and Philips, the Super Audio Compact Disc (SACD) is a CD-sized disc that can contain 2-channel and 6-channel surround-sound mixes with very high sound quality.

A key provision of SACD is the possibility for a single disc to play high-resolution digital audio on SACD players, and also deliver CD-quality sound when played on the installed base of more than 800 million CD players worldwide. This back-compatibility with CD players is made possible by a dual-layer "hybrid" disc in which one layer contains conventional 16-bit, 44.1kHz digital audio, and the second layer contains the high-resolution digital audio signal. The high-resolution layer is transparent to a CD player's laser beam, allowing the dual-layer SACD to function identically to a CD. But when played on an SACD player (or a universal DVD player that also provides SACD playback), the laser beam reads the high-resolution layer and delivers exceptional sound quality.

We saw how DVD-Audio uses sampling rates as high as 192kHz and word lengths up to 24 bits for better sound. SACD uses an entirely different system for representing music digitally. Called Direct Stream Digital (DSD), the technique samples the musical signal at a lightning-fast 2.8224 million bits per second. Each sample, however, generates just one bit of information. The amplitude of the audio signal is contained in the width of the 1-bit pulses. This is a radically different technique for encoding digital audio. DSD delivers an audio signal with 100kHz bandwidth (compared with 20kHz for CD), and a dynamic range of 120dB (compared with 96dB for CD). The sound quality from SACD is nothing short of spectacular, and vastly better than CD playback.

SACD is more of a high-end music format than is DVD-Audio. It doesn't connect to a video monitor, isn't a computer "convergence" product, and has no provision for a sonically compromised Dolby Digital mix.

Ideally, all DVD players will one day include playback of all optical media: CD, DVD-Video, DVD-Audio, and SACD. Consumers then wouldn't be concerned about what format a disc is—if it's a 5" optical disc, you can put it in any player and hear music or see video.

(For more detailed information about DVD-Audio and Super Audio CD, see my *The Complete Guide to High-End Audio*, Second Edition.)

Compact Disc and Vinyl Records

Although the Compact Disc (CD) player is an audio-only product rather than a home-theater component, chances are you'll want to play CDs through your home-theater audio system. As mentioned earlier, all DVD machines also play CDs as well as DVDs.

If you want the ultimate in sound quality, however, choose a separate CD player made by a specialist audio company. Contrary to what some mainstream publications say, all CD players do *not* sound alike. In fact, large sonic differences exist between brands of CD players. How much you enjoy music through your audio system can be affected by which CD player you choose.

The *worst* way to buy a CD player is to pick one from a list of units recommended in a mass-market consumer guide. Such publications' criterion for evaluating CD players is simple: whichever machine provides the most features for the least money. Unfortunately, such an approach often results in those units with the *poorest* sound quality receiving the *highest* ratings. Because adding features costs the manufacturer money, less money is available for parts or techniques that would improve the player's sound.

It's also a mistake to buy a CD player just because it carries the same brand name as your A/V receiver, DVD player, or television. There's no special "matching" that occurs between products of the same brand; virtually any audio/video product will work well with any other audio/video product. Some manufacturers will design a CD player with no care given to its sound quality. They know that many consumers will buy a player based on brand name or features alone, not musical performance. Conversely, other companies strive to design the most musically natural-sounding player possible for a given price. The engineers at such companies are music lovers who go to extraordinary lengths to make their CD players sound musical and enjoyable. The way to find these superior-performing players is to follow the product reviews in such magazines as *The Absolute Sound.*

You should also listen to candidate CD players for yourself with your favorite music. It doesn't take a "golden ear" to know which

CD player sounds best. If you listen carefully to several models, you'll be able to pick the one that sounds the most like music. For those home-theater enthusiasts who strive for the greatest possible musical performance, my book *The Complete Guide to High-End Audio* includes much more detail about choosing components and becoming a better listener.

There are, however, several advantages to buying a CD player of the same brand as the rest of your system. The main system's remote control will likely include controls for the CD player, obviating the need for a second remote cluttering your coffee table. Some remotes, however, are called "learning" remotes because they can be programmed to learn the commands from the remote control of a CD player made by a different manufacturer. Finally, some A/V systems' functions are integrated to simplify their operation. For example, if you push PLAY on the CD player, the A/V receiver or controller automatically selects the CD input for listening. This integrated function is possible only when using components made by the same manufacturer.

Fortunately, you can upgrade the sound quality of nearly any CD player by adding a component called a digital-to-analog converter, or DAC. The DAC takes a digital signal from your CD player and converts it to an analog signal that can feed your controller or A/V receiver. Every CD player contains a built-in DAC; an outboard converter replaces the integral converter with one of higher quality. All A/V receivers and controllers have a digital input that lets you connect the digital output of your CD player to the receiver or controller, which then functions as a D/A converter. The DACs inside your A/V receiver or controller perform the digital-to-analog conversion.

As the CD replaced the LP record, many listeners discarded their record collections and turntables in favor of the shiny disc. That was unfortunate; LPs can sound superb when played on a decent-quality turntable and phono cartridge. Moreover, if you're old enough to have been a record collector at any point in your past, much of your favorite music is probably on LP in your library. There's no reason to stop listening to vinyl. Pull out your turntable and record collection and keep enjoying the music.

Home Theater Software

The new home-theater enthusiast often sees for sale a film he's always wanted to own, and buys it. After all, a film is a film is a film. But many factors influence the quality and artistic merit of prerecorded films, whether on DVD, satellite, or VHS tape. Several versions of the same film may be available that vary dramatically in technical quality and fidelity from the filmmakers' vision.

Let's take a look at two extremes of the way in which a film is presented to the consumer. We'll start with the way many viewers experience a film on VHS tape, or as broadcast on commercial television.

Director's Cuts and Aspect Ratios

Appearing at the beginning of many VHS films and television broadcasts is a disclaimer that reads something like this: "This film has been edited for content, reduced in length to fit the time allotted, and formatted to fit your television." In other words, this piece of art (at least *some* films qualify as art) has been hacked in length so that the evening news can start on time, or portions have been removed so as not to offend an eight-year-old girl in the Midwest, or the picture's left and right edges have been cut off in order to force the image to fill your television screen—or *all* of the above.

Conversely, another release of the same film on DVD may be a "director's cut"; i.e., the director has re-edited the film to reflect his or her original creative vision, not the film studio's commercial considerations. Instead of being inferior in content to the original film, as in our first example, this version is usually better than the theatrical release. Moreover, the director, cinematographer, sound designer, and other artistic/technical contributors supervise the entire film-to-video process to ensure that the consumer release is of the highest technical quality and artistic merit.

On the technical side, the high-quality version will be presented in the film's original theatrical *aspect ratio*. This term describes the ratio between the width and height of the projected image seen by the audience. The aspect ratio is chosen by the film's director and cinematographer to best convey their vision. (Aspect ratios may vary slightly between the original image on film and the theatrical release.) The theatrical aspect ratio of films made after 1953 is almost always wider than a conventional television screen's aspect ratio of 1.33:1 (also expressed as 4:3). Original theatrical aspect ratios range from 2.66:1 to 1.33:1, with most films falling between 2.35:1 and 1.35:1. Many films have an aspect ratio of 1.85:1, which is very slightly wider than the 1.78:1 of a 16:9 widescreen HDTV. (1.78:1 is the same as 16:9.) Fig.3-8 shows common aspect ratios.

If the original widescreen aspect ratio is left intact, we see black bars above and below the image when viewed on a conventional 4:3 TV set. Movie studios are concerned that viewers will think something is wrong with the disc or tape if they see these black bars, or that they're somehow being cheated because the image doesn't fill the screen. In reality, both filmmakers and viewers are being cheated if the left and right edges of the image are chopped off to fit the television's 1.33:1 aspect ratio. Changing the aspect ratio is nothing short of butchering the filmmakers' creation.

Fig. 3-8 Films can be formatted in different aspect ratios. Widescreen television has an aspect ratio of 16:9, which is equivalent to 1.78:1. Conventional television has an aspect ratio of 4:3, which is equivalent to 1.33:1.

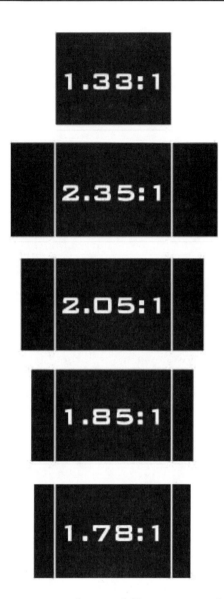

High-quality consumer releases of films are sometimes called *widescreen* or *letterbox*, two identical terms indicating that the film retains its original theatrical aspect ratio, or at least an aspect ratio very similar to the original. Films made without this fidelity to the original aspect ratio are called *pan&scan*. A pan&scan movie has had its left and right edges cut off so that the image fills the frame of a conventional TV set.

Nearly all high-definition televisions (and most projection screens in front-projection systems) are "widescreen" with an aspect ratio of 1.78:1 (16:9). The 16:9 aspect ratio has been chosen as the standard for High-Definition Television. A widescreen television will present feature films in their original aspect ratios, with narrower black bars above and below the image. When watching television or films formatted to a conventional television's 1.33:1 ratio, however, the widescreen television will show black bars on the left and right sides of the image, a condition called "windowboxing."

Widescreen televisions have been the norm in Japan for several years, and are only now becoming commonplace in the United States. The driving force behind the move to widescreen televisions is largely DVD, which virtually always contains a widescreen presentation.

Anamorphic, or "16:9 Enhanced," DVDs

A problem with widescreen presentations is that the image doesn't occupy all of the 480 usable scanning lines in a video frame. The image may use only 360 scanning lines, with the black bars above and below the image consuming (and wasting) the other 120 lines. The result of wasting a third of the picture to transmit the black bars is fewer lines for the image and lost resolution.

Delivering widescreen aspect ratios without losing resolution is made possible by the *anamorphic* format. DVDs presented in the anamorphic format are also labeled by the less technical names "16:9 Enhanced," "Widescreen Enhanced," or "Enhanced for 16:9 Televisions." All three terms mean the same thing. In an anamorphic presentation, the widescreen image is squeezed horizontally until it fills the standard 1.33:1 frame. Think of putting your hands on either edge of the widescreen image and pushing your hands together until the black bars above and below the image are gone. The picture will be distorted geometrically (actors will look tall and skinny), but now the picture uses all 480 lines of video information.

An anamorphically squeezed image must be "unsqueezed" on playback in the DVD player or video display to restore the correct picture geometry. Think of putting your hands on the top and bottom of the squeezed image and pushing them together until the picture returns to its original height. This picture can then be displayed on a widescreen projection device such as a front projector, or a direct-view television or rear projector with a 16:9 aspect ratio. The DVD player's setup menu lets you tell the player that you have a widescreen display. The anamorphic presentation maintains the film's original aspect ratio while preserving full vertical resolution by using the full 480 lines of video available.

The improvement in picture quality afforded by such "16:9 Enhanced" discs is substantial. The number of scan lines in the image is increased by about a third, which is clearly apparent as finer resolution of detail and a more continuous, filmlike image. Unfortunately, not all studios enhance their widescreen DVD titles, although the practice is becoming standard procedure now that 16:9 televisions are becoming prevalent.

As described in Chapter 7, some 4:3 HD-ready televisions have a feature that vertically compresses the raster (the illuminated picture area) so that all the set's scanning lines are used to produce the image. The anamorphic image is fed to the TV, which restores the correct geometry through this raster compression and takes advantage of the increased vertical resolution conferred by the anamorphic format. Through this technique, anamorphic widescreen images can be displayed on a 4:3 television.

DVD Transfer Quality and Supplemental Material

In addition to the film's theatrical aspect ratio, several other technical factors influence the quality of a consumer release. The process of converting film to video, called *telecine*, is an art form in itself that must be performed with care and dedication. The telecinist controls the picture's brightness, black level, color, tint, and every other aspect of picture quality. If a telecine transfer isn't performed with skill and care, the picture quality will suffer. This so-called "transfer quality" varies enormously from disc to disc. Similarly, the soundtrack should be transferred to the consumer-release format with the highest audio quality.

Many DVD releases include supplemental material not available on the VHS releases. This material may include the film's original theatrical trailer(s), the director's narration, extra footage ("Never before seen!"), a short "Making of" documentary, production still photographs, and/or a booklet with production notes and photographs.

With an anamorphic presentation in the original theatrical widescreen aspect ratio, a high-quality transfer, director's cut restoring original material, director commentary track, "Making of" documentary, and other supplemental material, the DVD format exploits the technical and artistic possibilities of viewing movies at home—quite a difference from "This film has been edited for content, reduced in length to fit the time allotted, and formatted to fit your television screen."

Superbit DVDs

In late 2001, Sony introduced a premium line of DVDs called *Superbit* that maximize picture quality. To understand the concept behind Superbit, you should know that the greater the number of digital bits that encode the picture, the better that picture will look. You can think of a DVD as a "bit bucket" of a fixed size. The disc's authors can add supplemental material to that bucket, but fewer bits will then be available to encode the picture. Superbit sacrifices all the extras possible on DVD so that the picture can be stored with a higher bit-rate. Most DVDs are encoded with a bit-rate of about 3Mbs (3,000,000 bits per second);

Superbit DVDs are typically encoded at 6-8Mbs. The difference in picture quality is significant, particularly on a high-quality video display.

THX Certification of Software

The THX program devised by Lucasfilm is a set of technologies and performance criteria for audio quality that a movie theater must meet in order to call itself "THX Certified." THX certification was expanded to include home-theater products and, more recently, to encompass home-theater software. A THX-certified laserdisc or DVD has been made to exacting standards of quality, from the telecine transfer all the way to disc replication. Quality-control procedures during the manufacturing process ensure that a THX-certified release meets certain criteria for the technical quality of both picture and sound. Although some VHS tapes have been THX-certified, I think the THX software program should be reserved for only high-quality formats such as laserdisc and DVD. You can expect a THX-certified release to look and sound good, but non-certified releases can also be superb. Some companies simply choose not to participate in the THX program or pay the THX license fee. Software that has been THX-certified carries the THX software logo.

4 Audio/Video Receivers

Introduction

The audio/video (A/V) receiver is the brain and muscle of a home-theater system. It performs many functions, from selecting which source you want to watch to amplifying the signals that drive your loudspeakers. The A/V receiver is the component you'll interact with most, either through its front-panel controls or via the receiver's remote control.

An A/V receiver, also called a *surround receiver*, is similar to the conventional "stereo"receiver with which you're probably familiar, but with several important differences. Although both stereo and A/V receivers select between sources, control the system's playback volume, and amplify signals to drive your loudspeakers, the A/V receiver is unique in three respects: it 1) includes some form of surround-sound decoding; 2) can handle multiple channels (rather than a stereo receiver's two channels); and 3) has video inputs and outputs.

You can see from fig.4-1 that the A/V receiver is the central switching point that controls the entire home-theater system. Its other main job is decoding the soundtrack read from VHS tape, DSS transmission, or DVD. Decoding means taking the raw signal from the source component and converting it into left, center, right, and surround left and right analog audio signals (receivers with THX Surround EX and DTS-ES also generate back-surround signals). The A/V receiver also performs digital signal processing to create multichannel surround sound from 2-channel music sources such as CD, and also to split up the frequency spectrum to send bass to the subwoofer and midrange/treble to the rest of the loudspeakers. Finally, the A/V receiver incorporates five, six, or seven power amplifiers to drive your five home-theater loudspeakers.

Fig. 4-1 An A/V receiver is the central switching point of a home-theater system.

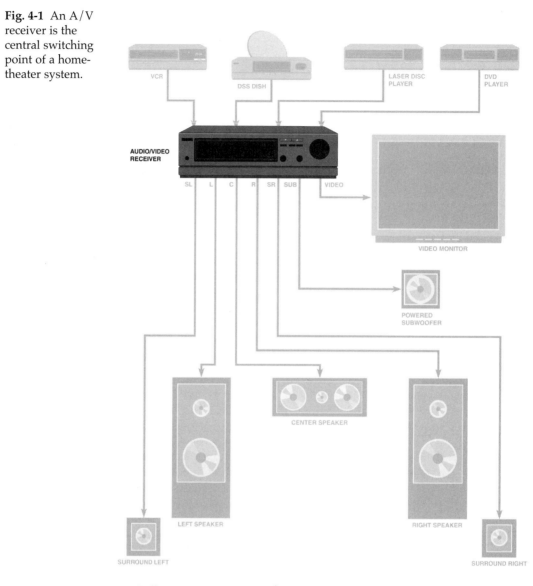

Following is a list of all the functions performed by the A/V receiver. I'll discuss each of these in detail later in the chapter. The A/V receiver:

- receives video and audio signals from various source components (HDTV set-top box, VCR, DSS, DVD) and selects which are sent to the video monitor and home-theater loudspeakers (a function called *source switching*);

- performs surround decoding, whether Dolby Pro Logic, Pro Logic II, Dolby Digital, THX Surround EX, or DTS;

- picks up AM and FM radio broadcasts;

- controls the playback volume;

- makes adjustments to the system setup, such as fine-tuning the individual channel levels;

- directs bass to the appropriate loudspeakers and subwoofers (called *bass management*);

- performs THX processing (if so equipped); and

- amplifies the five, six, or seven signals to drive your left, center, right, surround left, and surround right loudspeakers (and back-surround speakers in system with Dolby Digital EX decoding).

What the A/V Receiver Does

With that overview of what an A/V receiver is and does, let's look at each function in more detail.

Source Selection, Inputs and Outputs, and Video Connections

First and foremost, the A/V receiver takes in audio and video signals from various source components and allows you to select which are sent to your loudspeakers and video monitor. Selecting which source is sent to the rest of your system is accomplished by pressing a button on the remote control or on the A/V receiver's front panel. A front-panel display often tells you which source is selected, or an LED illuminates next to the selected button. Fig.4-2 shows the front panel of an A/V receiver.

Fig. 4-2 A receiver's front-panel display sometimes shows the selected source.

Courtesy Denon Electronics

A/V receivers vary in the number of source components they can accommodate. Some accept perhaps three A/V sources (audio and video signals), one audio-only source (such as from a CD player), and have one A/V tape loop for connecting a VCR. An A/V tape loop is just like the tape loop on a stereo receiver, but with the addition of a video input and video output. Top-of-the-line A/V receivers may have as many as eleven A/V inputs and provision for connecting three VCRs.

An A/V receiver will also have audio-only inputs for CD players and audio-only tape loops for cassette decks. If you want to play LPs, the A/V receiver should also have an input marked PHONO.

All the analog audio inputs and outputs will be on connections called *RCA jacks*. These are the familiar connectors found on conventional stereo components. Video connections, however, can be made via RCA jacks or a newer connector, called *S-video*. An RCA jack carries what's called a *composite-video* signal; the S-video connector carries the video signal's color and brightness information separately. The only components that benefit from S-video connection are DSS decoder boxes, DVD players, and S-VHS tape machines playing S-VHS tapes (which are rare). If you have a DSS dish, DVD player, or S-VHS machine, you should choose a receiver with S-video inputs and outputs for better picture quality. To take advantage of S-video connections, your video monitor must also have S-video inputs. Many A/V receivers duplicate their video inputs with both composite and S-video jacks, allowing you to choose the connection format. Fig.4-3 shows an A/V receiver's rear-panel input and output jacks.

Fig. 4-3 An A/V receiver's rear panel has RCA audio input and output jacks, S-video and RCA (composite) video jacks, and loudspeaker connection terminals.

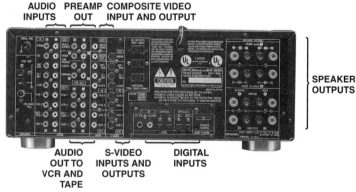

Courtesy Denon Electronics

Most newer A/V receivers also have two or three component-video inputs and one component-video output. Component-video connection, found in better DVD players and video monitors, offers the highest picture quality. A receiver with component-video switching will probably have two component-video inputs and one component-video output. Any component-video connections from source components to the A/V receiver require a component-video connection from the A/V receiver to the video monitor.

Be aware that some A/V receivers compromise picture quality because their component-video switching circuits lack sufficient bandwidth to pass video signals without removing high-frequency video information. This high-frequency video information contains picture details; therefore, a receiver with inadequate bandwidth will soften the picture. The vital specification is the receiver's video bandwidth; a typical bandwidth of 27MHz (megahertz) will not pass high-definition video without reducing picture detail. A receiver with a video bandwidth of 10MHz will compromise the picture quality of a progressive-scan DVD player. Look for a video bandwidth of at least 50MHz if you plan to switch HD video signals through the receiver's component-video switching circuits. (Component video is covered in Chapter 7.)

The A/V receiver will have five, six, or seven output terminals for connecting the receiver's amplified outputs to your loudspeakers. In receivers with Dolby Digital and DTS decoding (those lacking Dolby Digital Surround EX or DTS-ES decoding) the five terminals correspond to the left, center, right, surround left, and surround right channels. A sixth output, marked SUBWOOFER OUT, is for connecting an optional subwoofer. Unlike the powerful signal at the five loudspeaker terminals, the SUBWOOFER OUT jack provides only a low-level signal, which must be amplified by a separate amplifier. Most subwoofers have a built-in amplifier so they can accept this low-level subwoofer output signal.

Receivers that can decode a back-surround channel have an additional amplifier channel and output terminal to drive a back-surround speaker. These so-called "6.1" receivers use a generic decoder to extract the back-surround signal from film soundtracks. True THX Surround EX receivers (those certified by THX) employ two additional amplifier channels to drive two back-surround speakers, for a total of seven amplifier channels.

The A/V receiver has a video output, called MONITOR OUT, that feeds one of the video inputs on your video monitor. Whatever video source you've selected on the A/V receiver will be sent to this monitor output jack. The monitor output jack can be composite, S-video, or component-video; most A/V receivers offer composite and S-video, with higher-end models providing component-video output as well.

There's one quirk in all A/V products than can throw you if you don't know about it. If you have a source component connected to your A/V receiver with an S-video cable, but a composite-video cable from the A/V receiver's monitor output to your video monitor, you won't be able to see a picture. Any S-video connections from source components to the A/V receiver require an S-video connection from the A/V receiver to the video monitor.

Receivers also have digital audio inputs that receive the digital audio outputs from your source components. The receiver's digital audio inputs are usually offered on either RCA jacks or TosLink optical connectors. The RCA input, also called the *coaxial* input, accepts the digital audio signal from a source component in electrical form. The *TosLink* connector accepts the digital audio signal from source components as pulses of light traveling down a fiber-optic cable. Despite the apparent "high-tech" nature of TosLink connection, it is sonically inferior to the coaxial electrical connection.

Some older receivers, or recent top-of-the-line models, have an additional type of digital input marked AC-3 RF, which means it accepts the RF-modulated Dolby Digital signal read from a laserdisc (see Chapter 3 for a full explanation). The other digital inputs accept an unmodulated Dolby Digital bitstream, such as that output from a DVD player. Some receivers have a single Dolby Digital input and automatically switch between modulated and unmodulated decoding. In addition, the unmodulated input will automatically switch between PCM and Dolby Digital input signals.

Note that the "RF-modulated" form of Dolby Digital was a temporary measure that allowed Dolby Digital to be put on a laserdisc. All current formats with Dolby Digital audio (DVD and HDTV, for examples) output the "unmodulated" or "bitstream" Dolby Digital signal.

Surround Decoding

In addition to selecting which source you listen to and watch, the A/V receiver always includes surround decoding. Virtually all A/V receivers have Dolby Pro Logic, Dolby Digital, and DTS decoding. Some higher-end models also sport the newer THX Surround EX and DTS-ES decoding. A new version of Dolby's venerable Pro Logic, called Pro Logic II, has also become ubiquitous. A basic, entry-level A/V receiver provides Dolby Pro Logic, Dolby Digital, and DTS. Just a few years ago, only upper-end models featured Dolby Digital and DTS decoding. A top model will offer all the following surround-sound decoding formats: Dolby Pro Logic, Pro Logic II, Dolby Digital, DTS, THX Surround EX, DTS-ES Matrix, DTS-ES Discrete, DTS Neo:6 Music, and DTS Neo:6 Cinema.

Virtually all modern A/V receivers use Digital Signal Processing (DSP) chips to perform Dolby Pro Logic, Dolby Digital, and DTS decoding. A DSP chip is an integrated circuit that manipulates the audio signal by performing mathematical computations on the digital ones and zeros that represent the audio signal. The DSP operates according to instructions programmed in the receiver's software. For example, when decoding a Dolby Digital source, the DSP is controlled by one set of instructions for decoding Dolby Digital; when fed a DTS signal, the same DSP is controlled by the instructions for DTS decoding.

Similarly, the same DSP chips also create the "soundfield" modes that process 2-channel sources for surround-sound playback over multiple loudspeakers. These soundfield modes attempt to simulate the acoustics of various venues, from jazz clubs to stadiums, by adding simulated acoustic reflections to the signal and delaying signals sent to the surround loudspeakers.

After the signal has been decoded and processed by the DSP chips, the digital signal is converted to analog by the receiver's six, seven, or eight integral digital-to-analog converter circuits. These stages take the ones and zeros representing the audio signal and convert it to a continuously variable voltage that can drive the receiver's next section, the power amplifiers.

Power Amplification

An A/V receiver incorporates multiple power amplifiers to drive your home-theater loudspeaker system. Unlike a stereo receiver, which has two amplifier channels (left and right), an A/V receiver usually has five amplifier channels (left, center, right, surround left, surround right). Receivers with generic back-surround decoding typically have a sixth amplifier channel to drive a back-surround speaker, and receivers with full THX Surround EX and DTS-ES decoding have seven amplifiers channels, with the two additional channels driving two back-surround speakers.

Amplifier power is rated in watts per channel (Wpc), with power ratings in A/V receivers ranging from a low of about 25Wpc up to 140Wpc. Some older A/V receivers provided more power to the front channels than to the surrounds. For example, a receiver may be specified at 70Wpc into each of the three front channels, but at only 35Wpc into each of the surround channels. Reducing the power to the rear channels is feasible because the surround loudspeakers reproduce much less of the system's total sound output than do the front channels. Moreover, in the Dolby Surround format, the signal driving the surround loudspeakers is limited in its frequency response to the range of from 100Hz to 7kHz, rather than the full audio bandwidth of 20Hz–20kHz. Because the surround loudspeakers don't have to reproduce bass, they can be driven by less powerful amplifiers.

This trend was justified by Dolby Surround's virtual domination of the marketplace. But with the ubiquity of the Dolby Digital and DTS formats and their full-bandwidth surround channels, A/V receiver manufacturers now offer identical power output in all five channels. Virtually all A/V receivers now provide as much power to the surround loudspeakers as to the front loudspeakers.

Some A/V receiver manufacturers scrimp on the center-channel power amplifier in the mistaken belief that the center channel carries less signal than the left or right. Manufacturers may also have thought they could offer less center-channel amplifier power because most users would consider only a receiver's left- and right-channel power ratings. But as consumers have become more savvy, manufacturers have started to provide equal, or nearly equal, power to all three front channels. In fact, the center channel is the workhorse of the home-theater system, reproducing nearly all the dialog, some music, and many effects. One factor that reduces the need for center-channel amplifier power is that many center-channel loudspeakers can't reproduce bass below about 100Hz, and bass management filters low bass from the signal driving the center-channel speaker.

How to Choose an A/V Receiver

A/V receivers start in price at about $200 and go as high as $3800. Above this price level is the realm of separate controllers and power amplifiers (described in the next chapter). A $200 receiver's performance, features, and flexibility will differ greatly from those of a $3800 model. Here are the main differences between entry-level and higher-end A/V receivers:

- number of inputs

- type of inputs (S-video, direct digital audio inputs, component-video switching, etc.)

- power output (number of watts per channel)

- surround decoding format (Dolby Pro Logic, Dolby Pro Logic II Dolby Digital, DTS ,THX Surround EX, DTS-ES)

- circuit quality (which translates to sound quality)

- build quality

- THX certification

Choose Enough Inputs for Your System

Looking first at the number of inputs, a basic A/V receiver may provide just two A/V inputs, one A/V VCR loop, and one audio input. This product could therefore accommodate a DVD player, DSS dish, one VCR, and a CD player—but no more. Such a product would limit your ability to expand your system. If you have a PVR, DVD player, and DSS satellite dish, you need a minimum of three A/V inputs. Add a camcorder and you'll find yourself needing four A/V inputs. A good rule of thumb for determining the number of A/V inputs your receiver should have is to estimate the number of A/V sources your system will have when completed, then add one. That way, you're covered for future system expansion. If you ever think you'll want two VCRs, choose an A/V receiver with two A/V loops.

A top-model A/V receiver will provide as many as eleven A/V inputs, six audio inputs (also called line inputs), and two (or even three) A/V VCR loops. Some receivers have an A/V input on the front panel to make connecting a camcorder easy. If you have a turntable and a record collection, make sure the A/V receiver has a phono input. A phono input is unique in that it must equalize the signal from the phono cartridge to achieve a flat response. You can't connect a turntable to a normal line input.

In addition to the number of inputs, the *type* of input is also important. All A/V receivers have conventional analog inputs to accept audio and video signals from your source components, as well as digital audio inputs. As described earlier in this chapter, these digital inputs let you connect the digital audio output of a digital source component directly to the receiver's internal digital circuitry. Digital inputs come in two varieties: coaxial on a standard RCA jack, or optical on a TosLink connector. If you have the choice, use the coaxial connection. In technical terms, the coaxial connection has a wider bandwidth, which produces less jitter (timing inaccuracies) in the digital signal. Even though both coaxial and optical connectors faithfully transmit the same digital ones and zeros, the optical connection's narrower bandwidth compromises sound quality.

If you're considering an older used A/V receiver that doesn't have an internal Dolby Digital decoder, it's a good idea to select one that is "Dolby Digital Ready" (also called "5.1-Channel Ready"). This means the receiver has six separate line inputs that will accept the six line outputs from a Dolby Digital decoder inside some DVD players. Such DVD players have six analog outputs that connect to the six separate analog inputs on a "5.1-Ready" receiver. If you use a DVD player with an integral Dolby Digital decoder, you'll still need an A/V receiver with Dolby Digital decoding if you have other Dolby Digital sources, such as DSS (in the future) or HDTV broadcasts. This option is like an expansion port that will allow you to upgrade your receiver to the latest decoding format simply by adding an outboard decoder, rather than selling your receiver and starting over.

There's another reason to choose a receiver with a 6-channel analog input: DVD-Audio and SACD players have six analog outputs to deliver surround-sound music. Unless your receiver has a 6-channel analog input, you won't be able to play multichannel DVD-Audio and SACD discs though your receiver.

Which A/V Receiver Features are Important?

Today's A/V receivers are loaded with features. Some of these are vital to getting the best performance from your system; others are useless gimmicks. Oddly, some of the most important A/V receiver features aren't always included in otherwise excellent products.

Below is a list of several useful A/V receiver features, with explanations of why each feature is important.

1) *Analog bypass.* As we've just learned, A/V receivers work internally in the digital domain, meaning that they process digital signals rather than analog ones. For example, the receiver spits up the frequency spectrum to send bass to the subwoofer, and midrange/treble to the other speakers, by performing mathematical calculations on the digital ones and zeros representing the audio signal. That means that analog signals feeding the receiver (such as from a turntable, tuner, or CD player) are converted to digital as soon as they enter the receiver. The receiver then processes those digital signals, and converts them back to analog just before the power amplifiers. These conversions reduce sound quality.

The solution is a feature sometimes called "analog bypass" or "straight" mode. This mode allows analog signals fed to the receiver to be passed directly to the receiver's power-amplifier stage without digital conversions. No signal processing is possible in this mode. The analog bypass mode is an important feature to ensure the purest music reproduction from analog sources.

Ideally, the receiver would have analog bypass on its analog inputs, as well as on the discrete six-channel input. The stereo analog inputs can accept and pass analog signals from a tuner or phono preamplifier (if you listen to records); the six-channel analog input takes in the six-channel analog output from multichannel SACD and DVD-Audio players.

2) *Automatic surround-mode switching when you change sources.* Let's say you're watching a movie on DVD one night with Dolby Digital decoding and THX processing. The next day you play a CD and switch the input from DVD to CD. The CD should be played back in straight stereo mode, with no decoding and no THX processing. Unfortunately, most receivers will process the CD with whatever processing was last used, degrading the CD's sound quality. That's why a nice feature is the ability to assign a certain surround mode to each input. For example, the CD, TUNER, and PHONO inputs could be put in straight stereo bypass mode, the DVD input would switch to Dolby Digital decoding with THX processing, and the VCR input can be set to Dolby Pro Logic decoding. This would be done automatically every time you switch inputs on the receiver.

Some receivers take this concept a step further by automatically memorizing all the conditions associated with an input, then calling up those settings when you select that input.

3) *Preamplifier-out and power-amplifier–in jacks.* These RCA jacks on the receiver's rear panel let you convert your A/V receiver to either a controller or a multichannel power amplifier.

If you're satisfied with your A/V receiver's surround decoding and user interface but want more amplifier power, you can connect a separate multichannel power amplifier to the receiver's preamp-out jacks. (You can see these jacks in fig.4-3.) This feature lets you increase your system's power output without getting a new receiver. All of your receiver's functions—source switching, surround decoding, volume control—still work; you've simply bypassed the receiver's power amplifiers. Your A/V receiver has just been converted into a controller.

Conversely, if you want to upgrade the controller section of your receiver (to add, say, a Dolby Digital or DTS decoder) and are happy with your receiver's power output, you can connect a separate controller to your receiver's power-amplifier–in jacks. Your A/V receiver has just been converted into a multichannel power amplifier.

Finally, the preamp-out and power-amplifier–in jacks let you put a subwoofer crossover in the signal path. A few subwoofers can be connected this way rather than via the receiver's subwoofer out jack. The subwoofer crossover removes bass from the left and right channels and feeds it to the subwoofer.

Without preamplifier-out and power-amplifier–in jacks your upgrade possibilities and connection options are limited.

4) *24-bit/96kHz DACs.* Newer A/V receivers can accept 24-bit, 96kHz digital audio signals from DVD players, which offer better sound quality than 16-bit, 44.1kHz signals. In addition to being able to receive and process high-resolution 24/96 signals, the DACs of a "24/96" receiver will be able to convert such signals to analog.

5) *Component video switching.* As described in Chapter 7, component video connection offers vastly better picture quality than composite video or S-video connection. Component video, carried on three separate cables, is available on DVD players and some video monitors. A select few A/V receivers provide the ability to connect several component-video sources into the receiver, and select which one is sent to the video monitor. Without this feature, you must connect the DVD player directly to the video monitor and switch the input on the video monitor before watching a DVD source.

6) *Multi-room capability.* Some A/V receivers are "multi-room"–capable, meaning they will play music in two rooms at the same time. The front left and right channels typically power two speakers in the "main" room, and the surround amplifier channels power two speakers in the "remote" room. To take advantage of this feature, your home must be wired for multi-room operation. This feature isn't important if all your listening will be in the same room.

7) *Equalization.* In addition to the familiar bass and treble knobs, A/V receivers can offer extensive equalization options. A built-in equalizer

lets you adjust the frequency balance of your system to overcome acoustical problems in your room or deficiencies in your loudspeakers. It's easy to set an equalizer incorrectly, however, and get worse sound. And you can't force low bass out of a small loudspeaker by cranking up the bass on an equalizer. An equalizer is the least important of the features listed here. Most users will never need an equalizer.

8) *Separate center-channel delay control.* As described in Chapter 9, the front three loudspeakers should be arranged in a semicircle with the center-channel loudspeaker set back behind the left and right loudspeakers. This placement puts all three loudspeakers the same distance from your ears. If the three loudspeakers were in a straight line, you'd be sitting closer to the center-channel speaker and the soundstage would be appear to be less spacious.

This is where the center-channel delay control comes in. If your setup mandates putting the three front speakers in a line, a receiver's center-channel delay control lets you delay the signal to the center channel so that it arrives at your ears at the same time as the sound from the left and right loudspeakers. Because sound travels at the speed of about 1 foot per millisecond (0.001 second), a center-channel delay of 2ms is like moving your center-channel loudspeaker back by two feet. This is a nice feature, but not essential. A more elaborate version of this feature, often found in THX-certified products that also include Dolby Digital decoding, lets you delay the sound from the left and right speakers in installations where the center speaker is placed behind a projection screen.

9) *Dynamic-range compression.* Available only with Dolby Digital–equipped receivers and when playing Dolby Digital sources, dynamic-range compression lets you listen to a movie at a lower peak level without losing clarity. If you want to watch a movie late at night and family members are sleeping elsewhere in the house, you don't want explosions to wake them. But if you simply turn down the volume, you won't be able to hear dialog and low-level sounds. A dynamic-range compressor boosts quiet sounds and reduces loud sounds so that you hear all the clarity at a low listening level.

Note that this boosting of quiet sounds and reducing the volume of loud sounds isn't arbitrary. The film-sound mixers insert codes in the Dolby Digital signal that control the compression of the dynamic range in a way that doesn't degrade the viewing experience.

Compressing a movie's dynamic range can be a good thing even when listening at a loud level. Some film soundtracks hype explosions and effects to the point that you find yourself reaching to turn down the volume during loud parts, then turning it up again to hear the dialog clearly. A dynamic-range compressor can overcome these problems.

10) *"5.1-Channel Ready."* As described earlier in this chapter, a "5.1-Channel Ready" receiver will connect to a separate surround decoder.

This feature lets you upgrade a Dolby Pro Logic receiver to Dolby Digital or DTS decoding.

Not all 5.1-Channel Ready receivers handle the signal identically. Some provide no filtering of bass from the main channels when you're using a subwoofer. The receiver manufacturer is counting on the separate surround decoder to filter the signals before they get to the receiver. Unfortunately, not all surround decoders have filtering—their manufacturers count on the receiver to provide filtering. It is therefore possible that certain surround processors and 5.1-Channel Ready receivers won't work well together. A 5.1-Channel Ready receiver with subwoofer filtering is preferable to a receiver without filtering. In addition, some THX-certified 5.1-Channel Ready receivers no longer perform THX processing when used with an external decoder. This limitation varies from model to model; check the receiver's specifications before making a purchase.

As mentioned previously, a "5.1-Channel Ready" input is also called a discrete 6-channel input, which means it can accept the six analog outputs of a DVD-Audio or SACD player.

11) *Record-out selector.* This feature lets you send one source to the tape-output jacks while you listen to another source. You can thus record one program while listening to a different program.

User Interface

An A/V receiver can be easy to set up initially and a joy to use on a daily basis. Or it can be a confusing nightmare that makes you feel lucky to get any sound at all from your speakers—never mind fine-tuning the receiver for the best performance.

Which of these situations comes to pass is determined by the receiver's *user interface*, a term that encompasses the front-panel controls and display, the remote control, and the onscreen display. Some products are easy and intuitive to use; others are frustrating and complex. Choosing an A/V receiver with a well-thought-out user interface makes a big difference not only in how easy the product is to use, but also in the sonic performance you'll get from the receiver. If you understand and can easily control the receiver, you're much more likely to set it up optimally. Poor user interface is, in my view, the biggest impediment to enjoying home theater. You want to turn the system on, put in a disc, press PLAY, and enjoy the film—there's nothing worse than fiddling with controls in the dark two minutes into a movie. Unfortunately, most consumers don't consider the user interface—until they get the unit home and try to set it up.

One dead giveaway of a poorly designed user interface is a remote control with a forest of identically sized and shaped black buttons against a black background. If the remote control is poorly realized, it doesn't bode well for the rest of the user interface.

Some remote controls have as many as 75 buttons, with little or no grouping of similar functions. A well-designed remote should use colors to identify groups of controls: input switching in one color group; level controls and surround modes in another group; CD and DVD player controls in another; and so on. Different shapes also help decipher what a button does. The shapes of a pair of triangular buttons, one pointing up, the other down, suggest their functions: volume up and down. Similarly, the PLAY command for a DVD player may be a triangle pointing to the right. Infrequently used controls should be hidden behind a small flip-open panel to reduce confusion. Conversely, frequently used controls (overall volume, for example) should be larger in size, and located beneath your thumb as you hold the remote. Some remotes offer buttons that glow in the dark for easy location. Other remotes light up with the push of a button.

Another factor to consider is whether the remote control operates by sending IR (infrared) signals, or by RF (radio frequency) signals. IR remotes must be pointed at the component they are controlling; RF remotes work without pointing. Some IR remotes are more directional than others; that is, they work only when the remote is pointed right at the component. RF remotes can also be bi-directional, receiving information from the component as well as sending the component commands. These bi-directional RF remotes, however, quickly consume batteries.

The receiver's front-panel display should be easy to read, tell you what source is selected, what surround mode is invoked, if THX processing is engaged (on THX-certified products), and the volume setting. Some receivers have a numerical readout of volume; others have a small red light in the volume-control knob that rotates with the knob. Source selection is usually via a row of buttons marked LD, DVD, TUNER, or PHONO; selecting which source you want to watch/hear is simply a matter of pushing the appropriate button. Other receivers have a system in which you push the input-select button several times to scroll through the various inputs until the input you want appears in the display. The direct-access pushbutton method is easier—except in the dark, when you have to read the remote's markings to find the right button. It's also helpful if the display readout tells you the name of the source, such as PVR or DVD rather than just VIDEO 1 and VIDEO 2.

Many of an A/V receiver's setup and control functions are performed through the receiver's *onscreen display* (*OSD*). Your video monitor will usually show a menu system that lets you tell the system whether or not you have a subwoofer, at what volume to set each of the channels, if the center-channel loudspeaker is large or small, how much surround-channel delay you want, and a host of other parameters. This type of onscreen display uses text exclusively to guide you through the setup. You interact with the text-based systems by moving a cursor and pressing an ENTER key to input commands.

Other products have a graphical, icon-based system that is much easier to use. For example, the onscreen display may show you an illustration of a room with a video monitor and five loudspeakers (plus an optional subwoofer). The left and right loudspeaker icons will flash on and off as the display asks you whether the left and right loudspeakers are large or small. Similarly, the individual channel levels may be represented in a bar-graph form that allows you to quickly and easily see how the individual channel levels are set, and to adjust them. And rather than ask you to INPUT DELAY TIME IN MILLISECONDS, the onscreen display has a place for you to enter the distance in feet you sit from each loudspeaker. The system then sets the optimum delay time, based on those distances. One panel of an excellent, icon-based onscreen display is shown in fig.4-4.

Fig. 4-4 A/V receivers are set up and adjusted through an on-screen display.

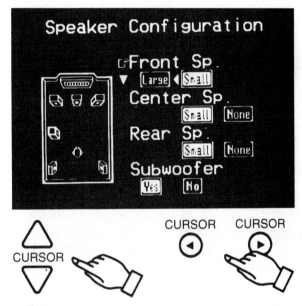

Courtesy Denon Electronics

The onscreen display is helpful in setting up an A/V receiver. It can also be a nuisance when you're watching a movie. Let's say you're ten minutes into a movie and you discover that the dialog is a little hard to hear. The solution is to increase the center-channel level by 2–3dB, which makes the dialog clearer and more intelligible. You want to press a button on the remote control to effect this center-channel boost but not disturb the flow of the movie. If an onscreen display obscures the picture every time you adjust a parameter, the experience is interrupted for everyone watching the movie.

The best solution is a receiver that either lets you turn off the OSD, or never turns it on in the first place when you're making minor changes to frequently adjusted parameters. The only functions you're likely to change when watching a movie are overall volume level, center-channel volume, and surround volume. These should not be accompanied by onscreen displays.

Some receivers have two video monitor outputs: one overlaid with an OSD, the other with no OSD. After configuring and setting up the system with the monitor connected to the output with an OSD, you simply switch one cable so that the monitor is driven by the signal that never contains an OSD. In addition to keeping the OSD from distracting from a film, the output with no OSD sometimes gives slightly better video quality.

How do you determine whether or not a particular receiver has a good or bad user interface? First, ask the salesman to take you through the setup menus and controls. If *he* has a hard time, watch out. Second, get out the owner's manual and remote control in the store and go through the setup yourself. Is the system simple and intuitive, or complex and frustrating? Trying the product yourself also gives you the advantage of letting you ask questions while you're in the store rather than after you've taken the product home. Finally, you should read reviews that describe the product's user interface. In my A/V receiver reviews for *The Perfect Vision* (888-475-5991, www.theperfectvision.com) I always comment on the quality of the receiver's user interface.

The remote control that comes with your A/V receiver is probably what's called a "learning remote." This means that it will learn the commands of your other remote controls (such as a PVR, VCR, or DVD machine) so that one remote can control the entire system. You can also replace the receiver's stock remote control with a third-party model that makes controlling your system much easier. The Marantz RC2000 (fig.4-5) is a good example of how an entire home-theater system can be controlled by an intuitive learning remote. The unit also includes an illuminated display that tells you the system's status. And to make using the controls easier in the dark, the buttons are illuminated.

Fig. 4-5 Add-on remote controls can make using your home-theater system easier.

Courtesy Marantz America

One other type of user interface does away with lots of buttons on a remote control. Instead, the remote control has just one button. You interact with the system through a graphic display on the video monitor by moving the remote control to navigate a cursor to the desired icon (VOLUME UP, for example) and clicking the remote's single button. For example, the onscreen display might show the controls of a VCR. To start the VCR playing, you position the cursor on the "button" with a forward arrow, then click the remote control's button. This system has the advantage of a single button, but requires a large and intrusive display on your video monitor every time you want to make *any* adjustment.

Finally, some remote controls provide a touchpad screen instead of buttons. The touchpad remote can be easier to use, but uses batteries quickly. These remotes also provide two-way communication between the A/V receiver and remote control, rather than simply sending commands from the remote to the receiver.

Surround-Sound Decoding Formats

Virtually all A/V receivers incorporate Dolby Pro Logic decoding. As described in Chapter 2, Dolby Pro Logic is a better decoding method than straight Dolby Surround. Because Pro Logic is used in so many products (thus lowering its cost), it has largely superseded Dolby Surround decoding.

Starting in 1997, many receivers incorporated Dolby Digital decoding in addition to Pro Logic. As Dolby Digital receivers have sold in ever-larger numbers, the price has dropped dramatically. Today, even entry-level receivers include Dolby Digital and DTS decoding; the same DSP chip can be quickly and easily reprogrammed to decode DTS.

As described in Chapter 2, several new surround-sound formats have been introduced recently, notably Dolby Digital Surround EX and DTS-ES. Before buying an A/V receiver, consider whether you think it's worth paying a premium for these new decoding formats, as well as going through the trouble of installing a back-surround speaker or speakers behind the listening position.

Should You Buy a THX-Certified Receiver?

Choosing a THX-certified A/V receiver has many advantages. First, THX's signal processing (surround decorrelation, timbre matching, re-equalization, subwoofer crossover) is of unquestionable benefit in reproducing film soundtracks in the home. Second, you know that the receiver has achieved a certain level of technical performance. Third, a receiver with THX certification will likely have all the output power you'll ever need. Finally, using a THX-certified receiver with THX-certified loudspeakers and subwoofer takes the guesswork out of matching the receiver to the loudspeakers. (THX certification for loudspeakers is described in Chapter 6.)

However, you should know that there are many excellent A/V receivers on the market that *don't* bear the THX logo; their manufacturers simply decided not to participate in the THX licensing program"or pay Lucasfilm the THX royalty on each unit sold.

Given the choice between two products of roughly equal quality, only one of which was THX-certified, I'd choose the THX product. I'd even pay a premium for THX certification. But I'd never buy a product solely because it was THX-certified. When choosing an A/V receiver, weigh all the factors described in this chapter.

Power Output: How Much Do You Need?

A receiver's power-output rating is sometimes the only criterion consumers use when choosing an A/V receiver. But power output is only one of many factors that reveal a product's quality. Moreover, power output isn't always an indicator of how loudly your home-theater system will play. In fact, the loudspeakers connected to the A/V receiver have as much influence on the system's volume capability as does amplifier power.

Specifically, loudspeakers vary in their *sensitivity*, a measure of how much sound they produce for a given amount of input power. To come up with a loudspeaker's sensitivity rating, its *sound-pressure level (SPL)* is measured while the loudspeaker is being driven with one watt of power. The SPL is specified in decibels, or dB. For example, loudspeaker A may have a sensitivity of 83dB/1W/1m. The "1W" means that the speaker was driven by one watt of power; "1m" means the speaker's sound output was measured from a distance of one meter; and "83dB" means that the speaker produced a sound-pressure level of 83 decibels under these conditions. A very sensitive speaker, which we'll call speaker B might have a sensitivity of 95dB/1W/1m.

What does this sensitivity difference mean in the real world? A lot. Every 3dB *decrease* in loudspeaker sensitivity requires a *doubling* of amplifier power to achieve the same loudness. That means that speaker A (83dB sensitivity) would need 16 times the amplifier power to produce a given sound-pressure level compared to speaker B (95dB sensitivity). That's right: 160W driving speaker A produces the same volume as 10W driving speaker B.

This relationship between loudspeaker sensitivity and amplifier output power was dramatically illustrated in an unusual demonstration conducted more than 50 years ago. In 1948, to show how true to life his speakers sounded, loudspeaker pioneer Paul Klipsch conducted a live vs. recorded demonstration with a symphony orchestra and his Klipschorn speakers. His amplifier power: 5W. The Klipschorns are so sensitive (an astounding 105dB/1W/1m) that they will produce very high volume with very little input power.

We've seen that every doubling of amplifier power yields an increase of 3dB. Consequently, there's a 3dB difference between a 10W amplifier and a 20W amplifier, but also between a 500W amplifier and a 1000W amplifier. Although the output power is vastly greater between 500W and 1000W than between 10W and 20W, the difference is still 3dB. When comparing power-amplifier ratings, consider the ratio of output powers, not the number of watts. This means that you can choose a lower-powered (and less expensive) receiver if your loudspeakers have a high sensitivity (89dB or higher).

Other factors to consider in determining your power-amplifier needs are the size of your home-theater room, its acoustical character-istics, and how loudly you like to play movies. The larger the room, and the more sound-absorbing material in it (drapes, padded furni-ture), the more power you'll need. And if you like to hear movie soundtracks reproduced at room-shaking volumes, choose a receiver with high output power.

Now for some concrete numbers. Let's say you have loudspeakers of average sensitivity (87dB/1W/1m) in an average-size room (3000 cubic feet), and like to listen at loud but not blasting sound-pressure levels. A receiver with 70Wpc is adequate for such conditions. And remember that if you have a 70Wpc receiver and want to play the system 3dB loud-er (a perceptible but not significant increase), you'll need a receiver with 140Wpc to achieve the 3dB increase in volume.

Yet another factor influences how powerful a receiver you need: whether or not you have a subwoofer with a built-in power amplifier. When using a subwoofer, low bass is kept out of the front three chan-nels, which reduces the amount of amplifier power needed to drive the main loudspeakers. Low bass requires more amplifier power to repro-duce than do midrange and treble frequencies. By directing the bass to the subwoofer and away from the front speakers, the receiver's power amplifiers don't have to work as hard. Adding a powered subwoofer reduces the receiver's power-output requirements by about 20%. (Other benefits of adding a subwoofer to your home-theater system are described in Chapter 6.)

Power-Output Claims: Why All "100W" Receivers are Not Created Equal

When manufacturers made the transition from 2-channel stereo receivers to multichannel A/V receivers, they were faced with a dilemma. Consumers were used to high power ratings from 2-channel receivers, sometimes several hundred watts per channel. But the requirement of five, six, and even seven amplifier channels in a single chassis no bigger than a 2-channel receiver forced manufacturers to cut back on output power per channel. To avoid making the new A/V receivers appear under-powered, many manufacturers resorted to "specsmanship" to make their products seem more powerful than they really were.

How much output power a receiver can produce depends on the conditions under which it was measured. These conditions are described in the jargon that follows a power-output rating. For example, a receiver's spec sheet may say "xWpc continuous RMS power into 8 ohms from 20Hz to 20kHz with no more than x% THD, all channels driven." This is an honest specification. Products that include this detailed description as part of the output power rating can be directly compared with each other.

To understand how power ratings can be fudged, we need to understand what each of these elements means. First, the word "continuous" means that the amplifier can deliver its rated power continuously, not just over a short period of time. Next, the letters "RMS" stand for "Root Mean Square," a mathematical formula that best describes an amplifier's usable output power. Some manufacturers rate the output power as "peak" power rather than RMS, which exaggerates the power-output claim by about 30%.

The impedance into which the power is generated should be specified. A receiver will always put out more power when measured into a 6 ohm or 4 ohm load than into a standard 8 ohm load. Manufacturers will sometimes try to sneak by a power rating into a 6 ohm load when specifying the center- or surround-channel output power. This technique makes the receiver seem more powerful than it really is.

The next part of the specification tells you over what *bandwidth* (range of audio frequencies) the amplifier can deliver its rated power. An honest specification will measure the amplifier's output power from 20Hz (the lowest audible frequency) to 20,000Hz (or 20kHz, the highest audible frequency). Watch out for power ratings made at "1kHz." Obviously, an amplifier that can deliver its rated power over the entire audio range is more powerful than one that can deliver its power only over a narrow frequency band. Another trick to watch out for is the specification that says "40Hz–20kHz." By excusing the receiver from reproducing low bass (from 20Hz to 40Hz), its power output is made to look larger.

The next element in the specification is the amount of THD (Total Harmonic Distortion) the receiver produces at its rated output power. A low THD figure doesn't mean the receiver has a cleaner sound, only that the receiver wasn't unfairly overdriven when its maximum output power was measured.

The final element of the specification, "all channels driven," tells you that the receiver put out its rated power when all five, six, or seven channels were driven simultaneously. This is a difficult condition to meet in a multichannel A/V receiver, but one that indicates the receiver's fundamental power abilities. After all, a film soundtrack doesn't contain sounds in only one channel at a time, but in many channels simultaneously. Testing for THX certification is performed with all channels driven.

Next time you compare power-output ratings, look closely at the fine print.

Binding Posts

One feature related to a receiver's output power is the binding posts that provide the connection to your loudspeakers. Some manufacturers take the cheap route of supplying spring-clip terminals: You hold in a tab and insert the speaker wire into a tiny hole; when you let go, a spring clamps down on the wire. This is the worst possible termination for connecting your loudspeakers to the receiver. First, the contact area between wire and spring clip is tiny, and can restrict current flow from receiver to loudspeaker. Second, the clip and exposed copper wire will oxidize, thus degrading the connection. Third, the spring clip is fragile and easily broken.

A much better termination is called the binding post. The binding posts on most A/V receivers accept speaker cables terminated with banana plugs, which simply slide into the binding post. The best termination of all is the "five-way" binding post, which accepts banana plugs and spade lugs. (Cables and terminations are described in Chapter 8.)

Build Quality and Sound Quality

Reviews of A/V receivers make reference to a product's *build quality*. This term describes the solidity of the mechanical construction, parts quality inside the unit, and electrical construction techniques. Build quality also encompasses such things as: whether or not the RCA jacks are gold-plated to resist corrosion; the quality of the loudspeaker binding posts; the thickness of the chassis metal (or if plastic is used); and if the unit appears to be made as cheaply as possible, or if the designers did what they could within their design budget to improve the product's quality.

For example, I've reviewed A/V receivers whose manufacturers took every possible shortcut to save money. In one product the loudspeaker terminals were spring clips, the unit used a single amplifier channel to drive both surround loudspeakers, the power transformer was undersize and lightweight, the electronic circuitry was made from integrated circuits rather than separate transistors, the chassis bottom panel was plastic, and the heatsinks that keep the circuitry cool were marginally adequate. This receiver carried a list price of $1095.

Another A/V receiver—this one priced at $699—featured high-quality binding posts for loudspeaker connections, an oversize power transformer, a separate power supply for the center-channel amplifier to improve performance, high-quality electronic parts such as resistors and capacitors, all-transistor circuitry rather than cheaper integrated circuits, copper shielding inside to electrically isolate subsections from each other, large heatsinks, and a sturdy, all-metal chassis.

Looking inside the first receiver, it was obvious that the manufacturer cut as many corners as possible to maximize profit. It was equally obvious from looking inside the second receiver that the designers had really tried to make a quality product. The marketplace embraces a huge range of value for money; without knowing what to look for, it's difficult for a consumer to judge build quality. That's one reason product reviews in reputable magazines are invaluable in choosing an A/V receiver. This range of build quality also points to why it's a mistake to buy the "most watts per dollar" in an A/V receiver.

If the receiver you're considering hasn't been reviewed, here's a down-and-dirty way to judge build quality: Compare the weights of the competing receivers. Assuming comparable power ratings, the product with the better build quality will often weigh more than the more cheaply built one. The most expensive—and heavy—single component of an A/V receiver is the power transformer. This is where manufacturers typically scrimp to save money. You can also get a feel for a product's quality by looking at its binding posts. Spring clips are a good indicator that the manufacturer tried to reduce the manufacturing cost rather than make something of lasting value. Conversely, some manufacturers cut corners on the chassis so they can put more of the build budget into better-quality parts inside. These products often provide superior sound at a reasonable price.

A/V receivers also vary in their sound quality from brand to brand. Some products sound better when reproducing film soundtracks and music than do other products. A high-quality A/V receiver will have a smooth and natural-sounding treble; listen to cymbals and dialog sibilance (*s*, *sh*, and *ch* sounds) for a metallic or irritating sound. If the treble seems to stand out from the rest of the music or film soundtrack, that's an indication that the receiver's sound quality is poor. This test assumes that the loudspeakers have a smooth treble response. Always compare receiver sound quality through the same loudspeakers. The higher the loudspeaker quality during listening evaluations, the more differences you'll hear between receiver brands and models.

Receivers also vary in their bass quantity and quality. Some receivers, particularly those with large power transformers, have a deeper, more extended bottom end that adds solidity and impact to the sonic presentation. A good test of bass dynamics and power is the opening song from the Eagles' DVD *Hell Freezes Over*. It starts with a huge unaccompanied bass drum that can quickly separate the solid-performing receivers from the low-quality models.

You should also listen for the quality of the spatial presentation on both film soundtracks and music-only recordings. On music, a solo vocalist should appear as a focused aural "image" directly between the front two loudspeakers, and you should be able to point to the exact location of instruments in the music. When reproducing soundtracks, the better A/V receivers will produce a greater sense of envelopment and diffusion. Also, listen for detail in the surround channels. Do you hear individual raindrops, for example, or just a smeared, continuous rain sound? To judge these qualities, however, you must connect the receiver to a properly set-up loudspeaker system.

Better receivers also localize sound better. That is, they let you hear the source of a sound with greater precision. One sound is right here, another clearly over there. Dialog intelligibility also varies between models. Some receivers present clear and easily understandable dialog that rises above the music and effects. Other products tend to bury the dialog and make it hard to hear. There's nothing more fatiguing than straining to hear dialog. These spatial aspects are largely the result of differences in the quality of the Dolby Pro Logic or Dolby Digital decoding circuits. Not all such circuits are implemented equally well.

FM Tuner Performance

The tuner performance in A/V receivers is another quality variable. Unlike other home-theater specifications, which tell you little about sound quality, an FM tuner's specifications are revealing. If you live far from radio transmitters, the tuner's *sensitivity* is of paramount importance. Sensitivity is expressed in microvolts (μV); the lower the number, the easier it is for the tuner to pick up distant radio stations. If you live in an urban area whose airwaves are crowded with stations, the tuner's *alternate-channel selectivity* is more important. This specification indicates how well the tuner can reject strong stations near the desired station. The higher the selectivity, the greater the tuner's ability to reject unwanted adjacent or alternate stations.

When a tuner receives two signals, it must suppress the weaker one and capture the stronger one. A tuner's *capture ratio* indicates how well the tuner can capture the desired station; the lower the number, the better the performance.

A vital element in tuner performance is the quality of the antenna connected to your A/V receiver. A tuner is only as good as the signal it picks up. That's why it's hard to compare FM tuner performance in a showroom: the different receivers may have different antennas, or one antenna may be better oriented than another.

How *Not* to Choose an A/V Receiver

Many consumers buy receivers or power amplifiers based on their output-power ratings. This "most watts per dollar" mentality usually results in the consumer getting the *worst* sound for the money. Some mass-market manufacturers make the receiver as powerful as possible for a given price, even at the expense of overall performance. They know that many consumers will buy a product based on its spec sheet, not personal listening experience. A product that looks good on paper often disappoints when you get it home.

Similarly, many consumers judge a receiver by the amount of *Total Harmonic Distortion* (THD) the product has. THD has nothing to do with sound quality. In fact, receivers with very low THD figures probably sound worse than receivers with higher THD figures. Here's why: THD can be reduced by using a design technique called *negative feedback*, in which a portion of the output signal is fed back to the input. The greater the amount of negative feedback, the lower the THD (all other factors being equal). Although negative feedback lowers the THD, it introduces all kinds of other problems that degrade a receiver's sound quality. It's a perfect example of trading away sound quality to achieve a better specification that is actually meaningless, but is perceived by the general public to be an important indicator of sound quality.

Another trap is choosing a receiver based on the number of "surround modes" offered. These signal-processing circuits attempt to simulate various acoustical environments, accessible via such settings as STADIUM, ROCK CLUB, or CONCERT HALL. In reality, these signal-processing modes are useless gimmicks that actually degrade the fidelity to the original source. Nonetheless, virtually all A/V receivers include some form of such signal processing. Ironically, higher-end A/V receivers have fewer surround modes than budget models. The manufacturers know that the entry-level buyer is more easily influenced by the number of surround modes than is the more sophisticated buyer of top-end A/V receivers.

The best place to begin your search for a high-quality A/V receiver is by reading competent and honest magazine reviews. Some of the "consumer" magazines are undoubtedly unbiased, but their reviewers lack the skills and experience necessary to fully evaluate such sophisticated products. Moreover, the testers for these magazines aren't enthusiasts, and consequently have very low standards of what constitutes good performance. If the reviewers don't care about performance improvements, how can they value them? And if they've never experienced truly high-end home theater, how can they put the receiver's performance in its proper context?

Conversely, some magazines employ competent reviewers, but the magazines themselves are advertiser-driven—they won't say anything bad about a product made by a company that advertises in their pages. A few magazines are uncompromising in their editorial integrity, and employ veteran writers with a passion for their subject. Read a magazine for a few months before following their recommendations. You'll know which ones to trust.

But the best way to ensure that you're buying a quality product is to do business with a specialty audio/video retailer who considers you a long-term customer. How to find such a retailer is discussed in Chapter 8.

5 Audio/Video Controllers and Power Amplifiers

Introduction: Should You Buy an A/V Receiver or Separate Components?

Most home-theater enthusiasts will choose an A/V receiver as the heart of their systems. The A/V receiver is cost-effective, easy to set up and use, and consumes the least amount of space. A good-quality A/V receiver can provide satisfying performance.

If you want to take the next step up in sound quality and upgrade flexibility, however, home-theater *separates* are the way to go. Rather than combine a controller, multichannel power amplifier, and FM tuner in the same chassis, separates divide these functions among individual components (fig.5-1). The controller section of an A/V receiver performs surround decoding, source switching, and digital signal processing. With separates, these functions are performed by a standalone product called a *controller*, also known as an A/V preamplifier or surround-sound processor. Because "controller" best describes the product's function, we'll use that term throughout this book.

Separates generally offer better performance than A/V receivers for several reasons. First, the designer isn't constrained by the need to fit lots of electronics into a single chassis. The product can be designed for optimum performance or maximum power-amplifier output power, not economy of chassis space. Second, separating the various functions improves sonic performance—the electronic subsystems can't interact with each other when they're in separate chassis. For example, a power amplifier's large power transformer can radiate noise into a receiver's sensitive controller circuits, but is unlikely to do so if the controller is in a separate chassis. Third, separates offer greater upgrade flexibility com-

Fig. 5-1
Ambitious
home-theater
systems use a
separate A/V
controller and
multichannel
power amplifier
instead of an
A/V receiver.

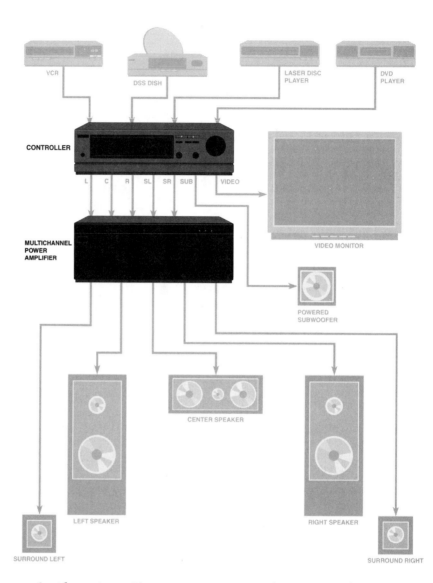

Fig. 5-1
Ambitious home-theater systems use a separate A/V controller and multichannel power amplifier instead of an A/V receiver.

pared with receivers. If you want to increase the power to the surround channels, for example, you can simply buy a more powerful rear-channel amplifier. In addition, separates are more easily adaptable to changing technology. Finally, all the cutting-edge electronic design in home-theater electronics is done in separate components, not receivers.

The higher performance of separates comes at a price. An entry-level controller and multichannel power amplifier will set you back about $2200. Although this is about the same price as better-quality A/V receiver, the separates will probably offer less output power and fewer features. A separates package with the same features and power output as a top-quality A/V receiver will generally cost about 20% more than a comparably equipped receiver. The higher price of a separate controller and multichannel power amplifier is partially because the manufacturer must make two chassis instead of one, and provide two power cords, two shipping cartons, two owner's manuals, and so forth. Fig.5-2 shows a high-end controller and 5-channel power amplifier.

Another option is the *controller/tuner*, a component that combines a controller and AM/FM tuner in one chassis. The controller/tuner provides many of the advantages of separates, but doesn't require that you buy an additional component to hear radio broadcasts.

Fig. 5-2 A high-end controller and 5-channel power amplifier.

Courtesy Classé Audio

Proceed AMP 5 photo courtesy Madrigal Audio Laboratories

The Controller

No product better exemplifies the fundamental shift in home-entertainment technology than the controller. The controller is an entirely new product category that combines many diverse functions in a single chassis. To understand what a controller is and does is to understand the technologies that are transforming the way we reproduce sound in our homes.

A modern controller replaces as many as four separate components in your music and home-theater system: the source-switching functions of a preamplifier, a surround-sound decoder, six (or eight) channels of digital-to-analog conversion, and an electronic crossover to split up the frequency spectrum. Moreover, the rapidly increasing computing power of today's controllers points to a future in which they will incorporate even more functions and capabilities, such as digital signal processing for loudspeaker and room correction. While power amplifiers and loudspeakers change relatively little over time, the controller represents a radical new path to the future by seamlessly merging a diverse array of sophisticated processing and controls to provide nearly transparent interoperability to the user.

Most of the description of an A/V receiver in the previous chapter also describes how a controller works. The only difference is that the controller feeds a separate amplifier or amplifiers. To recap, a controller:

- receives video and audio signals from various source components (PVR, VCR, DSS, DVD) and selects which are sent to the video monitor and home-theater audio system (this function is called "source switching");

- performs surround decoding, whether Dolby Pro Logic, Pro Logic II, Dolby Digital, DTS, THX Surround EX, or DTS-ES;

- controls playback volume;

- makes adjustments in system setup, such as the individual channel levels;

- directs bass to the appropriate loudspeakers or subwoofers (called bass management); and

- performs THX processing (if so equipped).

A controller has multiple audio and video inputs to accept signals from your source components. It then performs surround decoding to create a multichannel signal for output to the separate power amplifiers. Controllers with Dolby Digital decoding have six line-level outputs, those with THX Surround EX and DTS-ES have eight line-level outputs. As mentioned in Chapters 2 and 4, one of these outputs is marked LFE (Low-Frequency Effects), the ".1" channel in 5.1-channel sound that carries additional bass signals for high-impact, very low bass sounds, such as explosions. The LFE output is connected to a powered subwoofer. Bass from other channels can be selectively added to form the subwoofer drive signal. For example, if you have small front speakers, you can direct the front-channel bass to the subwoofer along with the LFE channel. Fig.5-1, shown earlier, illustrates how a controller is connected to a multichannel power amplifier and a subwoofer.

The controller is the master control center of your home-theater system. When you first set up a controller, its onscreen display will guide you through selecting such things as whether or not you're using a subwoofer, if your surround loudspeakers are large or small, and calibrating individual channel levels and delay times. You will also control the system on a day-to-day basis through the controller's front panel and remote control. This includes source selection, volume adjustment, and the setting of individual channel levels (described in Chapter 9).

As described in Chapter 2, some controllers are THX-certified, meaning that they incorporate certain types of signal processing to better translate film sound into a home environment and meet a set of specific technical criteria. To recap, THX processing in a controller includes re-equalization, surround decorrelation, and timbre matching. Re-equalization removes excessive brightness from film soundtracks for home-theater playback. Surround decorrelation improves the sense of spaciousness from the surround channels by introducing slight differences between the two surround signals. Timbre matching compensates for the fact that the ear doesn't hear the same tonal balance of sounds in all directions. The THX timbre-matching circuit ensures that sounds from the front and rear have the same timbre (tonal balance). To keep their products' prices low, some manufacturers of budget controllers license only the THX re-equalization circuit from Lucasfilm. Such controllers cannot, however, be billed as "THX-certified."

A THX-certified controller will also include a crossover circuit to separate the bass from the rest of the audio spectrum when a subwoofer is connected to the system. The crossover keeps bass out of the front-channel signals, and filters mid and high frequencies from the subwoofer output. A THX crossover has a specified *cutoff frequency* of 80Hz. (The cutoff frequency is the frequency below which bass is sent to the subwoofer output and higher frequencies are sent to the front-channel outputs.)

How to Choose a Controller

Choosing a controller involves many of the same considerations described in the previous chapter. These include making sure the controller has enough inputs for your system, provides your preferred surround-format decoding (THX Surround EX and DTS-ES, for example), offers a friendly user interface, has THX processing and certification (if desired), is well-built, and has good sound quality.

Inputs, Outputs, and Source Switching

Let's start with the controller's most basic function: selecting the source you listen to or watch. The controller accepts audio or A/V (audio and video) signals from all your source components and lets you select which source signal is sent to the power amplifiers and video monitor. A basic controller will offer two analog-audio inputs (for a tuner and CD player, for example) and perhaps four audio/video (A/V) inputs. In addition to the main outputs that drive your TV and power amplifiers, two record outputs are often provided, to drive two VCRs or a VCR and an analog tape recorder.

When choosing a controller, make sure its array of inputs matches or exceeds the number of source components in your system. Your system is likely to expand in the future, so look for a controller with at least one more input than you need right now.

All controllers have inputs for digital audio signals as well as for analog. These inputs receive the digital-audio output of a DVD player, HDTV set-top box, DSS receiver, or CD transport. The signals carried on these digital connections include Dolby Digital, DTS, Dolby Surround, and 2-channel PCM (Pulse Code Modulation) signals, such as from a CD transport.

If you're an old hand at home theater, you probably own a laserdisc player with Dolby Digital output. Further, you know that to get Dolby Digital (once called AC-3) onto a laserdisc, the signal had to be encoded in radio frequency (RF). If you don't want to immediately replace your cherished laserdisc collection with DVDs, you'll probably need a controller that can decode those RF-encoded Dolby Digital discs. If your controller doesn't have an RF digital input (typically labeled AC-3 RF), you'll need an external RF demodulator box. This device converts RF Dolby Digital to bitstream Dolby Digital, which can then be fed to one of the controller's standard digital inputs.

Don't forget the controller's responsibility for handling the video signal. Look for S-video input jacks on all A/V inputs and outputs. Most controllers offer both composite video (on RCA connectors) and S-video jacks. Better models also include component-video switching. Controllers can degrade video quality, and some have better-quality video processing than others.

As more DVD players and video monitors incorporate component-video inputs and outputs (described in Chapter 7), controllers are now offering component-video switching. That is, the controller may have two component-video inputs and one component-video output, allowing you to select which component-video source is displayed on your video monitor. If your controller lacks this feature, you'll need to run the component-video output from your DVD player directly to the component-video input of your video monitor. Some video-switching circuits don't have a wide enough bandwidth to pass HDTV signals without removing high-frequency information. Because fine picture detail is contained in high frequencies, controllers without sufficient video bandwidth can make an HD picture look soft. Note that this problem is avoided by connecting source components directly to the video display, bypassing the controller.

Unlike receivers, with their RCA jacks for inputs and outputs, higher-end controllers sometimes have what are called *balanced* inputs and outputs. A balanced cable, shown in fig.5-3 along with an RCA cable, is found only on higher-end separates. An RCA cable, also called an *unbalanced* or *single-ended* cable, carries the signal on one conductor plus a ground conductor. A balanced cable carries the signal on two conductors, plus a ground. Balanced cables are used in professional audio, and have some advantages over unbalanced cables. Controllers with balanced inputs and outputs will usually offer both balanced and unbalanced connection jacks to ensure compatibility with a wide range of power amplifiers and source components. To use a controller's balanced inputs, your source components must have balanced output jacks. And a controller's balanced output jacks work only with a power amplifier with balanced input jacks. If your source components or power amplifier lack balanced jacks, you can still connect them through the unbalanced (RCA) connections.

Fig. 5-3 Some high-end controllers and power amplifiers can accept either unbalanced cables (top) or balanced cables (bottom).

Courtesy AudioQuest

2-Channel Bypass Modes

For the music lover shopping for a controller that will also serve as a 2-channel preamplifier for his system, one of the most significant considerations is its performance with 2-channel analog sources (especially if you have an extensive vinyl collection) and signals from an SACD or DVD-Audio player. In that case, you'll want a controller that has an *analog bypass* mode. Without an analog bypass mode, the analog signal will be converted to digital and back to analog as it passes through the controller. Digital conversion is far from sonically transparent, so the sound will suffer.

There are two catches to look out for regarding the bypass mode. First, the controller must have an analog volume control. Most modern controllers adjust the volume digitally in their DSP (digital signal processing) chips, which usually don't sound as good as an old-fashioned volume knob. Second, whenever you engage bass management, even a controller with a bypass mode will convert the analog signal to digital because bass management is performed by the DSP chips. If you have a subwoofer with satellite speakers and use the controller's crossover to divide the frequency spectrum, the bypass mode won't remove the A/D and D/A conversions from the signal path. This is a serious limitation for music lovers who demand the ultimate in sound quality.

One novel approach, used by a few manufacturers, is to split the incoming analog signal and filter bass from the left and right outputs with an analog filter. This signal, which has never been digitized, drives the left and right channels. The other half of the split signal is digitized and processed through the controller's bass management, which derives a subwoofer signal. It's not pure analog bypass because the signal driving the subwoofer has been digitized, but bass frequencies are much less likely to be degraded by digital conversions.

If you've found a controller that meets your home-theater needs but lacks an analog bypass mode, you can still enjoy uncompromised music performance by adding an analog preamplifier to your system. Your analog source components connect to the analog preamplifier, as do the left and right outputs from the controller. In essence, the preamplifier is inserted in the signal path between the controller and left- and right-channel power amplifiers. When playing movies through the controller, the analog preamp acts as if it's not there, and has no effect on the signal. With this technique, your analog sources never go through the controller.

Some preamps have a feature (called something like "cinema pass-through") that sets their gain (volume) at a predetermined level when you play movies, so that you don't have to adjust the preamp's volume control to achieve correct volume from the left and right loudspeakers in relation to the other loudspeakers.

Digital Signal Processing (DSP)

The availability of powerful *Digital Signal Processing* (*DSP*) chips has revolutionized controllers in the past few years. DSP chips are the heart and brain of the controller, performing surround-sound decoding, signal processing (equalization, crossovers), and THX post-processing (if the controller is THX-certified). Today's advanced controllers boast the computing power of a late-1980s mainframe computer.

The first job of the DSP chip is decoding; that is, converting a stream of digital data into separate digital signals that can be converted to analog audio. Virtually all controllers today decode the three major surround-sound formats: Dolby Digital, Digital Theater Systems (DTS), and Dolby Surround, as well as their variations, Dolby Digital EX, DTS-ES, Dolby Pro Logic II, and DTS Neo:6.

Even inexpensive A/V receivers sport DSP chips, although they have less computing power than those in high-end controllers. Consequently, high-end controllers offer better implementations of surround-sound decoding, more flexible features, and higher sound quality. (More powerful DSP chips allow greater precision in the mathematical computations performed on the audio signal.)

A DSP chip is a number cruncher that operates on specific instructions (the software) controlling it. When decoding a Dolby Digital source, for example, the software tells the DSP how to decode Dolby Digital. When decoding DTS, the same DSP operates under the instructions for decoding the DTS bitstream. A DSP chip is only as good as the software it is running. That's why some high-end companies write all their own software in-house rather than rely on stock software that performs a given task. As DSP chips grow increasingly more powerful and less expensive, controller capabilities increase proportionately.

Beyond decoding the surround-sound signal, DSP chips provide advanced signal processing that creates such artificial acoustic environments as "stadium" or "concert hall." Such artificial environments are the parlor tricks of DSP.

The Future-Proof Controller: Software Upgrades and Modular Construction

Because of this software control, some controllers can be updated simply by downloading new software into the machine. As new technologies arrive or refinements in existing systems are discovered, you simply install new instructions for the DSP chips. Such "software-based" controllers can be thought of as general-purpose DSP devices that happen to be running the software for Dolby Digital, DTS, and Dolby Pro Logic decoding.

The Proceed AVP is a good example of a software-updatable controller. The unit has an RJ-11 port (a telephone jack) on the rear panel that connects to a computer's RS232 port. A Proceed dealer can download the latest software from the Internet, connect his computer to your AVP (either in your home or his shop), and update the AVP's flash memory. The process takes about eight minutes, can be performed with the AVP installed in your system, and doesn't erase your setup and configuration settings.

New software can add capabilities such as DTS decoding (by changing the DSP code), refining the user interface (by updating the operating system), or configuring the unit to accept formats not available when the product was designed (by changing the input-receiver software). The AVP's input receiver (the chip that receives, identifies, and decodes the incoming bitstream) is custom-made, which allows the AVP to work with future formats whose interface protocols have not yet been established. Updating software in this way reduces the likelihood of needing expensive hardware changes.

Another method of heading off controller obsolescence is "modular" construction, exemplified in the product shown in fig.5-4. Rather than build all the electronics onto a single circuit board inside the controller's chassis, the modular controller is built more like a computer. The modular controller's slotted motherboard accepts plug-in boards that perform specific functions. For example, a modular controller may provide Dolby Pro Logic, Dolby Digital, and DTS decoding on one plug-in board. If you ever decide you also want THX Surround EX or DTS-ES decoding, you simply plug in an additional decoder board.

Fig. 5-4 A modular controller can be updated to new technology simply by plugging in a circuit board.

Courtesy Meridian Audio

The modular controller is a basic platform that can be customized to fit your particular system, expanded as your system grows, or configured to be compatible with future technology. Rather than scrap your controller and start over when technology inevitably marches on, the modular controller is simply reconfigured by plugging in a new board. Modular controllers are also more reliant on software than on hardware. The benefit is that your system never becomes obsolete, and will probably cost less in the long term. The only disadvantage to modular controllers is their higher initial cost.

Some modular controllers (from Theta Digital, for example) also give you the option of choosing the quality of circuitry inside. Every controller has digital-to-analog converter chips that turn digital ones and zeros into analog signals that appear at the controller's six line-level output jacks. The quality of the converters influences sound quality; by specifying the converter quality, you can tailor the modular controller for your budget and system. For example, you may start with basic D/A converters, then upgrade the converters on the front channels as budget permits—simply by removing a board and installing another one.

Bass Management Flexibility

An important controller function performed within the DSP chips is *bass management*, the subsystem that lets you selectively direct bass information in the soundtrack to the main loudspeakers or to the subwoofer. Bass management allows a controller to work correctly with a wide variety of speaker systems. For example, if you have five small loudspeakers and a subwoofer, you tell the controller to filter bass from each of the five channels and to direct it, in sum, to the subwoofer. With a Dolby Digital or DTS movie, the bass from the left, center, right, and surround channels is mixed with the LFE channel to drive the subwoofer. The bass management in most controllers lets you direct the full frequency range to the left and right channels (including the LFE channel), but filter bass from the center and surround channels.

A feature of the most advanced controllers is their ability to specify the crossover frequency and slopes between the subwoofer and main speakers. The crossover is implemented in the digital domain with DSP. That is, the audio spectrum is divided by performing mathematical computations on the ones and zeros representing the audio signal. Splitting the frequency spectrum into bass and treble in the controller is a vastly better approach than subjecting the analog audio signal to the capacitors, resistors, and inductors found in the crossovers built into subwoofers.

The most sophisticated controllers let you specify the crossover frequency (40Hz, 80Hz, 120Hz, for examples), as well as the crossover slope or phase characteristics. The greater the flexibility in specifying crossover frequency, slope, and phase, the greater the likelihood that you can seamlessly integrate the subwoofer with the main speakers. (Crossover slope and phase are described in Chapter 6.)

Keeping low bass out of smaller loudspeakers confers large advantages in the speakers' power handling, dynamic range, midrange clarity, and sense of ease. When the woofer doesn't have to move back and forth a long distance trying to reproduce low bass, the midrange sounds cleaner and the speaker can reproduce loud peaks without distortion.

High-Resolution Digital Audio Decoding and 6-Channel Analog Input

Many controllers today feature the ability to accept digital input signals with word lengths of up to 24 bits and a sampling frequency of 96kHz. This allows them to decode high-resolution digital audio output from a DVD player that can deliver 24/96 digital signals. The selection of 24/96 discs is small, and until a digital interface with a copy-protection system is in place, don't expect many DVD players to provide access to the 24/96 bitstream. That's because manufacturers are sensitive to the music industry's concern about providing consumers access to a recordable, high-resolution digital bitstream that can produce near-perfect copies of the professional master.

A more useful feature for taking advantage of the high-resolution multichannel formats about to come on the market (DVD-Audio and Super Audio CD, or SACD) is a 6-channel analog input on the controller. Until the digital-interface issue is resolved (which may take a long time because it is inextricably linked to the copy-protection problem), DVD-Audio and SACD players will have six analog outputs for reproducing multichannel music discs. Unless your controller has a discrete 6-channel analog input, you won't be able to play high-resolution multichannel music through your system until the copy-protection dust has settled. The 6-channel analog input approach has its drawbacks: You're paying for six DACs in the DVD-A or SACD player and for six DACs in the controller. It would obviously be better and more cost-effective if multichannel DVD-A or SACD was provided to the controller in a single digital datastream. Until then, the most important thing to look for is that the analog bypass is available for the DVD-A and SACD signals. Adding extra layers of conversion will only degrade the sound. The issue becomes more complicated when you add bass management to the mix, since bass management is done in the digital domain.

In early 2002, several manufacturers of A/V equipment began selling DVD-Audio players with a 6-channel, high-resolution digital output, and A/V receivers and controllers with a 6-channel, high-resolution digital input. The interface between the two is a proprietary encrypted format. This means that you can't mix and match brands of DVD-Audio players and receivers; a manufacturer's DVD-Audio player will work only with its own A/V receiver or controller for playing high-resolution multichannel recordings through the digital interface. This lack of standardization is a temporary situation that will exist until a universal, copy-protected format is adopted and approved by record companies.

Digital-to-Analog Conversion

Built into every 5.1-channel controller are six digital-to-analog converters (DACs) and six analog output stages. Controllers with THX Surround EX and DTS-ES capability have eight DACs and eight analog output stages. The DACs convert the digital data for each channel into analog signals. The quality of these DACs and the subsequent analog output stage (which drives the power amplifier through interconnects) is crucial to realizing good sound quality. DACs vary greatly in their sound, and a poor-sounding DAC (or a poor implementation of a good one) can ruin an otherwise excellent controller. More expensive controllers use higher-quality parts and design techniques, including metal-film resistors, polystyrene capacitors, four-layer circuit boards, and exotic circuit-board material. Also look for analog stages made from discrete transistors instead of inexpensive operational-amplifier (or op-amp) chips. Some high-end companies now have considerable expertise in designing cutting-edge digital converters, expertise they can apply to building multichannel digital controllers.

Don't be swayed by marketing hype that touts DACs as "24-bit." Although the DAC may have 24 resistor "rungs" on its "ladder," that doesn't mean it has 24-bit resolution. The last four bits often contain only noise, not real information. Because real-world DAC technology is limited to about 20 bits, those last four bits are known cynically in the industry as "marketing bits."

The best minds working today in digital conversion cite the historical "two bits per decade" rule of converter advancement; that is, it takes an entire decade for DACs to increase their resolution by two bits. Assuming this rate of progress continues, consider this: A 24-bit converter has a theoretical noise floor of –144dBV, but the thermal noise produced by a single 1000-ohm resistor (generated by the random movement of electrons) at room temperature is –125dBV—a noise floor 19dB higher than a 24-bit converter's theoretical limit. I doubt that converter technology will advance beyond 21 bits without a fundamental breakthrough employing new DAC architectures.

In the future, controllers may not need to incorporate digital-to-analog conversion. That's because amplifiers and loudspeakers that accept and operate on digital signals may one day be commonplace. The controller would output digital signals to six digital loudspeakers that process the signal in the digital domain, convert the signals to analog within the loudspeaker, then amplify those signals with power amplifiers built into the loudspeakers. A system based on digital loudspeakers requires only a controller and the digital loudspeakers. Digital power amplifiers are covered later in this chapter.

7.1-Channel Playback from 5.1-Channel Sources

Some home-theater receivers and controllers provide 7.1-channel playback from 5.1-channel sources such as Dolby Digital and DTS. These products have eight channels (seven channels plus a subwoofer) rather than the six channels of most Dolby Digital– and DTS-equipped products. The two additional channels drive two extra speakers placed behind the listener, augmenting the two surround speakers at the sides of the listening location. The eight speakers in a 7.1-channel system are front left, center, and right, surround left and right, back surround (x 2) , and a subwoofer.

Making effective use of the additional surround speakers requires sophisticated signal processing in the controller. For example, the Logic 7 mode in Lexicon's MC-1 digital controller attempts to create the illusion of eight independent channels by cleverly manipulating the signals driving the side and rear speakers.

Here's how it works: When reproducing 5.1-channel sources (Dolby Digital and DTS) with Logic 7 and seven loudspeakers, the MC-1 sends the right surround signal to the right side and right rear speakers, and the left surround signal to the left side and left rear speakers. This is identical to wiring two surround speakers to each surround channel. But as sound effects are panned toward the rear, the Logic 7 algorithm uses equalization to "steer" surround signals between the two side and two rear speakers. Specifically, effects moving from the left to rear pan smoothly from the left front loudspeaker to the left side, then from the left side to both left and right loudspeakers. When effects are moving toward the rear, Logic 7 adds a 3dB treble cut (shelf filter) to the side speaker. As the sound pans farther to the rear, the treble cut becomes greater. When the sound is fully to the rear, a 6dB/octave, 400Hz low-pass filter is applied to the side speakers. The result is an apparent separation between the side and rear channels that heightens the feeling of envelopment, and of sounds in motion. In my experience, Logic 7 processing is surprisingly effective at creating the illusion of being surrounded by a more continuous soundfield.

Other techniques are available for playing 5.1-channel soundtracks through seven loudspeakers plus a subwoofer, although they tend to be less sophisticated than Logic 7.

Controllers with THX Ultra2 processing incorporate a circuit that creates a 7.1-channel signal from any source, allowing you to use your entire 7.1-channel loudspeaker system on all source material, not just on those movies that have been THX EX or DTS-ES encoded.

User Interface

The ease or difficulty of day-to-day operation of your system is determined by the *user interface*. Choosing a controller with a well-designed user interface can make the difference between being completely comfortable using your home-theater system or feeling frustrated by it. What to look for in a controller's user interface is identical to what you'd look for in an A/V receiver (discussed in depth in Chapter 4).

Power Amplifiers for Home Theater

The power amplifier is the workhorse of your home-theater system. It takes in line-level signals from the output of your controller and amplifies them to powerful signals that will drive your home-theater loudspeaker system. A power amplifier has line-level inputs to receive signals from the controller, and terminals for connecting loudspeaker cables. The power amplifier is the last component in the signal path before the loudspeakers.

A separate multichannel power amplifier can offer higher output power than the power amplifiers found in A/V receivers. The most powerful receivers can have outputs of 140 watts per channel; separate power amplifiers offer as much as 350Wpc.

A power amplifier is described by the number of amplifier channels in its chassis. The most common home-theater power amplifiers have five channels for powering the left, center, right, surround left, and surround right loudspeakers. The next most common number of channels is three. A 3-channel amplifier can power the front three loudspeakers, leaving a 2-channel amplifier to handle the two surround loudspeakers. If you already have a stereo (2-channel) amplifier, you can update your system for home theater by adding a 3-channel home-theater amplifier. Alternatively, a 3-channel amplifier can power the center and two surround channels, leaving your stereo amplifier to drive the left and right loudspeakers. As the THX Surround EX and DTS-ES formats become more popular, power amplifiers with seven channels are becoming increasingly available. Note that if you upgrade your controller to a 7.1-channel unit, you can augment your 5-channel power amplifier with a stereo amplifier to power the back-surround speakers.

Some home-theater power amplifiers, called *monoblocks*, drive only one amplifier channel per chassis. The monoblock approach lets you upgrade more easily by buying power for only as many channels as you need. Monoblocks have the potential of better sonic performance, but also cost more than the same number of amplifier channels in a multichannel power amplifier.

How to Choose a Home Theater Power Amplifier

High-quality multichannel power amplifiers are big, heavy, and can be expensive. The more output power provided by the amplifier, the bigger, heavier, and more expensive it will be. Output power, measured in the familiar "watts per channel" (Wpc) units, describes the power amplifier's ability to deliver electrical voltage and current to your loudspeakers. The flow of electrical current is what makes a loudspeaker's cones move back and forth to create sound. If the amplifier's flow of electrical current is restricted, the sound will be restricted as well. When an amplifier runs out of power, the sound becomes strained, hard, even distorted. If you buy an amplifier without enough power for your system, you'll never hear the dynamic impact and clean sound of today's film soundtracks. Moreover, an underpowered amplifier can more easily damage or destroy your loudspeakers.

Conversely, an amplifier with more power than you need will waste your precious home-theater dollars. It follows, then, that one of the most important criteria for choosing a power amplifier is its output power.

Typical power-output ratings of separate home-theater power amplifiers range from 60Wpc to as much as 350Wpc. Contrary to popular opinion, a power amplifier's output rating doesn't tell you everything about how loudly the system will play. Many variables affect a home-theater system's ability to present film soundtracks at realistic volume levels, with wide dynamic range and without distortion; amplifier power is only one of these variables.

As described in Chapter 4, loudspeakers vary in how much of their electrical input is converted to sound. This specification, called the loudspeaker's *sensitivity*, has as much influence on the system's ability to play loudly without strain as does the amplifier's output power. To reiterate from Chapter 4, a loudspeaker sensitivity rating might be listed as "87dB/1W/1m." This means that the loudspeaker produced a sound-pressure level of 87 decibels (dB) when driven by 1 watt of amplifier power, measured 1 meter in front of the loudspeaker. Every 3dB increase of loudspeaker sensitivity is equal to doubling the amplifier power. A loudspeaker rated at 90dB sensitivity would therefore need only half the amplifier power to reach the same listening volume as a loudspeaker with a sensitivity of 87dB.

Other variables in deciding how much power you need include room size, the room's acoustic character, and how loudly you like to play your system. The bigger and more acoustically absorbent the room is, the more amplifier power you need. The relationships between amplifier power, room size, speaker sensitivity, and room acoustics are shown in fig.5-5.

Most home-theater enthusiasts listen at moderate levels to loudspeakers of average sensitivity (85–88dB) in rooms of average size (3000–4500 cubic feet) with average furnishings (carpet, some drapes), and so will need a minimum of about 70W for each of the five, six, or seven channels.

Another important factor in deciding how much amplifier power you need is whether or not you have a subwoofer connected to the system. Without a subwoofer, the main left and right loudspeakers have the job of reproducing all the bass. Consequently, the left and right channels

Fig. 5-5 The relationship between loudspeaker sensitivity, room size, room acoustics, and power-amplifier output power.

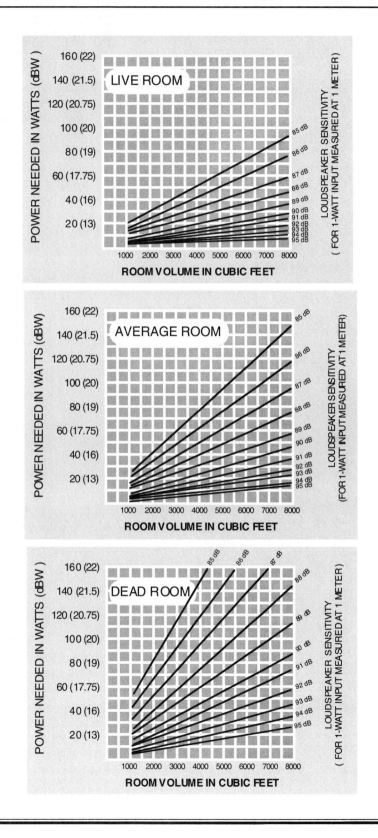

of your power amplifier must carry the burden of amplifying bass frequencies. The accurate reproduction of bass requires much more power than the reproduction of midrange and treble frequencies. Conversely, connecting a subwoofer relieves the left and right loudspeakers from reproducing bass, and the left- and right-channel power amplifiers from driving the speakers' large woofer cones. This leaves more power to amplify the midrange and treble frequencies. In short, if you have a powered subwoofer, you can get by with a lower-powered amplifier.

If your home-theater power amplifier lacks sufficient output power, loud peaks in the soundtrack such as explosions, musical crescendos, and sound effects will sound strained. A home-theater system with sufficient amplifier power gets louder gracefully, and reproduces peaks with more dynamic impact and realism. The last thing you want, when the film soundtrack gets intense, is to hear the system sound distorted or compressed as the amplifier runs out of power. When you're suddenly aware of the sound system, the illusion a home-theater system creates is momentarily shattered.

Finally, the loudspeaker system must be capable of handling the full output power from your amplifier. If the loudspeaker distorts before your power amplifier reaches its power limit, some of your amplifier power is wasted.

Build and Sound Quality

Separate home-theater power amplifiers are generally better made than the power amplifiers found in A/V receivers. The parts in separate power amplifiers are usually more heavy-duty than in receivers, even in products of comparable power ratings.

A crucial element of a power amplifier is its *power transformer*, the large metal block or cylinder inside the chassis that accounts for most of a power amplifier's weight. All of the current that the power amplifier delivers to your loudspeakers must pass through the transformer. All other factors being equal, the larger the transformer, the more current available to drive the loudspeakers.

Let's consider the example of two home-theater power amplifiers, identically rated at 100Wpc into an 8 ohm loudspeaker. All power amplifiers increase their power output when driving impedances of fewer than 8 ohms. That's because a loudspeaker of lower impedance (resistance to flow of electrical current) pulls more current from the power amplifier, which increases the amplifier's power output. How much an amplifier can increase its output power when driving 4 ohms tells us a lot about its build quality.

If we connect 4 ohm loudspeakers to the first amplifier, it may be able to increase its output power from 100Wpc to perhaps 150Wpc. But the second amplifier can deliver 200Wpc when driving 4 ohms. Although these two amplifiers look identical on paper when specified with an 8 ohm speaker, they have very different performances in the real world. The first amplifier could sound anemic, and distort on loud peaks when used with 4 ohm loudspeakers, or with 8 ohm speakers that have an impedance dip at a certain frequency. The second amplifier would reproduce those same peaks without a hint of strain. Moreover, the ability to increase power into 4 ohms is associated with a deeper and better-defined bass reproduction.

This difference is directly related to the power amplifier's ability to deliver current to the loudspeaker. This is where the power transformer's size and weight tip us off to how powerful the amplifier really is. The first amplifier probably had the smaller power transformer. In addition, the first amplifier's heatsinks (the metal cooling fins on the amplifier's side or rear panels) would probably be less beefy. A large, heavy transformer doesn't guarantee good performance, but its size and weight are fairly reliable indicators of the amplifier's fundamental build quality.

Two terms associated with power amplifiers that you should know about are *discrete* and *IC*. A fully discrete solid-state amplifier uses separate transistors in all its circuitry, from the low-level input stages all the way to the big transistors that actually drive current through your loudspeakers. An IC-based amplifier uses integrated circuits somewhere in its signal path. The least expensive power amplifiers use ICs throughout, even for the output devices that power your loudspeakers. Fully discrete power amplifiers usually offer better sound quality and are more robust than amplifiers using integrated circuits.

Power amplifiers also vary in their sound quality. The differences in sound between amplifiers include bass "tightness," treble smoothness, and the ability to re-create the illusion of a 3-dimensional soundstage.

Bridging Power Amplifiers

Some 2-channel amplifiers can be "bridged" to function as a more powerful single-channel monoblock power amplifier. Bridging changes the amplifier's internal connections so that one channel amplifies the positive half of the waveform and the other channel amplifies the negative half. The loudspeaker is connected as the "bridge" between the two amplifier channels instead of between one channel's output and ground.

In theory, bridging results in a four-fold increase in output power. That's because bridging doubles the amplifier's maximum output voltage, and, according to Ohm's Law, quadruples the power. (Power equals voltage squared divided by resistance, or $P=V^2/R$.) In practice, however, bridging roughly doubles an amplifier's 4 ohm power rating, due to the amplifier's current-output limitations. Amplifiers that only marginally increase their output powers into 4 ohms (compared with their 8-ohm rating) will not come close to quadrupling their 8-ohm ratings when bridged.

Bridging is most beneficial when the power amplifiers are asked to drive low-sensitivity, high-impedance (8 ohms nominal) loudspeakers.

High-impedance speakers are driven more by voltage than by current. Conversely, low-impedance speakers demand more current from the power amplifier. A bridged amplifier's maximum output power is limited by its ability to deliver current. Moreover, connecting a 4-ohm speaker to a bridged power amplifier causes the amplifier to "see" a current-hungry 2-ohm load, further stressing the amplifier's current capacity. The result can be amplifier overheating, which will either damage the amplifier or cause its protection circuit to shut it down.

THX Certification of Power Amplifiers

Separate power amplifiers can be THX-certified if they meet the performance criteria established by Lucasfilm. As described in Chapter 2, Lucasfilm holds separate power amplifiers to a higher standard than the power-amplifier sections of A/V receivers. The higher standards for separate power amplifiers are for power output only; all other criteria are the same. A THX-certified power amplifier will probably have more output power than a THX-certified A/V receiver. In addition, THX certification ensures that the amplifier will drive THX-certified loudspeakers (and nearly all other loudspeakers) to levels that deliver the full dynamic impact, volume, and clarity of movie theaters and film dubbing stages.

Digital Power Amplifiers

Some newer power amplifiers on the market operate on digital, rather than analog, signals. They accept the digital outputs from a controller, amplifying and converting the digital signal to analog in the same step.

The heart of a digital amplifier is a DSP chip that converts Pulse Code Modulation (PCM) audio signals—which have a sampling rate of perhaps 48kHz and a word length of perhaps 20 bits—to a high-frequency bitstream with just two levels, high and low. This bitstream then fully turns on or fully turns off the output transistors. The transistors therefore amplify digital pulses rather than a continuous analog waveform, as in conventional amplifiers. The pulse widths in the digital code determine the amplitude of the final output signal. A low-pass filter just after the output switching transistors smoothes the pulses into a continuous analog signal.

A digital amplifier removes from the signal path the digital-to-analog converters in the controller, along with all the circuitry inside a conventional power amplifier. Such an amplifier produces very little heat, and can sound spectacular because it removes so much analog circuitry from the signal path. At the time of this writing, digital power amplifiers are very expensive, but I expect them to drop in price as the technology becomes more widely used.

6 Home Theater Loudspeakers

Introduction

Of all the components in a home-theater system, the loudspeaker's job is by far the most difficult. The loudspeaker is expected to reproduce the sound of chirping birds, the human voice, a symphony orchestra, and the liftoff of *Apollo 13*—all at the same time, and all with the same level of believability. A home-theater loudspeaker system should transport you from the depths of the ocean floor to the far side of the galaxy—and everywhere in between. Moreover, it should do this without ever calling attention to itself. The best loudspeaker is the one you *don't* "hear."

Loudspeakers are also the most misunderstood component of a home-theater system. The unwary buyer often chooses loudspeakers for all the wrong reasons—and winds up compromising the system's performance, paying too much, or both. The world is full of poor-quality loudspeakers masquerading as "top brand" models, often with sky-high price tags. There is often little relationship between price and quality when it comes to home-theater loudspeakers. What's more, some very bad loudspeakers are expensive, while superlative models may sell for a fraction of the inferior model's price. From my experience reviewing loudspeakers for *The Perfect Vision* and *The Absolute Sound*, I would estimate that only one loudspeaker system in fifty is worth owning.

In addition, carefully matching the loudspeakers to the rest of your system can give you better performance *and* save you money. But before we get to specific advice about buying loudspeakers, let's take a look at the role of each loudspeaker in a home-theater system.

Fig. 6-1
Loudspeakers
are the last link
in the home-
theater playback
chain.

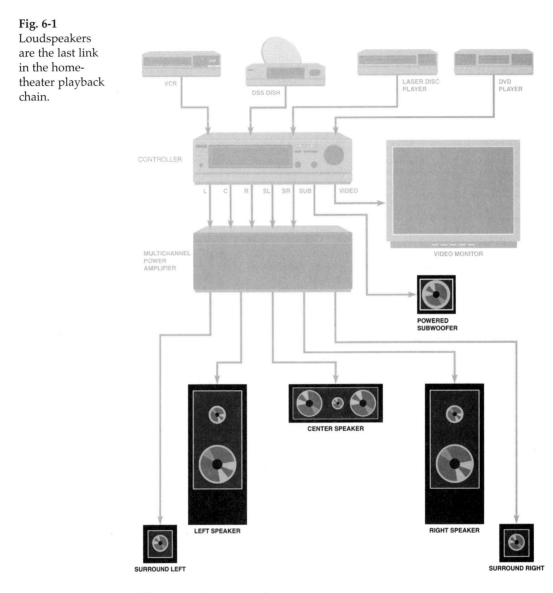

The Center-Channel Speaker

Though the center-channel loudspeaker carries a large part of the film soundtrack—nearly all the dialog, many effects, and some of the music—only recently have center-channel speakers moved from being considered afterthoughts to being recognized as the anchor of the entire home-theater loudspeaker system.

The center speaker is usually mounted horizontally on top of the video monitor. It can also be placed beneath the video monitor or mounted inside a wall above the video display; or, if you're using a front-projection system, behind an "acoustically transparent" screen. Fig.6-2 shows the typical center-channel loudspeaker placement.

Fig. 6-2 The center-channel speaker is usually placed on top of the video monitor.

Courtesy Infinity Systems, Inc.

Because a stereo system uses only two loudspeakers—left and right—across the front, you may be wondering why you need a third loudspeaker between them for home theater. The center-channel loudspeaker provides many advantages in a home-theater system. First, it anchors dialog and other sounds directly associated with action on the screen in the center of the sonic presentation. When we see characters speaking, we want the sound to appear to come from their visual images. Similarly, when sounds are panned (moved from one location to another) across the front, we want the sound to move seamlessly from one side to another. For example, if the image of a car travels from the left side of the screen to the right, the sounds of the car's engine and tires should travel with it, precisely tracking the car's movement. Without a center speaker, we may hear a gap in the middle as the car sounds jump from the left loudspeaker to the right. The center speaker makes sure on-screen sounds come from the screen.

A 2-channel stereo system is, however, capable of producing a sonic image directly between the two speakers. This so-called "phantom" center image is created by the brain when the same signal is present in both ears. A sound source directly in front of us in real life produces soundwaves that strike both ears simultaneously. The brain interprets these cues to determine that the sound source is directly in front of us. Similarly, two speakers reproducing the same sound send the same signal to both ears, fooling the brain into thinking the sound is directly in front of us.

For two loudspeakers to create this phantom center image, they must be precisely set up, and the listener must sit exactly the same distance from each of them—if you sit off to the right, the center image will pull to the right. In addition, creating a phantom center image from two loudspeakers may be a learned skill; some listeners may never hear a phantom center image. There's also evidence that the work the brain must perform to conjure up this phantom center image is distracting and fatiguing.

These problems are overcome by putting a center-channel speaker between the left and right speakers. Dialog and onscreen sounds are firmly anchored on the screen for all listeners, not just those sitting in the middle. With three speakers across the front, someone sitting way off at the left end of the couch can still hear dialog coming from the area of the screen—not just from the left loudspeaker. The center speaker also prevents the entire front soundfield from collapsing into the speaker closest to where you're sitting. Moreover, the center speaker provides a tangible sound source directly in front of you; your brain doesn't have to work to create a phantom image between the left and right speakers. Finally, the center speaker reduces the burden on the left and right loudspeakers. With three speakers reproducing sound, each can be driven at a lower level for cleaner sound.

Center-Channel Modes: Phantom, Wide, and Normal

Not every home-theater system uses a center speaker—it's possible to reproduce the front soundfield with just left and right speakers. In fact, A/V receivers and controllers can be configured for systems without center speakers. A/V receivers provide a PHANTOM (or NONE) mode that directs center-channel sounds equally to the left and right loudspeakers. If you want to use your existing stereo speakers for home theater before taking the plunge into a full home-theater speaker system, be sure to set your receiver to the PHANTOM mode; if you don't, you'll never hear the phantom center image. The receiver's Pro Logic or Dolby Digital decoder will remove the center-channel information from the left and right speakers and send it to the missing center speaker, leaving a big hole in the sound. Running your home-theater system without a center speaker should, however, be a temporary measure until you can add a third speaker across the front.

Older A/V receivers and controllers provide two other settings that relate to the center speaker: WIDE and NORMAL. The terms describe the bandwidth (range of frequencies) sent to the center speaker. When set to WIDE, the receiver sends to the center speaker the full range of audio frequencies. When set to NORMAL, the signal sent to the center speaker has no bass frequencies. The NORMAL selection keeps low bass out of the center speaker to avoid overloading it. Because most center speakers are made small enough to sit atop a video monitor, they can't handle much bass. The WIDE position should be used only in rare instances when the center speaker is a large, full-range type.

All modern A/V receivers ask you whether your center speaker is "large" or "small"; answering "small" is identical to putting the receiver in NORMAL mode. These three possibilities"PHANTOM, WIDE, NORMAL"are collectively called the *center-channel mode*. When you see the receiver button or menu display that says CENTER CHANNEL MODE, you'll know what it means.

Adding a Center Speaker to Your System

Some television sets have an input that purports to turn your TV's internal speakers into a center-channel speaker for home theater. I recommend against using this feature. The TV speaker's sound quality will be so different from that of the left and right speakers that the overall sound will likely be degraded. In addition, the speakers in most TVs are located at the left and right edges of the cabinet, too close to the left and right speakers to do any good. If you don't have a separate center-channel speaker, set the receiver to the PHANTOM center-channel mode and forget about using the TV's speakers.

Although you can add a different brand of center speaker to your existing left and right speakers, you're better off with three matched speakers across the front of your home theater. Speakers all sound different from one another. No matter how good the quality of a speaker, it will have some *coloration*, or variations from accuracy, in its sound. I mentioned earlier that you want to hear a seamless movement of sounds across the front soundfield. If the center speaker has a different sound from the left and right speakers, you'll never achieve a smooth and continuous soundfield across the front—when sound sources move from one side to another through the center speaker, the sound's character will abruptly change.

Let's go back to our earlier example of a car driving from the left side of the soundfield to the right. If the center speaker has a different sound from the left and right speakers, the car will have one sound character as it starts moving, a different sound as it is reproduced by the center speaker, then return to its original sound as it is reproduced by the right speaker. The mismatched center speaker destroys the seamless soundfield we want to create.

The solution is to buy three matched front-channel speakers. Their identical tonal characteristics will not only provide smooth panning of sounds, but also produce a more stable and coherent soundfield across the front of the room. If you already have high-quality left and right loudspeakers that you want to keep, buy a center-channel speaker made by the manufacturer of the left and right loudspeakers. They probably won't be as well-matched as a three-piece system, but the added center speaker is much more likely to sound similar to your existing left and right speakers. Separate center speakers sometimes use the same drivers (the raw speaker cones themselves) and other parts as the stereo speakers from the same manufacturer.

For state-of-the-art home theater, the three front loudspeakers should be identical. Although most home-theater enthusiasts will use a smaller center speaker that will fit on top of a television set and doesn't reproduce much bass, more ambitious systems use large, full-range center speakers. These speakers are hard to position, and are generally used only with front-projector systems; the center speaker can be placed behind a perforated projection screen, just as in a movie theater.

Center-Speaker Placement Tips

Although loudspeaker placement is covered in depth in Chapter 9, it doesn't hurt to reiterate a few center-speaker placement tips. Here's a simple one that will greatly improve the sound of your system for both home theater and music listening.

Rather than position the three front speakers in a line, put the left and right speakers slightly forward of the video monitor. This creates an arc, with the center speaker in the middle. This placement has two advantages over putting the three speakers in a straight line. First, pulling the left and right speakers forward puts all three front speakers the same distance from your ears. With the three speakers in a straight line, you're sitting closer to the center speaker and hearing its sound slightly before the sound from the left and right speakers. The result is that the soundstage tends to pull in from the sides to the center speaker; the soundstage is narrower and less expansive. But moving the left and right speakers forward makes the soundstage wider.

This placement also reduces acoustic reflections from your video monitor. Some of the sound you hear comes directly from the speakers; some is bounced off nearby reflective objects. As we'll see in Chapter 9, these reflections reduce sound quality. By moving the left and right loudspeakers slightly in front of the video monitor, you hear more direct sound from the speakers and less reflected sound.

Here's another little tip on positioning the center speaker: Line up its front edge with the front edge of the video monitor. This correct placement, seen in fig.6-2 earlier, reduces the amount of sound reflected from the video monitor. The result is clearer and more intelligible dialog.

Left and Right Speakers

The left and right loudspeakers carry the majority of the film's musical score and many of the effects. And if you aren't using a subwoofer, nearly all the bass will be reproduced by the left and right speakers. Consequently, left and right speakers are often the largest speakers in a home-theater system. Where a center speaker may use two 5" cones and a tweeter (treble speaker), left and right speakers typically feature large woofers of perhaps 8" or 10" in diameter to reproduce bass. Left and right loudspeakers will also use small drivers and a tweeter, as in center speakers, so that they can reproduce the full frequency range. Speakers that can reproduce bass as well as midrange and treble frequencies are called *full-range* speakers. If they sit on the floor, they are called *floorstanding*. Full-range, floorstanding left and right loudspeakers are the most common. The left and right speakers in fig.6-2 are full-range, floorstanding models.

Left and right speakers can also be small units that sit on speaker stands or on an entertainment cabinet. If that's the case, the small speakers must be used with a subwoofer to reproduce bass. The small left and right speakers reproduce the midrange and treble frequencies and the subwoofer handles all the bass. Such a system, called a *subwoofer/satellite* system, is ideal if your available space is limited, or if you want the left and right loudspeakers to better blend into your decor. Satellite speakers can be small and unobtrusive, and the subwoofer can be tucked out of the way. If you build the three front speakers into a wall in a custom installation, they will most likely be satellites. All THX-certified loudspeaker systems use a subwoofer.

Surround Speakers

The surround loudspeakers are completely different in design and function from left, center, and right speakers. Their job is to re-create a diffuse atmosphere of sound effects to envelop us in a subtle sonic environment that puts us *in* the action happening on the screen. Unlike front and center speakers that anchor the sound onscreen, surround speakers should "disappear" into a diffuse "wash" of sound all around us.

A good example of how surround speakers create an atmosphere comes from the film *Round Midnight*. Toward the beginning of the movie the character François is outside a Paris jazz club in a driving rainstorm, listening to Dexter Gordon's character playing inside. The scene cuts between the intimate sound of the jazz club and the rainy Paris street. Inside the club, the sound is direct and immediate to reflect the camera's perspective of just a few feet from the musical group. When the scene cuts to the street, we are surrounded by the expansive sound of rain, cars driving by, people talking as they walk past—in other words, all the ambiance and atmosphere of a rainy night in Paris. This envelopment is largely created by the surround speakers. We don't want to hear the rain and street sounds coming from two locations behind us, but to be surrounded by the sounds, as we'd hear them in real life. The surround speakers perform this subtle yet vital role in home theater.

Surround speakers envelop us by their design and placement in the home-theater room. They are best located to the side or rear of the listening position, and several feet above ear level. Because they don't have to reproduce bass, surround speakers can be small and unobtrusive, and are often mounted on or inside a wall.

Dipolar and Bipolar Surround Speakers

Most of the surround speakers' ability to wrap us in sound comes from their *dipolar* design. Dipolar simply means that they produce sound to the front and rear equally. While front speakers have one set of drivers that project sound forward, dipolar surround speakers have two sets of drivers, mounted front and back. This arrangement produces a directional pattern that fires to the front and back of the room (fig.6-3).

Fig. 6-3 Most loudspeakers fire sound only toward the front (left diagram); dipolar speakers fire sound equally to the front and rear (right diagram).

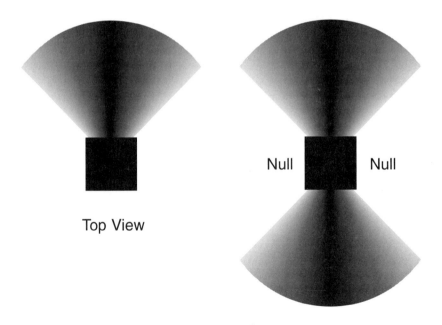

Top View

Null   Null

Because the surround speakers are positioned to the sides and fire to the front and back of the room, we hear no direct sound from them. The listener sits in the surround speakers' "null"—the point where they don't directly project sound. Instead of hearing direct sound from the surround speakers, we hear their sound after it's been reflected, or bounced off the room's walls and furnishings. The surround speakers' dipolar directional pattern makes their sound diffuse and harder to localize. You shouldn't be able to tell where a properly set-up surround speaker is just by listening.

You may see surround speakers called either *dipolar* or *bipolar*. Although both produce sound equally from the front and rear, the bipolar speaker produces sound from the rear that is in-phase with the front sound. A dipolar produces sound from the rear that is out-of-phase with the front sound. In-phase means that the front and rear waves have the same polarity—when the front-firing woofer moves forward to create a positive pressure wave, the rear-firing woofer also moves forward. The opposite is true in a dipole—when the front-firing woofer moves forward, the rear-firing woofer moves backward. In a dipole, the front and back waves are identical, but have the opposite polarity. Both bipolar and dipolar achieve the objective of enveloping the viewer/listener in the film's aural ambiance, but the dipolar type is preferred because it creates a greater "null," or reduction in sound, at the side of the speaker that faces the listener.

A true dipolar or bipolar surround speaker can't be flush-mounted inside a wall. Instead, it must be mounted *on* the wall so it can radiate sound toward the front and rear of the room. Some surround speakers approximate a dipolar radiation pattern by mounting small drivers on an angled baffle. Although not true dipoles, these flush-mounted surround speakers accomplish the goal of creating a diffuse ambiance *and* fit unobtrusively in your living room.

Surround speakers are also helped in their job by the surround decorrelation circuit found in all THX receivers and controllers. As described in Chapter 2, the surround channel in Dolby Pro Logic is monophonic; the same signal feeds both surround loudspeakers. This has the unwanted effect of localizing the surround speaker's sound at the listening position rather than creating a diffuse soundfield. THX surround decorrelation slightly changes the signal fed to the left and right surround speakers to provide a greater sense of envelopment.

The amount of sound produced by the surround speakers is adjustable through the receiver's or controller's remote control. Their volume level should be set so that you never hear them directly; but if you turned them off, the soundfield would collapse toward the front. All too often, consumers set surround speaker levels too high—their thinking seems to be that if they *bought* speakers, they should be able to *hear* them. We'll talk more in Chapter 9 about how to correctly set the surround speakers' volume level.

Surround Speakers with Dolby Digital and DTS

The widespread availability of Dolby Digital and DTS surround sound has changed the role of surround speakers. You may recall from Chapter 2 that the surround channels in Dolby Digital are considerably different from those generated by a Dolby Pro Logic decoder. Instead of having a monophonic surround channel that has no low bass and no treble, Dolby Digital's surround signals are full-bandwidth and comprise two separate channels. Some contend that Dolby Digital soundtracks should be reproduced by full-range, point-source loudspeakers (those that aren't dipolar or bipolar). Using point-source speakers as surrounds provides greater directionality of rear-channel sounds, but less sense of envelopment.

I've experimented with point-source and dipolar surrounds with both Dolby Pro Logic and Dolby Digital sources, and firmly believe that dipolar surrounds provide a more involving home-theater experience with both Dolby Pro Logic and Dolby Digital soundtracks. Other respected experts, however, disagree. They argue that the role of a loudspeaker system is to accurately reproduce the signals recorded on the source (such as a DVD). By "smearing" the surround channels with dipolar speakers, we are departing from the goal of accuracy of reproduction, the argument goes.

The other issue is whether small surround speakers designed for Dolby Pro Logic's limited-frequency-range surround signals work with the full-range Dolby Digital surround signals. The answer is yes and no. Generally, Dolby Digital's surround signals contain very little bass energy. The film's mixers make the decision of whether or not to put low bass in the surround channels. If you use small surround speakers and have a Dolby Digital decoder and Dolby Digital sources, you should keep low bass out of them by selecting the appropriate settings on the receiver's setup menu. You have the option of keeping bass out of the surround speakers, and directing the surround-channel bass to a subwoofer. Either of these methods will prevent the surround speakers from being overloaded, sounding distorted, or even damaged by Dolby Digital soundtracks that have low bass in the surround channels.

Back-Surround Speakers for THX Surround EX and DTS-ES

As described in Chapter 2, the THX Surround EX and DTS-ES formats add one or two additional surround speakers behind the listener. THX recommends that two speakers be used, and that their radiation patterns be dipolar. According to Lucasfilm, the surround channels are best reproduced by four identical dipolar speakers. The two surround speakers remain at their normal position (normal for 5.1-channel reproduction), which is 110°, or slightly behind the listener on the side walls. The back surround speakers are located at 150° as shown in Chapter 9.

The two back-surround speakers should be arranged so that their facing sides are in-phase with each other. That is, the side of the dipole that would face the back of the room if mounted on a sidewall should face toward the room's centerline when the speaker is mounted on the rear wall. This arrangement keeps the drivers of two back-surround speakers that face each other in-phase, contributing to their ability to create an image between them directly behind the listening position.

Subwoofers

A subwoofer is a speaker that reproduces only low bass. Subwoofers are usually squarish or rectangular cabinets that can be positioned nearly anywhere in the home-theater room (fig.6-4). A good subwoofer adds quite a bit of impact and visceral thrill to the home-theater experience.

Most subwoofers for home-theater use are *powered* or *active* subwoofers. These terms describe a subwoofer with a built-in power amplifier that drives its large woofer cone. The powered subwoofer takes a line-level output from the jack marked SUBWOOFER OUT on your A/V receiver or controller, and converts that electrical signal into sound. Because powered subwoofers have built-in amplifiers, they must be plugged into a wall AC outlet.

You can use a subwoofer in two ways. First, the sub can augment the bass produced by full-range left and right loudspeakers. The subwoofer and the left and right loudspeakers all reproduce bass for greater bass output. As a side benefit, the subwoofer usually can generate frequencies lower than those your left and right speakers can reproduce. In fact, the term "*sub*woofer" means it reproduces frequencies *below* that of the woofer found in full-range left and right speakers. In this arrangement, bass isn't kept out of the left and right speakers.

Fig. 6-4
A subwoofer reproduces low bass frequencies, and adds impact and drama to the home-theater presentation.

PSB photos courtesy Lenbrook Industries, Ltd., Pickering, ON, Canada

The second way of adding a subwoofer is to let the subwoofer handle all the bass, leaving your left and right speakers to reproduce only midrange and treble frequencies. Nearly every subwoofer has a *crossover network* that splits the frequency spectrum into bass and midrange/treble. Bass is sent to the subwoofer, and the midrange/treble is sent to the left and right speakers.

Using this connection method is essential if the left and right speakers are small and can't reproduce bass on their own. But it also grants benefits even if your left and right speakers are full-range. Keeping bass out of the front speakers has many important advantages. For a loudspeaker to reproduce bass, its cones must move back and forth a great distance (the cone's movement is called *excursion*). The lower the frequency the speaker is reproducing, the greater the excursion, and the more amplifier power is required to move the speaker cone back and forth. Most speakers are limited in how loudly and cleanly they will play by the amount of their cone excursion; at some point, the speaker cone runs out of room. In addition, the high power needed to move the cone back and forth generates heat inside the speaker that can damage it. These constraints set the limit on how loudly the loudspeaker will play; the more bass the speaker is reproducing, the more strain it is under. Moreover, a power amplifier doesn't sound as clean when it's working so hard. In addition, a cone trying to reproduce low bass as well as midrange frequencies adds something called *Doppler distortion*, which degrades sound quality. Finally, making the subwoofer the sole source of bass reproduction avoids the problem of bass from the subwoofer and bass from the left and right speakers combining in unpredictable ways and creating large amplitude peaks and dips in the bass response.

But by adding a subwoofer that keeps low bass out of the left and right speakers, the speakers can cruise along with minimal excursion and amplifier power. Neither the speakers nor the amplifier has to work very hard. The burden has been shifted to the subwoofer, which is better equipped to handle large excursions and high amplifier power. And because the left and right speakers have been relieved of reproducing low bass, their midrange and treble sound is cleaner. Moreover, they can now handle much more power because all their power-handling capability hasn't been consumed by trying to reproduce bass. The power amplifier has much more power reserve, which makes it sound cleaner and gives it some room to reproduce loud peaks such as explosions without running out of power. This is one reason why adding a subwoofer increases the system's dynamic range (ability to reproduce loud peaks without distortion). In addition, the subwoofer's built-in power amplifier adds to the total power available to drive the loudspeaker system. The result is a cleaner, more dynamic sound that will go louder without distortion.

Subwoofer Power Amplifiers and Phase Adjustments

Virtually all subwoofers have built-in power amplifiers to drive their cones. You can often see the subwoofer power amplifier's black-finned heat sinks on the sub's rear panel. As described in Chapter 4, A/V receiver manufacturers often resort to audacious "specsmanship" to make their products appear to have more power than they actually have. In comparison with subwoofer power-amplifier claims, however, receiver manufacturers are downright conservative. Consequently, you'll see inexpensive subwoofers with an 8″ cone touted as having an integral "1000W" power amplifier. There's no way the tiny amplifier in such a product could produce 1000W, and even if it could, it would immediately melt the 8″ driver's voice coil (the part of the speaker through which amplifier current flows). When looking at subwoofers, it's best to ignore the manufacturer's power-output claims and judge the subwoofer using the listening criteria described later in this chapter.

Subwoofer power amplifiers don't need to be large and heavy to generate lots of power. A switching power amplifier can be small, run cool, and output high wattage. A switching power amplifier, sometimes called a "Class D" amplifier, operates very differently from conventional "linear" power amplifiers.

A subwoofer may have several controls on its rear panel. The most obvious control is VOLUME, which sets how much sound the subwoofer produces for a given input level. This control is adjusted in conjunction with the receiver or controller subwoofer adjustment to achieve the correct amount of bass.

Another control is the *phase adjustment*, which can be a switch marked "±180°" or a continuously variable knob. The switch inverts the polarity of the subwoofer's acoustic output to achieve a better blend between the subwoofer and the main speakers. In some room locations, the subwoofer will blend better with the main speakers when this control is set to the "0°" position, and in other locations you'll hear a smoother transition when in the "180°" position. The continuously variable phase adjustment is significantly more useful than the switch because it lets you fine-tune the phase relationship between the subwoofer and the main speakers.

To better understand the function of the phase adjustment, think of your subwoofer and main speakers both reproducing a bass frequency at, say, 80Hz, the crossover point between them. Let's say the subwoofer and main speakers are exactly the same distance from your ears. If the subwoofer's phase control is set incorrectly, the subwoofer's cone and the woofer (or midrange) in the main speaker won't move in perfect unison—one cone will either lead or lag the other. There is a slight phase (time) difference between the two sound waves.

When playing music or film soundtracks, the slightly out-of-phase acoustic outputs of each cone combine in the air, causing a cancellation at some frequencies and a reinforcement of other frequencies. We hear this as "lumpy" bass as some bass frequencies seem to "stick out" while others are reduced in volume.

A phase adjustment is required because the subwoofer's location relative to the main speakers is variable. In some setups, the sub will be farther away from the main speakers, and closer in others. The phase adjustment lets you dial in the timing relationship between the sub-woofer and the main speakers. As you can see, a continuously variable phase control is much more useful than a simple "±180 degree" switch. (Chapter 9 details a technique for perfectly setting a subwoofer's phase adjustment.)

Anatomy of a Loudspeaker

Before we get to the important business of choosing home-theater loud-speakers, let's look at how a loudspeaker is constructed. A little knowl-edge of what goes on inside the speaker will help you weed out impres-sive-looking but poor-performing products.

A loudspeaker converts an electrical signal into sound. The speaker has two or more *drivers*—the round cones or domes that move back and forth to create sound. The large driver, called the *woofer*, is usually between 8" and 12" in diameter. The middle-sized driver, called the *midrange driver*, is typically about 4" in diameter and reproduces midrange frequencies such as dialog. The smallest driver, the *tweeter*, handles the treble frequencies.

A circuit inside the speaker, called a *crossover*, splits up the audio fre-quency band into two or more segments. The crossover sends bass to the woofer, mid frequencies to the midrange driver, and highs to the tweeter.

So far, I've described a three-way speaker. This term means that the speaker splits up the frequency spectrum into three bands—bass, mid-range, and treble. A two-way speaker splits the frequency spectrum into two bands, which are reproduced by a woofer and a tweeter. The vast majority of home-theater speakers will be either two- or three-way.

You can't tell if a speaker is two-way or three-way from counting the number of drivers in the cabinet. Many speakers use two small woofers instead of one large one, along with a tweeter. Such a speaker is still a two-way design. The two-way designation refers to the number of frequency bands created by the crossover, not the number of drivers in the speaker.

The driver cones are made from paper or a special plastic material. Attached to the back of the cone is a coil of wire (the *voice coil*) suspend-ed in a magnetic field created by a large magnet on the back of the dri-ver. The flow of electrical current through the wire coil creates a magnet-ic field around the coil that interacts with the permanent magnetic field generated by the driver's magnet. The magnetic forces pull and push the coil of wire—and, with it, the speaker cone—to produce sound.

The drivers and crossover are mounted in the speaker's *enclosure*. The enclosure plays a vital role in loudspeaker sound quality. It should be rigid and vibration-free. When the driver cones move back and forth, some of that energy is put into the cabinet, making it vibrate. A vibrating cabinet acts like another cone, creating sound. The sound generated by the cabinet has a different frequency response than the sound from the driver, changing the speaker's tonal balance. This change in tonal balance varies with volume; the speaker's sound quality changes during loud passages. Moreover, the sound produced by the cabinet is slightly delayed in time relative to the sound generated by the drivers, smearing the time relationships in music and film soundtracks. You can easily hear a poorly designed speaker cabinet by the sense of strain on loud peaks. As the music or soundtrack gets loud, the sound congeals into a roar rather than maintaining separation between instruments. That's why good loudspeakers all have solid, inert cabinets. (An example of a well-made speaker cabinet is shown in fig.6-5. Notice the internal bracing to keep the cabinet's side walls from vibrating. The crossover network is also visible in the photograph.)

Fig. 6-5 High-quality speakers use well-braced cabinets for better sound.

Courtesy Thiel

The enclosure also plays a large role in the speaker's design. Some enclosures are *sealed*, which means that the box around the drivers forms an air-tight seal around the drivers. Sealed enclosures are also called *air suspension* or *infinite baffle* enclosures. A *ported*, or *reflex* enclosure has a hole in the cabinet front or back to channel bass from inside the cabinet to the outside, where it can be heard. Reflex loading has three advantages over a sealed enclosure. First, it increases a loudspeaker's maximum acoustic output level—it will play louder. Second, it can make a loudspeaker more sensitive—it needs less amplifier power to achieve the same volume. Third, it can extends the speaker's low-frequency cutoff frequency—the bass goes deeper. A speaker's cutoff frequency is the frequency at which its acoustic output is reduced by 3dB. These advantages are not available simultaneously; the acoustic gain provided by reflex loading can be used to increase sensitivity or extend the bass cutoff frequency, but not both.

The disadvantage of reflex speakers is that their bass tends to be less precise and articulate than the bass produced by sealed designs. And although a reflex system's cutoff frequency is lower than that of a sealed system (assuming the same woofer and enclosure volume), the reflex system's bass rolls off at a much faster rate. Specifically, a reflex-loaded speaker rolls off at the rate of 24dB per octave compared to the sealed enclosure's 12dB per octave. That means that in a reflex speaker, its bass output will be reduced by 24dB one octave below its cutoff frequency. The same driver in a sealed enclosure will produce an acoustic output that is reduced by only 12dB one octave below its cutoff frequency. Consequently, the sealed speaker's more gradual rolloff can provide a more satisfying feeling of bass fullness and weight.

Speakers made specifically for home theater are shielded; a metal shield inside the enclosure prevents the magnetic energy inside the speaker from getting out. This is important when you put a center speaker on top of your TV, and left and right speakers on either side. The speaker's magnetic energy will interfere with the TV's cathode-ray tube, producing all kinds of odd colors and distorting the picture.

The last element of the loudspeaker is the binding posts. These are the terminals through which you connect the speaker to the amplifier or receiver via a length of speaker cable.

How to Choose Home Theater Loudspeakers

Choosing just the right speakers for your home-theater system can seem like a daunting challenge. After all, there are so many models, so many marketing claims, and such a huge range of price of speaker systems. What's more, so many mediocre products are on the market that can easily fool the unwary consumer. There is often little relationship between price and performance. In fact, the heavily advertised brand most consumers consider a top performer is actually one of the worst-performing speaker lines.

This situation can, however, benefit the savvy shopper. If you know how much of your home-theater budget to spend on loudspeakers, how to match the speakers to the rest of your system, and how to spot the overpriced underperformers, you can wind up with excellent sound for not a lot of money.

The best place to begin shopping for loudspeakers is in the pages of a reputable magazine. As full-time professional reviewers, my colleagues and I hear hundreds of systems every year at trade and consumer shows. We weed out the majority of underachievers, choosing for review only the models that seem promising. Of the speaker systems reviewed, some are found to be unacceptably flawed, others offer good performance for the money, and a select few are star overachievers that clearly outperform their similarly priced rivals.

This is where reviews come in handy. You can survey the loudspeaker scene from the comfort of your own home and get familiar with brands, prices, and options. Be sure to read a magazine with high standards of what constitutes good loudspeaker performance. Be wary of magazines that give a favorable recommendation to every product they review. Not all loudspeakers are worth buying; therefore, not all reviews should conclude with a recommendation. The tone of the reviews—positive or negative—should reflect the vast range of quality and value in the marketplace.

After you've read the reviews, it's time to listen for yourself. Don't buy a loudspeaker system purely on the basis of a positive review. The reviewer's sonic priorities may differ from yours, and he will certainly have a different home-theater room and different electronics. Use reviews as a starting point for your own auditioning, not as the final word. *You're* the one who will live with the system after you've bought it. Make sure it suits your needs, sound-quality standards, budget, and home decor.

How Much Should You Spend on Speakers?

There's a common misconception that speakers are the most important link in the sound-reproduction chain. "After all," the thinking goes, "the speakers are what actually produce the sound. You should spend most of your home-theater budget on speakers."

I disagree. A home-theater speaker system is only as good as the signal fed to it. Putting high-resolution speakers at the end of a chain of mediocre electronics and source components only reveals the electronics' flaws. The best speaker system for the money is one that is well-matched in quality and characteristics to the electronics and home-theater room.

You should therefore spend about 35–40% of your total home-theater budget on speakers. Another way of looking at it is to spend at least as much on a speaker system as you spend on your A/V receiver, or separate controller and power amplifier.

Although you can buy a "home theater in a box" type of loudspeaker system for $199 at your local appliance store and get better sound than your TV offers, I recommend spending a minimum of $600 for a home-theater loudspeaker system. That amount of money may be a stretch at first, but it will save the inevitable disappointment of the "home theater in a box." It's false economy to buy an inferior system, sell it at a loss, and buy a better speaker system later. Do it right the first time.

Matching the Speakers to Your Living Room and Electronics

Your first consideration in choosing a home-theater speaker system is matching it to your room. The larger the room, the bigger the speakers the room will accommodate. It's a mistake to stuff a tiny room with large speakers that produce lots of bass. The result will be a thick, boomy sound that distracts from the home-theater experience.

You'll also need to consider what size speakers will fit in the room visually—the speakers should not dominate the room. Again, the larger the room, the larger the speaker the room will accommodate, visually as well as acoustically. Choose surround speakers that can be placed unobtrusively on the side walls. (Many surround loudspeakers have a white finish for a better blend with your living room.)

You can assemble just about any combination of VCR, DVD machine, A/V receiver, or video monitor and be assured that they'll work together virtually perfectly. But there are no such assurances when matching loudspeakers to an A/V receiver or power amplifier. Loudspeakers and amplifiers vary in their electrical properties; some combinations work better than others. Let's look at some variables.

The first consideration is the speaker's *sensitivity*. As explained in Chapter 4, a speaker's sensitivity specification describes how efficient the speaker is at converting electrical signals into sound. In fact, speaker sensitivity is sometimes (erroneously) called *efficiency*. A speaker's sensitivity specification may read: "86dB/1W/1m." This means that the speaker produced a sound-pressure level of 86 decibels (86dB) when driven by one watt (1W) of power measured from one meter (1m) away. The higher a speaker's sensitivity, the less amplifier power you need to drive it. Specifically, every 3dB increase in speaker sensitivity is the same as doubling the amplifier power. The speaker that is 3dB more sensitive is twice as efficient at converting amplifier power into sound.

Let's look at how speaker sensitivity affects your need for amplifier power. Say your next-door neighbor boasts of his new 250Wpc (250 watts per channel) home-theater power amplifier and invites you over for a demo. His new amplifier weighs 150 pounds, cost him $4000, and runs so hot that it can be used as a room heater in winter. After listening to his system, you bring him back to your house to listen to your home-theater system, which is based on a $350 A/V receiver that puts out 35Wpc. Much to your neighbor's surprise, your system plays *louder* than his, with more dynamic impact, no sense of strain on peaks, and a cleaner sound with only one-eighth the amount of amplifier power. The difference is explained by the fact that your neighbor has low-sensitivity speakers and you have high-sensitivity speakers. Your speakers simply convert more of the amplifier's electrical energy into sound.

I mentioned that every 3dB increase in speaker sensitivity is the same as doubling the amplifier's power. That means that 35Wpc driving a speaker with a sensitivity of 92dB will play louder than a 250Wpc amplifier driving a speaker with a sensitivity of 83dB. This range of sensitivity—83dB to 92dB—is about what you'll find in the marketplace. Most speakers, however, fall somewhere in the 85–88dB range. Still, that sensitivity difference equates to a doubling of amplifier power. Because amplifier power can be expensive, you can save yourself a lot of money by choosing high-sensitivity speakers. The home-theater speaker system shown in fig.6-2 has a sensitivity of a whopping 96dB/1W/1m. I've powered this system with as little as 10Wpc.

Another speaker specification affects the size of the power amplifier needed. *Impedance* describes a loudspeaker's resistance to letting electrical current from the amplifier flow through it. Most speakers are rated at either 4 ohms or 8 ohms impedance. An 8 ohm speaker presents twice as much resistance to the flow of electrical current as a 4 ohm speaker.

Just as pressure from your local water company pushes water through a garden hose, a power amplifier generates voltage that pushes electrical current through the speaker. Voltage is the water pressure, so to speak; electrical current is the flow of water, and the hose is the speaker. If you crimp the hose, thus increasing its resistance to water flow, less water flows through the hose (speaker).

You might think that more resistance (a higher impedance) makes the power amplifier's job of pushing current through the speaker more difficult. In fact, it is *low*-impedance speakers that give amplifiers problems. Low-impedance speakers demand more electrical current from a power amplifier. Just as uncrimping the garden hose lets more water flow, putting a low-impedance speaker on a power amplifier forces the power amplifier to deliver more current.

Though power amplifiers are limited in the amount of current they can deliver to the speaker, some aren't bothered by low-impedance speakers. These amplifiers, which can drive impedances as low as 1 ohm, are usually large and expensive. Other power amplifiers simply cannot drive low-impedance speakers. They overheat, shut down, or even *break* down if the speaker's impedance is too low. You can't tell which amplifier is which from looking at its power rating into 8 ohms; but if an amplifier is specified to drive 4 ohms, it probably can drive 4 ohm speakers. When choosing speakers, match their impedance to the power amplifier or receiver. Most separate multichannel power amplifiers can drive 4 ohm speakers with no problem. Some budget receivers won't work well with speakers of less than 6 ohms impedance.

Another factor in matching speakers to the power amplifier is the speaker's *power handling*. This specification describes how much power the speaker can take before it is overdriven. Some speakers sound distorted, or make a popping sound, at a relatively low volume. Others will keep playing louder and louder as you turn up the volume, and still maintain their clarity and low distortion. A speaker's power-handling specification doesn't always tell you how loudly the speaker will play before it is overdriven, but it can be a rough indicator. The best way to determine how loudly a speaker system will play is to turn up the volume until it is playing at the loudest level you would ever use. If the speaker keeps its cool and doesn't distort, it probably has enough power handling and maximum sound level for you. Make sure you use a powerful enough amplifier in this test; a power amplifier running out of juice will sound much like an overdriven speaker.

While we're on this subject, I'll dispel a common myth about speakers and amplifier power. Most people assume that a high-powered amplifier will blow up a speaker more easily than a low-powered one. In fact, a small, inexpensive receiver will more easily damage a speaker than will a massive, 1000Wpc power amplifier. It's not the power, but amplifier distortion that will send a speaker to an early grave. When an amplifier runs out of power, it distorts the audio waveform (a phenomenon called *clipping*). A 25Wpc amplifier overdriven into clipping will quickly blow up a speaker rated to handle 500W. Conversely, a speaker rated at 50W will usually take 100W without damage if that power is clean.

We've talked about matching a home-theater speaker system to your electronics and living room. But there's one other factor to which the speakers should be matched: your expectations. If you enjoy renting VHS tapes and just want to hear the dialog a little more clearly, the music score with more grandeur, the bass with a little more impact, and some sense of surround envelopment, a modest speaker system will do the job. But if you expect explosions to shake the couch, the *Apollo 13* launch to rattle windows, and the musical score to sound like an orchestra in your living room, you'll need to set aside significantly more money to achieve these goals. A speaker system that will play loudly, cleanly, and with deep bass extension is expensive.

THX-Certified Loudspeakers

The Home THX program described in Chapter 2 includes speaker systems as well as home-theater electronics. THX-certified speakers have certain characteristics that make them particularly good at reproducing film soundtracks. These characteristics include sensitivity and impedance, which we've just talked about. A THX-certified speaker has a specified sensitivity and impedance, so that when used with a THX-certified receiver or power amplifier, the system as a whole meets a film-sound engineer's expectations for loudness, dynamics, and other criteria.

THX-certified loudspeakers also have a specific directional pattern in the way they radiate sound. Because THX engineers discovered that reflected sound from the ceiling interferes with dialog intelligibility and clarity, THX speakers confine their sound to a more narrow directional pattern; they don't spray much sound upward to bounce off the ceiling, as some conventional stereo speakers do. THX-certified speakers do, however, have a wide horizontal dispersion pattern; that is, they disperse sounds to their sides. This characteristic widens the area over which listeners hear all the elements of the film soundtrack.

Another criterion for meeting THX standards is the speaker's frequency response, or range of frequencies it can reproduce. It must be able to not only reproduce low bass and high treble, but maintain a fairly consistent output across the frequency spectrum. In other words, the speaker can't have too much midrange, too little treble, or an exaggerated bass and still meet THX certification. An accurate speaker is often called "flat" because that's the shape of its frequency-response curve. A THX-certified speaker must adhere to a high level of accuracy.

Subwoofers can also be THX-certified if they meet certain criteria for impedance, sensitivity, bass extension (how low in frequency the subwoofer will play), and sound-pressure level. THX subwoofers also have a carefully specified crossover frequency and slope (how rapidly the signal amplitude decreases above and below the crossover frequency). This ensures that the THX subwoofer, when used with THX-certified front and surround speakers, and a THX-certified receiver or controller, will create a seamless transition from the subwoofer to the main speakers.

THX-certified loudspeakers are, however, not always ideally suited to music reproduction. Their directional characteristics compromise musical performance for accuracy in reproducing film soundtracks. If you plan on listening to music through your system, approach a THX-certified speaker system with caution. In response to the general criticism of THX-certified speakers for music reproduction, Lucasfilm has recently amended the performance criteria required to achieve THX certification.

The newer THX Ultra2 certification has addressed this issue by changing the specification to make THX-certified speakers perform well on both music and film soundtracks.

Build and Sound Quality: How to Spot Overpriced Underachievers

Of all the components in a home theater, the one you must be most careful in shopping for is the loudspeaker system. Not only must you match the speaker system to your room and amplifier power, you must also watch out for high-priced, under-performing systems masquerading as top models. Many loudspeaker companies make a good living by producing impressive-looking speakers with good marketing gimmicks, but that have poor sound quality and shoddy construction. It's easy to put lots of big drivers in a huge cabinet, make up some technical but irrelevant buzzwords, and sell them to unsuspecting consumers. This section will help you spot such products.

The general public believes that the more drivers in a speaker and the bigger its cabinet, the better the sound. In fact, there's often an *inverse* relationship between size/driver count and sound quality. Let's illustrate this by examining two speaker systems, each costing about $500 for the three front speakers.

Speaker A is a four-way design about 3' tall, with a 12" woofer and shiny chrome rings around the drivers. Speaker B is a two-way design only 15" tall, with a 6" woofer, and looks rather plain next to speaker A. Most consumers would think speaker A is the better value.

But let's look at what's inside each of these speakers. Speaker A must use inexpensive drivers—there are four of them in each cabinet—while speaker B uses two high-quality drivers. The four-way design of speaker A means that its crossover network has lots of parts in it, which means that the parts must be inexpensive. Speaker B's simple two-way crossover uses parts of much higher quality. Because Speaker A uses a large cabinet, it's probably made of thin material that vibrates when it reproduces sound. Speaker B's small cabinet is thick and well-braced inside to prevent the cabinet from degrading the speaker's sound quality.

If you were to hear Speaker A and Speaker B side by side, there would be little comparison. Through Speaker A, dialog sounds as if it's coming from a megaphone. Music is shrill and screechy, the bass a continuous mush and boom instead of clearly defined notes. The sound changes at loud volumes as Speaker A's cabinet starts to vibrate. The sound seems to come out of three separate boxes instead of as a smooth and continuous soundstage. Watching a movie with Speaker A in your system makes you feel a sense of relief as the closing credits scroll up— and you wonder why you have a headache.

Conversely, Speaker B reproduces dialog and the human voice in a natural and accurate way. The musical score is smooth, rich, and detailed. Bass sounds tight, clean, and quick, and not like a "boom truck." When the soundtrack gets loud, Speaker B shows no sign of strain. The soundstage produced by Speaker B envelops you, with precise localization of images and a huge, deep soundfield.

The company that makes Speaker A is marketing-driven. They don't care what the speaker sounds like, only that it offers *perceived* value and sells in large quantities. They will intentionally add colorations to the speaker to make it sound "better" in a quick demo. The bass will be made big and boomy, the treble overly bright to give the illusion of "clarity." The unwary may be impressed at first, but these colorations will quickly become fatiguing half an hour into your first movie.

Speaker B is made by a company founded by dedicated enthusiasts who strive to create the best-sounding speaker possible at a given price level. Their products are made for discriminating consumers who choose speakers based on how good they sound, not how impressive they look.

I'm not saying that a smaller loudspeaker is always better. But if two speaker systems are approximately the same price, and one is much bigger than the other and features more drivers, watch out. Buying a famous, nationally advertised brand name is no guarantee you won't waste your money on Speaker A. Many well-known companies produce inferior products.

If you're in the store evaluating speakers, here's a quick and dirty test for judging a speaker's build quality: rap your knuckles on the cabinet. If the cabinet produces a ringing tone, the speaker is probably not very well made. But if the rapping results in a dull thud, you can be fairly confident that the cabinet is solid. A thin, vibration-prone cabinet is a sure sign of a poorly built speaker. If the manufacturer has scrimped on the cabinet, you can be assured that they've cut corners elsewhere in the design. You can also pick up the speaker and feel how heavy it is. Does the speaker feel as if it's full of popcorn? Or does it seem as if it's made with solid bracing inside, like the cutaway photograph of fig.6-5?

How to Evaluate Speaker Systems in the Showroom

It always amazes me that so many people will buy a speaker system after only a brief demonstration—or no demonstration at all. You'll be living with your purchase for years; if you make a mistake now, you'll be stuck with the inferior system until you sell it and start over again. That's why you should carefully audition any home-theater system you're thinking of buying. The time to discover the speaker's flaws is in the showroom, not after you've taken the system home. And don't worry about taking up the salesperson's time; you're fully entitled to make sure you're buying the right speaker for you and your system.

No matter what your budget, ask to listen to the best speaker system in the store. Play both music and clips from films through the high-end model. This experience will provide you with a reference for evaluating the less expensive speaker system. After listening to the expensive system, play the same music and film clips on the speakers you're considering. Which of the speakers in your price range comes the closest to what you heard from the high-end speaker system?

Some other tips for finding the best speaker values: First, don't go for quick switching back and forth between speakers. These so-called "A/B" demos are worthless and misleading. Instead, listen to one system for 10 to 20 minutes, then play the same material on a second speaker system. Part of your evaluation should include listening to film clips with the video turned off—listening skills become less acute when so much brain power is engaged in watching. It's amazing how turning off the video (or closing your eyes) reveals flaws in a speaker system you didn't hear while watching.

Next, don't try to evaluate more than two systems at a time. If you're considering three systems, compare two of them, then put the winner up against the third system at a later time. Don't let the salesman distract you during the listening. Keep your focus on the job at hand: determining which speaker system does a better job of reproducing music and film soundtracks.

When evaluating speakers, use your ears—not the manufacturer's spec sheet, technical jargon, or the salesperson's pitch. If you follow these guidelines and listen for the characteristics described in the next section, you'll know which is the better-sounding speaker. It doesn't take a "golden ear" to know what sounds good. Trust yourself and your judgment.

What to Listen For When Evaluating Speakers

In this chapter we've talked about the various technical aspects of loudspeakers and how they affect performance. Although some technical background helps when choosing loudspeakers, *the best way to pick loudspeakers is by listening to them.* Careful and skillful listening prevents the speaker manufacturer from hiding behind marketing hype, advertising, claims of new technologies, and other hoopla. During a listening comparison, the speaker manufacturer cannot conceal the shortcuts made in building the product. Conversely, the speaker made by a conscientious, performance-driven company will become readily apparent by its superior sound quality.

Loudspeakers have several common flaws that you should listen for in the showroom. First, beware of thick or boomy bass. You should hear distinct pitches in bass notes, not a low-frequency "one-note" growl. If you've ever heard a "boom truck" cruising a downtown boulevard on a Saturday night, you know what bass should *not* sound like. Poorly reproduced bass becomes a constant annoyance that distracts from the home-theater and music-listening experiences. Although it may be tempting to choose the speaker with more bass during a brief audition, go to the next step of critically examining the bass *quality*. Can you hear individual bass notes? Or does the bass sound like mush? When it comes to bass, quality is more important than quantity.

It's a good idea to own a few movies so you can play the same clips in different stores. Find a few scenes that highlight different aspects of the sonic presentation. For example, the *T. rex* in *Jurassic Park* produces some incredibly low and powerful bass. Another classic bass test is the liftoff scene in *Apollo 13*.

You should also have in your repertoire a scene in which dialog competes with effects. Can you still hear the dialog, or is it hard to understand? Also listen for excessive dialog sibilance (*s, sh,* and *ch* sounds). Some speakers give the illusion of "clarity" by emphasizing the treble; they also accentuate dialog sibilance, which quickly leads to listening fatigue. The human voice is also revealing of a speaker's colorations, or departures from accuracy. Voices should sound natural, not as though the actors are speaking through cupped hands. In fact, dialog intelligibility should be high on your list sonic criteria because it's so important to a satisfying home-theater experience.

Listen for the spatial aspects of the sonic presentation. You should be wrapped inside a continuous soundfield, unaware that the sound is being reproduced by five separate sources. Listen for sounds that are panned (moved from one speaker to the other) to hear if the movement is smooth and continuous. You should also be able to precisely locate sounds from within the front soundfield. This, however, may have nothing to do with speaker quality, but speaker placement.

Finally, evaluate the loudspeaker's dynamic performance. A better system will reproduce transient (sudden) sounds with more impact. Also listen to the musical soundtrack during loud passages; does the sound become hard and strained? Or does the system maintain its sense of ease and clarity no matter what the volume? A loudspeaker system that correctly reproduces the full dynamic range (difference between the loudest and softest sounds) of music and modern film soundtracks delivers a much more thrilling and immersive experience than one that blunts the dynamic impact of high-level sounds.

Finding just the right speaker system is a challenging endeavor. Don't be in a hurry to buy the first system you hear. The more products you audition, the greater your chances of discovering the best value. You'll also discover that your listening skills become sharper with every system you audition. If you follow these guidelines, be discriminating and patient; your efforts will be rewarded with a good-sounding, well-made speaker system that fits your budget.

7 Video Displays: Direct-View and Rear-Projection HDTV, Plasma Panels, Front Projectors, Screens, and Image Scalers

Introduction

The video display is the central attraction of a home-theater system. While we want the sound-reproduction side of a home-theater system to "disappear" into the soundfield, the video monitor should assume a prominent position at center stage; it should be the focus of attention.

A home-theater video display can be anything from your old television set to a state-of-the-art front-projection system. You have a huge choice in video displays at all price levels, from about $400 to tens of thousands of dollars. Although sound quality is vital to the home-theater experience, it's the video display's quality and size that distinguish exceptional home-theater setups from average, middle-of-the-road systems. Good home theater is possible with a 32" TV, but there's nothing like the experience of a great front-projection system and a 10'-wide screen. In fact, with the new three-chip DLP technology, you can even watch movies on a 25' screen in your home—provided you have the space and budget.

This is an historic time for television and video displays; the new high-definition television (HDTV) technology has the potential of delivering vastly better picture quality than was possible with conventional analog television. This time of transition from analog to digital television is, however, marked by rapidly changing technology, consumer confusion, manufacturer marketing hype—and plummeting prices. Now, more than ever, it pays to be an informed consumer when shopping for a video display.

Fig. 7-1 A home-theater system's video monitor can be a conventional television set, rear-projector, or elaborate front-projection system.

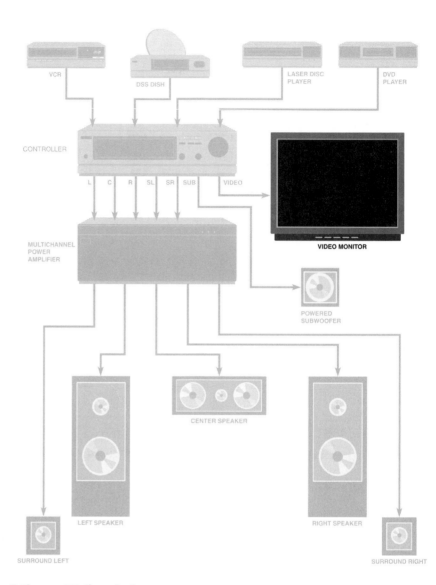

The Direct-View Television

Many home-theater systems will use a *direct-view television* as the video display. The term "direct-view" is just another name for the TV set with which we are all familiar. It's called direct-view because we see the image directly as it is created on the front of a *cathode-ray tube* (*CRT*). This is contrasted with rear- and front-projection sets, in which the image is projected onto a screen, either with mirrors (rear-projector) or across a room (front-projector).

A direct-view TV is described by the size of its screen, measured diagonally. The smallest screen size for a quality home-theater system is 32". Although 40" direct-view sets are available, they are disproportionately expensive and heavy. A 40" direct-view TV can cost—and weigh—more than a good 53" rear-projector.

Direct-view sets have many advantages: low cost, familiarity of use, easy setup, a relatively high contrast ratio with good color rendering, the ability to be viewed in higher ambient light than other video displays, and a wide choice of models in every price range. On the downside, direct-view sets are limited in their picture size to 40". If you want an image bigger than 40", you'll have to take the step of going to a rear- or front-projection set. Although a direct-view TV can be calibrated to have excellent picture quality, it is still limited in size and, thus, visual "impact."

How to Choose a Direct-View Television

Most people shop for a TV by going to the local appliance store and walking down a row of dozens of models, comparing the picture quality of a few sets in their price range. They then choose the one with the "best" picture. Such other factors as brand reputation, warranty, and features may also play roles, but the way the set looks in the store is often the overriding attribute.

But the picture quality you see in the store bears little resemblance to the way the set can look when properly calibrated. As described later in this chapter, TV sets' color, contrast, brightness, sharpness, and tint are often deliberately miscalibrated at the factory to be competitive on the showroom floor. The settings may not be accurate or produce a pleasing picture in the long run, but the miscalibration sells more TVs. In fact, picture quality is in some ways more dependent on proper calibration than on the set's intrinsic quality. That's why it's hard to compare pictures in a showroom to determine which set will provide you with the best picture quality. Smart home-theater enthusiasts learn how to make their sets look better and last longer through calibration.

Some magazine reviews of direct-view TVs report on a set's picture quality before and after calibration. Use these reviews as a guide in narrowing the vast range of choices in direct-view monitors.

As you ascend the price ladder for a given picture size, your money buys you either better picture quality or additional features. Go for the set that offers the best picture quality; the additional features on many sets are useless when the set is part of a home-theater system. For example, some direct-view TVs boast Dolby decoding and powerful audio amplifiers. But who needs them when you've got a much better Dolby Digital decoder and power amplifiers in your A/V receiver?

Similarly, don't be tempted by the set with the most input and output jacks—you won't need them when all the video switching is performed by your A/V receiver or controller. One feature you should insist on, however, is component-video input, a connection type described later in this chapter. Component-video connection between a DVD player and video monitor should deliver a significantly better picture than is possible from composite-video or even S-video connection. Component-video input is an absolute must if you plan to watch DVDs. If you have a DSS dish, a DVD player, an S-VHS recorder, or a HI-8 camcorder, an S-video input can be an advantage (more on this later). And if your A/V receiver lacks a front-panel A/V input, it's a good idea to have this feature on your TV. This lets you plug a camcorder into the TV without struggling to hook up cables behind the set. The newest high-definition models also offer an input called DVI, described later in this chapter.

Once you get past the bells and whistles of unnecessary features, look for technologies that make a difference in picture quality. One such recent trend in televisions has been toward flat-faced tubes. These new tubes don't have the traditional curved edges, which makes them look more modern, and, more important, also makes them easier on the eyes since they are less likely to reflect glare toward the viewer. Flat-faced tubes also reduce geometric distortion in the corners of the picture. However, flat-faced televisions are more difficult to manufacture and therefore more expensive. Flat-faced tubes are usually found only on the better-quality sets, not the commodity-level televisions sold in warehouse clubs.

Another thing to consider is the set's ability to separate brightness information, or *luminance*, from color information, or *chrominance*. Inexpensive sets often use an inferior circuit called a *notch filter* to do this. These are effective at removing dot crawl—the appearance of moving dots of color at the edges of color transitions—but in doing so filter out much of the picture's fine detail. Higher-quality TV sets and projectors use *comb filters* instead. Comb filters better preserve and display fine detail in the picture. *Digital comb filters* separate the brightness and color information with digital circuits, which results in a better picture.

A special test pattern on the *Video Essentials* calibration disc (described later in this chapter) helps the viewer determine the sophistication of a display's comb filter. A spectrum of color will be superimposed on the black-and-white test circle in the "Zone-Plate Test" as the circle moves around the screen. The amount of color that leaks onto this black-and-white image (and onto the stationary blocks around the circle) indicates how effectively the comb filter is doing its job. A rudimentary comb filter causes some black and white information to be interpreted as color, which is manifested as a swirling rainbow of color in the test pattern. More sophisticated comb filters reduce this effect noticeably. No set reproduces this test signal perfectly; just look for the one that causes the least distortion. (Try this test with composite, S-video, and component-video connections; you'll instantly appreciate the huge advantages of component video.)

Choose a set that lets you store combinations of settings such as brightness, color, tint, sharpness, and contrast for each input type (composite video, S-video) as well as for each input (Video 1, Video 2, etc.). After calibrating your set (described later), you can always return to the correct settings with the push of a button. Dual presets are even better; you can set one brightness level for daytime viewing and another for nighttime viewing. Another useful feature is the ability to turn off the set's *scan-velocity modulation* (SVM) circuit. SVM is a technique for making the picture brighter, but at the expense of accurate geometry and overall picture quality.

In short, forget useless frills and look for technologies that deliver a superior picture. The section on "Video Display Calibration" later in this chapter includes a description of how to judge picture quality.

High-Definition Direct-View Televisions

Before buying a new analog television, you should know that the federal government has mandated that all television stations stop broadcasting conventional analog television signals at midnight on December 31, 2006. This mandate, however, applies only if 85% of American homes can receive digital television broadcasts—an unlikely scenario. Still, it could mean that there will be no over-the-air signals to receive on your conventional TV by 2007. If you want to continue using your analog set past this date, you must buy a digital television (DTV) set-top box that can receive the new digital television broadcasts and convert them to analog. Although the set-top box may be able to receive and decode HDTV signals, your set's picture quality will be roughly the same as it is today. Downconverted HD signals will look at least as good as DVD when using a component-video connection between the digital-to-analog converter and your TV.

One way to avoid the coming obsolescence of your old analog TV is to buy an HDTV set now. The cost of HDTV sets has dropped dramatically since their introduction, and prices will continue to decline. Small direct-view HD sets are considerably more expensive than a comparably sized TV sold at a department store, but HD rear-projection televisions are only a few hundred dollars more than their analog counterparts. In fact, it makes no sense to buy an analog television today.

If you decide on a direct-view HDTV set, be wary of inflated marketing claims and confusing terminology. Many sets billed as "HDTV" don't have the full resolution required to display high-definition signals. Moreover, some sets described as "HDTV-Ready," "HDTV-Compatible," and "HDTV-Capable," lack an integral HDTV tuner, meaning that they require a separate set-top box (described in Chapter 3) before they can display true high-definition signals.

There are two key HDTV specifications. First is the number of vertical lines the set can display, called the set's *vertical resolution*. 480-line progressive (480p) is considered standard definition; 720-line progressive (720p) and 1080-line interlaced (1080i) are true high-definition. Second is the number of pixels on each line—the set's *horizontal resolution*. A pixel is the smallest piece of information in the picture; the greater the number of pixels, the higher the resolution, all other factors being equal.

This topic confuses even industry pros, so I'll state it another way. The horizontal resolution is the number of pixels the set can resolve on each horizontal line; the vertical resolution is the number of horizontal lines per video frame. In standard-definition NTSC television, the vertical resolution is absolutely fixed at 480 lines. That's the number of scanning lines that make up the picture. The horizontal resolution—the number of pixels the set can resolve on each horizontal line—varies with the quality of the set. In HDTV, the vertical resolution is absolutely fixed at either 720 lines or 1080 lines. That's the number of scanning lines that make up the picture. The horizontal resolution—the number of pixels on each horizontal line— varies with the quality of the video display. Vertical resolution is fixed by the format; horizontal resolution is a function of the video display.

There can be some confusion in the terms used to specify horizontal resolution. The term "pixel" is correctly used to refer to fixed-pixel displays or the resolutions of digital-television formats, while the term "TV Line" (TVL) is more appropriate when referring to an analog television's horizontal resolution. This specification is the number of vertical lines the television can resolve per picture height. If the set is driven by a signal of closely spaced alternating black and white vertical lines (think of a picket fence), we count the number of visually resolvable lines to determine the set's horizontal resolution. As those vertical lines become more closely spaced, they eventually turn into a gray blur. The threshold at which the individual vertical lines are still resolved is considered the set's horizontal resolution in TVL.

Don't confuse these vertical lines with the horizontal scanning lines of a television. The number of horizontal lines is fixed at 480 in NTSC video, and can be 720 or 1080 in HDTV. (NTSC is actually 525 lines, of which 480 contain picture information. The other 45 lines are black, and contain synchronization pulses and information such as Closed Caption data.) The 480 lines you see are called *active scan lines*.

There's one other source of confusion; the number of TV Lines the set can resolve is technically the number of lines across an area equal to the picture height. This requirement prevents widescreen sets from having an unfair advantage over conventional 4:3 sets. For example, even though the DVD format contain 720 pixels per horizontal line, we say its horizontal resolution is 540 lines because that's the number of pixels across an area equal to the picture height.

Many manufacturers grossly inflate their sets' horizontal resolution specification, with some even claiming the product can display the full 1920 x 1080 resolution of HDTV. When considering marketing claims of horizontal resolution, think about this: a professional direct-view HD monitor that costs $40,000 has a horizontal resolution of just 1400 lines. Moreover, its light output is so low (0.5 foot-lamberts, or one six-tieth the brightness of a conventional consumer monitor of the same size) that it must be viewed in a virtually pitch-black room. Even then, the image is still dim. There are no standards to which manufacturers are held when making claims of horizontal resolution, so take the number with a grain of salt.

Direct-view sets have the lowest horizontal resolution of all high-definition video displays. Pixels in a direct-view set are formed by phosphor stripes that emit light when struck by the scanning electron beam that traces each line of video. Small phosphors allow higher resolution, but at the expense of light output. Consequently, designers of HDTV sets must trade away some resolution so that the picture is bright enough. That's why the $40,000 professional monitor's light output is almost unusably low.

The highest-resolution HD signal is 1920 x 1080, meaning the image is composed of 1920 pixels on each horizontal line, with 1080 vertical lines per video frame. Multiplying these numbers gives us a pixel count of just over 2 million pixels. We've seen that direct-view televisions can't come close to resolving this number. But how much resolution is needed for the picture to be called "high-definition"? There's no exact threshold for calling a display "HD," but 1200 x 1080 pixels delivers about 1.3 million pixels, the point at which the video image makes the transition from looking very good to looking spectacular. (For comparison, a conventional analog television displaying a signal from VHS tape has a resolution of 240 TVL x 480.

Although a direct-view set's 1.3 million pixels falls short of HD's maximum resolution, it can still provide a picture of phenomenal resolution because of its relatively small size. The smaller the picture (and the greater the viewing distance), the fewer pixels needed to produce a great-looking image. When we get into larger-image video displays later in this chapter, we'll see how resolution becomes more important with large image size than with the relatively small images produced by direct-view TVs.

If you decide to delay buying an HDTV set, at least make sure the conventional set you buy has component-video inputs.

Displaying HD signals in their full glory brings us to the subject of our next section: a high-end rear- or front-projection display system.

The Rear-Projection Television

The rear-projection television (RPTV) is a popular choice for the home-theater enthusiast who wants a bigger picture size than is possible with a direct-view TV. Today's rear-projectors offer good picture quality, a narrow profile (so they don't stick out into your living room), and reasonable cost. Prices of high-definition rear-projectors have dropped dramatically in the last few years; good rear-projectors are available for less than $2000.

The main advantages of a rear-projector are picture size and price. A rear-projector provides a larger picture than a direct-view, but costs much less than a front-projector and screen. Whereas direct-view TVs top out at 40″, rear-projectors start at 40″ and go up to 70″ diagonal.

Rear-projectors have a few disadvantages, however. First, their light outputs are lower than those of direct-view TVs. This makes it harder to watch a rear-projection set in high ambient light conditions. Second, most rear-projectors have only a narrow "window" over which they disburse their light. You can see this for yourself by walking back and forth in front of an RPTV and watching the image brightness drop off as you move to the sides. You'll also see the color red shift to blue slightly when viewing from the side. Similarly, the rear-projector's light output drops if you're standing up or lying on the floor. All of the RPTV's available light output is concentrated in a narrow pattern directly in front of the screen. Another consideration is that if the three CRTs in a rear-projection television are not perfectly superimposed on each other (an adjustment called "convergence"), you'll see a separation of color around objects. Achieving good convergence over the entire screen is always a challenge.

How to Choose a Rear-Projector

If you decide on a rear-projector, the next choice you'll have to make is how large a screen you want. There are several factors you should consider when choosing the optimum picture size. First, you probably don't want to put a giant 60″ set in a small room. A cabinet that looks fairly large on a showroom floor can seem massive in a living room. Many of the new rear-projection sets have quite shallow front-to-back dimensions (as little as 16″), and so are less obtrusive in your living room. If you're tight on space, give careful consideration to the projector's depth. Keep in mind that a narrow cabinet can compromise picture quality, particularly the set's ability to maintain an even brightness over the entire screen.

Second, choose a picture size commensurate with your viewing distance. The closer you sit, the smaller the screen should be. If you sit too close to a large screen, you'll see the line structure and other flaws inherent in conventional standard-definition video. Conversely, sitting far away from a small screen produces a less dramatic image. Ideally, as much of your field of view as possible should be taken up by the picture without your noticing visible horizontal lines in the image. Specifically, the video image should subtend at least 30° of your field of view.

In theory a standard-definition, analog broadcast signal has only enough resolution to support a 10° field of view. More resolution is required to increase the amount of your visual area occupied by the picture. The high-definition television system was developed in part to provide enough resolution to make possible this 30° field of view.

You may be tempted by a giant 60″ or 70″ rear-projector that costs the same as a higher-quality 50″ set. But a huge picture isn't worth watching if the image is dull, fuzzy, lacks detail, and has poor color saturation. You're much better off with a smaller, better-looking set. Moreover, the rear-projector has only a finite amount of light output; when that light is spread over a larger screen, image brightness suffers. Expect to pay a hefty price for a 60″ set with a high-quality picture. I think 70″ rear-projectors push the capabilities of rear-projection technology too far; I haven't seen one that I would want to own. If you really want that big an image, consider taking the next step: buying a front-projector system.

As with a direct-view TV, don't spend your money on a rear-projector with a built-in, "high-quality" sound system.

If you like the idea of rear-projection and want the highest picture quality possible, the CRT projectors described later in this chapter can be configured to project their images from behind the screen. This custom-built approach is, however, considerably more expensive than buying a conventional "big-screen" TV from your local dealer.

High-Definition Rear-Projection Televisions

The rear-projection television is a great choice for displaying high-definition television signals, for many reasons: The RPTV's larger picture size benefits from the additional resolution in a high-definition signal; RPTVs can provide higher resolution than HD direct-view sets; and there's a wide selection of HD RPTVs in the marketplace.

Even if you live in an area without access to a wide range of HD programming, there's still a compelling reason to buy an HD RPTV: displaying the progressive-scan output from a DVD player. As described in Chapter 3, a progressive-scan DVD player outputs a signal with twice the number of scanning lines per unit time compared with a conventional interlaced DVD player. To take advantage of the superior picture provided by a progressive-scan DVD player, your video display must accept a 480p (480 line progressive) signal. All HD-Ready sets meet this criterion. The improvement in DVD picture quality when displayed on an HD-Ready set is alone worth the price of admission.

You'll notice that some HD rear-projection sets share a conventional television's 4:3 aspect ratio, while others have a 16:9 aspect ratio. Indeed, some manufacturers make two versions—i.e., with different aspect ratios—of what is essentially the same TV. Some consumers are reluctant to abandon the familiar 4:3 shape of a conventional television for the widescreen look.

There's no question that, as the world moves away from analog television toward digital TV, the widescreen aspect ratio will become increasingly common. A widescreen aspect ratio better fits humans' perception of motion, a fact reflected by the widescreen aspect ratio of movie-theater screens. Recognizing that television represents a large percentage of their incomes, filmmakers have wished that television would convert to a widescreen aspect ratio because it better matches the movie-theater experience.

Although we specify video displays as having either a 4:3 or 16:9 aspect ratio, these numbers get confusing when we talk about a film's aspect ratio. Video displays are specified as 4:3 or 16:9; films are specified as 2:1 or 2.35:1, for examples. Many films have an aspect ratio of 1.85:1, which nearly perfectly matches the 16:9 (1.78:1) aspect ratio of a widescreen television.

When watching a film with an aspect ratio of, say, 1.85 on a 4:3 (1.33:1) set, you see black bars above and below the picture. This condition, called *letterboxing*, is distracting to many viewers. Moreover, letterboxing reduces the image's vertical resolution, particularly on films with wide aspect ratios (2.35:1, for example). That's because some of the set's scanning lines are "wasted" on the black bars above and below the image, leaving fewer lines to produce the picture. Although letterboxing can reduce the vertical image size—and vertical resolution—by a third, it still better conveys the cinematographer's and director's framing of the film.

Displaying widescreen images on a widescreen HDTV set, however, fills more of the screen. A film with an aspect ratio of 1.85 displayed on a 1.78 set will produce very narrow black bars above and below the image. (In fact, the black bars are nearly imperceptible.) Widescreen sets are thus better suited to showing movies.

Another great benefit of a widescreen HD rear-projector is its ability to take advantage of *widescreen enhanced* DVDs. These DVDs deliver a third more vertical resolution when displayed on a widescreen set. (A full explanation of how they accomplish this feat appears in Chapter 3.) Conversely, a standard 4:3-aspect-ratio set cannot realize the tremendous improvement in resolution of such "16:9 enhanced" DVDs. Note, however, that some 4:3 HD sets incorporate a mode that shrinks the vertical area displayed to accommodate widescreen-enhanced DVDs as well as the 1.78 aspect ratio of HDTV. This feature, called "raster compression" or "vertical compression," squeezes all the set's available scanning lines into the widescreen picture area so that none of the scanning lines are wasted "drawing" the black bars above and below the widescreen image. These sets function as widescreen sets when displaying widescreen programming, with no loss of vertical resolution.

A related issue is whether the RPTV automatically locks into this compressed "anamorphic mode" when displaying an input signal with a resolution of 480p or 1080i. That is, some sets compress the raster whenever the input signal is anything other than 480i. The result is that non-anamorphic DVDs are displayed with incorrect geometry (the picture area is narrower than it should be, and actors are shorter and wider). Some sets allow you to manually turn on and off the anamorphic mode.

Now for the bad news about widescreen televisions: When watching television shows broadcast with a conventional 4:3 aspect ratio on a widescreen set, you see vertical black bars to the left and right sides of the picture. This condition, called *windowboxing,* can be annoying.

Moreover, prolonged display of windowboxed images can cause the phosphors in the image area to age faster than those in the black vertical bars on the left and right screen edges. The result can be permanent damage to the CRTs, causing a dimmer picture in the central 4:3 area of the screen. Most widescreen sets include several modes that "stretch" or "expand" the 4:3 image to fit the 16:9 screen, but such stretching distorts the picture. In practice, such geometrical distortion isn't as objectionable as it sounds. Note, however, that when 4:3 HD images in which the broadcaster has inserted the black bars are displayed, these stretching and expanding features are disabled, again introducing the potential for CRT damage. That's because the RPTV thinks it is displaying a widescreen image; the broadcaster has converted 4:3 to 16:9 by inserting the black bars.

There are ways of avoiding this potential damage while still displaying the correct geometry for any given source material. If the set's contrast is correctly calibrated (which is required to display the set's maximum resolution) the phosphors are less likely to be damaged over their useful life. Calibration can avoid damage from premature CRT "burn," but uneven phosphor wear is inevitable on a widescreen set displaying 4:3 images 90% of the time. (I've heard of a $40,000 projector being damaged in six months by children watching 4:3 cartoons all day.)

Nearly all RPTVs use three CRTs mounted inside the cabinet. These CRTs project their images into a mirror, which reflects the light onto the RPTV's screen. The size and type of focus system of the CRTs becomes a crucial factor in the resolution of high-definition RPTVs. Specifically, the larger the CRTs, the finer the resolution possible (all other factors being equal). Larger CRTs have more area in which to reproduce the resolution. RPTVs use CRTs ranging in size from 7" to 9", with the latter found only in the most expensive sets. Seven-inch CRTs, found in 95% of all RPTVs, are simply incapable of projecting the full horizontal resolution of 1920 pixels possible from high-definition signals. They can, however, display as many as 1200 horizontal TV Lines, which is a big improvement over conventional television. (HBO on DirecTV transmits its HD signals as 1280 x 1080.) A CRT's resolution is as dependent on the type of focus system used as on the size of the CRT itself. Not all RPTVs with 7" CRTs can deliver 1200 horizontal TV Lines across the width of the picture. Specifically, CRTs that are magnetically focused can achieve higher horizontal resolution than CRTs that are electrostatically focused.

High-quality rear-screen projection can also be achieved by projecting the image from a CRT-based front projector (described later in this chapter) onto a thin diffusion screen from behind that screen. These systems are usually custom-built and much more expensive than a cabinet-mounted RPTV, but provide better image quality. Such a system's picture quality can rival that of a front projector, and can maintain its contrast better in small amounts of ambient light. In addition, a separate

CRT projector mounted in a blacked-out room behind a screen isolates the projector noise from the viewing room.

Although the vast majority of RPTVs use three CRTs to generate the picture, an increasing number of sets use fixed-pixel technologies such as *Liquid Crystal Display* (LCD), *Digital Light Processing* (DLP) *Liquid-Crystal on Silicon* (LCoS), *Digital-Image Light Amplifier* (D-ILA), and *Fluorescent Liquid-Crystal Display* (F-LCD) technologies. These fixed-pixel-based RPTVs are much smaller and lighter than their CRT counterparts because their optical systems are smaller compared to CRT optics. Rear-projection televisions using fixed-pixel technologies have advantages and disadvantages similar to those of fixed-pixel front-projectors (covered later in this chapter). The fixed-pixel RPTV will have poorer black-level performance than a CRT projector, meaning that deep black is reproduced as a murky gray. This prevents the picture from having "snap," or vividness. In addition, LCD projectors currently on the market tend to have poor color uniformity, which can result in a blue sky having a different hue, depending on where on the screen the sky is displayed. But widescreen fixed-pixel RPTVs weigh little, have thin cabinets, and, when displaying windowboxed 4:3 images on their 16:9 displays, are not prone to the potential for CRT damage described earlier. As the resolution of fixed-pixel devices increases and prices drop, look for more rear-projection televisions to be based on fixed-pixel technology, particularly DLP.

Image Scalers in HDTV Sets

Although high-definition direct-view and rear-projection sets usually scan at the HD rate of 1080 interlaced scanning lines (1080i), conventional broadcast sources and interlaced-output DVD players output standard-definition signals at the 480i rate. Standard 480i video signals are called NTSC. The television must therefore perform an "upconversion" from 480i to the television's "native" scan rate, usually 1080i. This job is performed by a circuit inside the television called an *image scaler*, but known by a variety of trade names including Digital Reality Creation (Sony), Diamond Digital Pixel Multiplier (Mitsubishi), and Intelligent Digital Scan Conversion (Toshiba). Whatever the name, this circuit plays a crucial role in picture quality with standard-definition sources, which will probably constitute most of your viewing time.

A poor-quality scaler can introduce motion artifacts, seen as jagged lines on moving objects, particularly diagonal lines. In addition, a poor integral scaler can reduce apparent picture detail, blur slight gradations in color, and add an artificial or "plastic" cast to skin tones.

There's a simple test for judging the quality of an HDTV set's integral scaler: bypass the scaler by connecting a progressive-scan DVD player to the set. First, connect a good-quality progressive-scan DVD player to the television, and set the DVD player's output to "Interlaced."

When the HDTV set under test sees the DVD player's 480i signal, it will engage its scaler to convert the 480i signal to 1080i (or whatever the set's native scanning rate is). Look closely at the picture, paying particular attention to flesh tones and the smoothness of moving objects.

Now switch the DVD player's output to "Progressive" and watch the same scene again. You have just bypassed the HDTV set's internal scaler. If the picture quality is significantly better from the DVD player's progressive-scan output, the image scaler in the HDTV set is poor. Note that this test works only if the set scans at 480p. Many of the more modern HD sets also scan at 540p. If that's the case, the set's integral image scaler will not be bypassed in this test, and you can't use it to judge the set's scaler performance.

Most HD sets also include 3/2 pulldown removal for correctly displaying 24 frame-per-second film-based sources. This technique, described in Chapter 3, greatly improves the picture quality of images that were originally stored on film (rather than video).

This "Achilles' Heel" of HDTV sets (poor performance on standard-definition sources caused by low-quality image scalers) is becoming less of a problem as manufacturers improve the quality of image scalers built into HDTV sets. You can also add an external image scaler to improve the set's picture quality. Image scalers are described later in this chapter.

HDTV Shopping Checklist

Before visiting showrooms for a firsthand look at HDTV direct-view or rear-projection sets, consider the points on the following checklist.

1) Decide whether a **direct-view or RPTV** set best suits your living arrangements and needs. Direct-view sets have a slightly more vibrant picture, but are limited in picture size and resolution. Keep in mind that other display technologies are also available (plasma panels and front projectors, described later in this chapter), although they are considerably more expensive than direct-view or rear-projection televisions.

2) Choose a **picture size** commensurate with your viewing distance. A viewing distance of three-to-four times the picture *height* is a good range.

3) Decide whether a conventional **4:3 aspect ratio** or the new **16:9 widescreen aspect ratio** best fits your viewing habits. Although 4:3 sets will eventually become obsolete, there's an awful lot of 4:3 programming available—and some viewers object to watching 4:3 material on a 16:9 set with the attendant black or gray "windowbox" bars on either side of the image.

4) If you choose a set without **an integral ATSC (high-definition) tuner** that will pick up HD broadcast signals, be aware that you'll need an external set-top box if you want to watch high-def programming. (See Chapter 3 for more on ATSC tuners.)

5) Make sure the set doesn't automatically lock into widescreen anamorphic mode when feeding the set a 480p signal from a progressive-scan DVD player. Look for a feature called "**manual aspect-ratio control.**" Without this feature, non-anamorphic DVDs will be displayed with incorrect picture geometry.

6) Look for a set with **independent memory settings** for each input. This feature lets you calibrate the brightness, contrast, color, tint, and sharpness independently for each input for the best possible picture with a variety of sources. Without this feature, you're stuck with one setting for all inputs, which will cause variations in picture quality when switching among video inputs. Source components have different output levels, which can create differences in optimum video-display calibration for different sources.

7) Make sure the set has **enough inputs, and of the right type**, for your system. For example, a rudimentary input complement may include one RF (antenna), one composite, one S-video, one component, and one HD input. Better sets offer multiple RF inputs, six composite and S-video jacks, two component inputs, a separate RGB/HV input that accepts 1080i from a set-top box, and a 15-pin VGA connector for using the television as a computer monitor or for playing video games.

8) Check the set's **integral scaler quality** using the test described earlier in this chapter. Use both video and film-based sources for your evaluation. Look for a set that has a "Film" mode or other such name that identifies sets with 3/2 pulldown. Check the quality of the 3/2 pulldown; there are large variations between manufacturers.

9) Some RPTVs now offer an **automatic convergence** feature that aligns the red, green, and blue CRTs so that they produce images that perfectly overlap each other. You've probably seen a misconverged RPTV—a colored halo outlines objects, and white text appears to have a colored ghost image outlining it.

In addition to automatic convergence, RPTVs sometimes have an eight-point convergence feature, meaning that the convergence can be manually aligned at eight points over the screen. The best sets have as many as 64 convergence points, allowing a skilled technician to perfectly tune the convergence. The more points at which the convergence is adjusted, the better the image quality. Keep in mind that automatic convergence simply returns the set to its factory convergence setting. Between the factory's convergence calibration and your living room, the set has been jostled on four fork lifts and several trucks, which throws off the convergence. There's no substitute for on-site convergence adjustment.

10) If you choose a widescreen set, look at the **"zoom," "stretch," and "expand" modes** that make a 4:3 image fill the widescreen set. Some brands have better-looking stretch modes than others. These modes may save your picture tubes from uneven wear.

11) One indicator of quality is the **number of elements in the lenses**. More lenses means that each lens does less work, resulting (all other factors being equal) in a sharper and crisper picture.

12) Some models allow you to **update the set to accommodate new technology** by plugging in a circuit board. This is an increasingly important feature as integrated operation and control start to become widespread. This add-on board may have a FireWire (IEEE1394) connector, which allows the TV to communicate with the rest of your system. A FireWire-connected system functions as a single "smart" system that can be controlled by a single remote control. Manufacturers are increasingly including a Digital Visual Interface (DVI) jack on televisions for connection to set-top boxes and other high-definition source components.

13) Finally, check out the **user interface**. This includes things like how well the remote control fits in your hand, whether it is backlit (a great feature), how easy the set is to operate, and the general user-friendliness of the operation.

Front-Projection Systems

The ultimate home-theater experience is provided by the *front-projector*. If you want a really big image and you want that image to be bright, punchy, and detailed, a front-projection system is the usual way to get it. The leap into a front-projector shouldn't be taken lightly, however. Owning a front-projector requires a large commitment of money ($4000–$120,000), maintenance (periodic alignment and tube or bulb replacement), and a room that can be made dark enough to realize the projector's potential. A front-projector is for serious home-theater installations, not casual television watching.

As its name implies, a front-projector projects a video image onto a screen in front of it. The screen is typically located at one end of the room, the projector spaced back from the screen by a distance of 1.5 times the screen width. The projector can be mounted on the floor in front of the viewing position, or on the ceiling, out of the way.

You should rely on the guidance of a professional in choosing a projector and screen. The following information will give you a basic knowledge of projectors that will allow you to converse with a professional installer, but should not be considered a substitute for professional advice. And, because front-projectors are for the serious enthusiast, the following sections are more technical than the rest of this book. If you have a direct-view TV or rear-projector and aren't interested in the technical details of front-projectors, feel free to skip directly to the "Video Display Calibration" section of this chapter.

Before I describe the different front-projection systems, let's take a look at some general attributes of all front-projectors. First, it's important to realize that all the light you see in the video image—i.e., its brightness—is created by the projector. The more light the projector produces, the brighter the image, all other factors being equal. In practice, however, many things influence brightness. These include the screen size, screen gain (described later), and the amount of ambient light in the viewing room. The greater the amount of ambient light, the lower the picture's contrast ratio. The larger the screen, the less bright the picture from a given projector. As the projector's finite light output is spread over a wider and wider area, the picture gets dimmer.

The light output of projectors is rated in *ANSI lumens*. ANSI stands for American National Standards Institute, a regulatory body that sets measurement standards. Projector manufacturers are in a battle to provide the highest number of ANSI lumens for their products. But we don't look directly at the projector's output; we're more concerned with the amount of light reflected from the screen. The unit of measurement for screen-reflected light is the *foot-lambert (fL)*, a much more meaningful measure of image brightness than the projector's ANSI lumen rating. As we'll see, two projectors with identical outputs as measured in ANSI lumens can produce very different amounts of light as measured in foot-lamberts. A reference-quality movie theater will provide a brightness of 11 foot-lamberts. The minimum acceptable brightness is 8fL, with 10–11fL being excellent. Direct-view TVs provide 25–35fL, but over a relatively small area. They have to be that bright to compete with all the ambient light in most living rooms during the day.

How bright the image appears to the viewer is partially dependent on the amount of ambient light in the room. The expense of a high-quality projector and screen can be wasted if the viewing room isn't kept dark—the projector and screen must fight the ambient light to project a bright image. Any stray light will make the image look washed-out, with little contrast or dynamic range between black and white. Ambient light reduces the depth of black in the image, robbing the picture of its "snap" by reproducing black as gray. Indeed, one property that distinguishes a projector's quality is its ability to reproduce black as truly black. A projector can't "project" black, which is merely the absence of color; all it can do is project as little light as possible on the screen. If any light is projected where it isn't supposed to be, the blacks look gray and washed-out. High contrast—the ability to reproduce deep black accompanied by high light output—is associated with a three-dimensional-looking picture of maximum depth and visual impact.

In fact, high contrast ratio is one of the most important contributors to a great-looking picture. More specifically, the ability to reproduce black as truly black, a quality called "black level," is more important than a high numerical contrast ratio. If we take a picture and double the numerical contrast ratio by doubling the peak white level, the picture will show some improvement. But if we take that same picture and double the numerical contrast ratio by halving the amount of light in black areas, we'll see a vastly greater improvement. The contrast ratio was doubled in each example, but the eye responds more to deeper blacks than to brighter whites. That's one reason why the CRT projector produces the best image quality of all the projector types; it has by far the best black level.

With that basic background, let's look at five front-projection technologies currently on the market.

The CRT Projector

Until recently, the term "video projector" was synonymous with the cathode-ray tube (CRT) projector, which for years has been the undisputed king of high-quality video presentation in the home (fig.7-2). Only recently have other projector technologies like LCD, DLP, D-ILA, and LCoS (described later in this chapter) challenged the CRT projector. You can spend anywhere from $8000 to $50,000 for a CRT projector, but several good CRT projectors are available in the $10,000–$15,000 range.

A CRT projector works in much the same way as a direct-view television, but with three separate picture tubes, one each for the primary colors: red, green, and blue. Each cathode-ray tube projects its light through its own lens; when projected on a screen, the three outputs combine to form a single image. The lenses are 7" in diameter in budget projectors, 8" in mid-priced units, and 9" in top-end models. A projector using 9" tubes can cost twice as much as one using 8" tubes. What you get for the additional money is not more light output, but greater detail. A 9" projector may actually have lower light output than a projector using 8" tubes, but the 9" projector will deliver a sharper picture.

One way of creating a brighter image with a CRT projector is to use two projectors and superimpose their images on the projection screen. This technique of stacking projectors doubles the light output and creates a fabulous picture, but, as you can imagine, is very expensive. Nonetheless, it is sometimes done in high-end home-theater systems.

One factor to consider with CRT projectors is the need to periodically replace the projector's three tubes. The projector's light output, a crucial factor in image quality, drops during normal use. The light output can drop by as much as 50% in the first 20–30% of the tubes' operating life. As light output drops, picture contrast is reduced. Replacing a set of tubes can cost several thousand dollars.

This light fall-off of CRTs as they age is an important consideration when choosing a screen size. A new projector can illuminate a larger screen than when the projector's CRTs have aged. If you pick a smaller screen and operate the projector below its maximum light output, it will provide that light-output level for a much longer time. Conversely, if the screen is larger than the projector can comfortably drive, and the contrast is turned up to get a "bright" picture, the light-output capability will quickly drop. Most CRT-based projectors will not drive a 1.3-gain screen more than 7' wide.

Also keep in mind that higher-resolution projectors generally have lower light output. An expensive, 9" electromagnetically-focused projector probably won't drive as large a screen as will an inexpensive 7", electrostatically-focused projector.

Fig. 7-2 A CRT projector uses three CRTs to project an image onto a separate screen. It still offers the best image quality of all the projection technologies.

Courtesy Runco International

Another drawback to the CRT projector is the need for professional setup and calibration—getting the highest performance from a CRT projector is an art in itself. Moreover, the CRT projector needs to be fine-tuned as the tubes' light output decreases. A good installer will set up a service contract specifying that he will re-calibrate the projector every three to six months.

CRT projectors also have a fixed *throw distance*, or the distance between the projector and screen. The throw distance dictates the location of the CRT projector in your room, unlike the other projector technologies that allow a range of throw distances. Keep in mind that CRT projectors weigh several hundred pounds and are not easily moved.

If you're willing to part with a substantial sum of money, pay a professional installer to calibrate your projector, replace tubes periodically, and provide a dark room for viewing, the front-projector will reward you with state-of-the-art visual quality. Be aware that without a dark room and good technical support, CRT is not a wise choice.

The LCD Projector

LCD stands for *Liquid Crystal Display*, a technology popular in the displays of digital watches, notebook computer screens, and as the standard method of displaying presentation graphics in corporate meetings. Before 1996, LCD projectors just didn't have the picture quality to be seriously considered for high-quality video displays in home-theater systems, but recent technical advances have considerably improved their level of performance.

An LCD projector is vastly smaller, lighter, and easier to set up than a CRT-based front-projector. Some of them weigh less than 20 pounds and are no bigger than a slide projector. Unlike the challenging CRT front-projector, the LCD projector can be taken down and set back up again in a few minutes. Of course, like a CRT front-projector, an LCD projector requires a separate screen on which to project the image.

LCD projectors cost considerably less than CRT-based front-projectors. Quality units cost between $4000 and $10,000, with some excellent products available at the $7000 price level. Although more costly than a rear-projection television, the LCD projector can produce images of up to 100", measured diagonally. LCDs also have relatively high light outputs that provide a bright picture. An LCD projector's bulb should last for about 2500 hours. As the bulb wears out, its light output will steadily decrease. Replacement bulbs cost about $400—considerably less than the several thousand dollars it can cost to replace a set of CRTs, although light bulbs wear out much faster than CRTs.

All LCD projectors are inherently progressive-scan devices. They always include an integral *interlaced-to-progressive converter*, also called a line doubler, or image scaler. The quality of the LCD projector's internal image scaler greatly influences picture quality; some inexpensive projectors use inferior circuits that produce so-called de-interlacing artifacts that show up most obviously as extra motion in moving diagonal lines. Nearly all LCD projectors allow you to substitute an external scaler for the one built into the projector. Doing this often results in improved picture quality, but adds at least $700 to the installation cost. (Image scalers are described in more detail later in this chapter.) LCD projectors' high light output, built-in image scaler, light weight, ease of setup, and moderate cost make them a tempting alternative to the limited picture size and brightness of rear-projectors, and to the high cost and setup difficulty of CRT front-projectors.

Although capable of good video quality, LCD projectors still have some visible shortcomings compared with CRT projectors. First, they're less good at projecting deep black and at resolving different levels of black; the result is lack of detail in dark scenes. Dark areas tend to become patches of gray, with no gradations of shading. This characteristic can be seen on the gray-scale pattern on the *Video Essentials* calibration DVD.

Although we'll discuss setting the brightness and contrast adjustments later, it's important to note here that when the brightness or contrast are set incorrectly, you'll actually lose part of the picture. If you display a gray scale from a test DVD, you'll see a gray ramp and gray step. If the contrast control is set too high, some of the top steps in the gray scale will be missing. That is, the display cannot distinguish between shades of light gray, a condition called *white clip*. If the brightness control is set too low, some of the bottom steps will be missing: The display cannot distinguish between shades of dark gray (called *black clip*). As you move the brightness and contrast controls through their ranges, you'll see the ramp flattening out and steps in the gray scale disappearing. When adjusting the contrast control, you'll often see the top end of the scale changing color before the top steps disappear. Obviously, the contrast should be set below the point where any picture information is missing, and below a point where the color of white at the top end changes.

Another drawback of LCD projectors is that they can at times have difficulty producing uniform light distribution; that is, they often produce a bright spot in the center of the picture because the bulb is located in the center of the image-producing LCD array. Moreover, the lamp in an LCD projector generates a lot of heat, which must be removed from the projector housing with a fan. The noise generated by the fan can be distracting during quiet parts of film soundtracks.

An LCD projector's lens must be positioned on a line nearly perpendicular to the screen and aimed at the screen center. If the projector is placed on the floor projecting up to the screen, the image will be wider at the top, a phenomenon called *keystoning*. Unlike CRT projectors, most LCD units have no adjustment to compensate for keystoning. Similarly, an LCD projector mounted on the ceiling and pointing down will project an image that is wider at the bottom. LCD projectors must be located along a fairly narrow horizontal plane near the screen center. This means mounting the projector either on a stand to raise it closer to the center of the screen, or upside-down from the ceiling. Newer LCD projectors, however, may have a feature called *digital keystone adjustment*, which can compensate for a variety of projection angles. And, unlike CRT projectors, some LCD projectors offer lens options that can expand the projector-to-screen distance, such as zoom lenses to change the image size.

The LCD projector's light is generated by a powerful metal-halide lamp. The bulb's white light is split into the three primary colors: red, green, and blue. Each color is directed to its own LCD panel, which is controlled by electrical signals representing the red, green, and blue components of the picture. The LCD panels are composed of thousands of (or more than a million) tiny pixels, the smallest structure in a video image. The pixels act as valves that are turned on or off by the electrical signal. The pixels thus modulate the amount of light that passes through the LCD panel to the lens and, ultimately, to the projection screen. But this process isn't perfect; the "valves" don't block all the light, resulting in black being reproduced as gray. The reduction in contrast ratio caused by the LCD's inability to project true black results in a picture with less "snap," "punch," and "life" compared with CRT projectors.

An LCD array might have 640 x 480 pixels, or 307,200 pixels per panel, with three panels (one each for red, green, and blue) per projector. The greater the number of pixels, the higher the picture resolution. Better LCD projectors can have a resolution of 1024 x 768. Sony's VPL-VW-11HT (fig.7-3) features a 16:9 LCD panel with a resolution of 1366 x 768, which maximizes resolution when displaying widescreen images. Because the LCD projector uses a panel of pixels to create the image, it is called a "fixed-pixel display." This is contrasted with the CRT projector, which operates more as an analog device.

Fig. 7-3 Today's LCD projectors are an affordable alternative to CRT projectors for high-quality home theater.

Courtesy Sony Electronics Inc.

LCD projectors are rated by their light outputs, measured in ANSI lumens. Lower-end LCD projectors can have light outputs of 350 ANSI lumens; top models reach 1000. As with CRT projectors, the light-output specification is only a guideline. The "white clip" described earlier can occur long before a projector reaches its maximum light output. High light output is especially important when the projector is asked to produce a large image, or to compete with ambient light.

Newer LCD projectors—not re-packaged corporate-graphics displays, but designed from the ground up for home-theater use—incorporate features that not only improve picture quality, but make the projector easier to use in a home-theater system. For example, modern LCD projectors offer video memories for storing different picture-control settings, allowing you to program separate, optimum settings for VHS, DVD, and TV.

The DLP Projector

An entirely new method of projecting video images was introduced commercially in 1997. This technology, called *Digital Light Processing* (*DLP*), has been under development for more than 20 years by Texas

Instruments. Now that DLP is a commercial reality, Texas Instruments is licensing the technology to many manufacturers of video projectors. DLP projectors (fig.7-4) are lightweight, easy to set up, portable, priced below CRT projectors, and can provide good picture quality. Like LCD projectors, the DLP projector is a fixed-pixel display device.

Fig. 7-4 A DLP projector using the Texas Instruments 1280 X 720 Digital Light Processing chip.

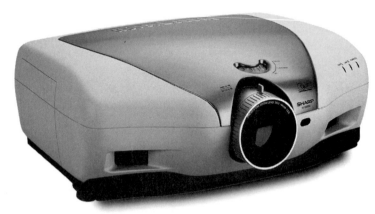

Courtesy Sharp Electronics

DLP was originally called *Digital Micromirror Device* (*DMD*) technology, a term that better describes how it works: A semiconductor, similar to a computer chip, is made with hundreds of thousands (or more than a million) tiny mirrors on its surface, each mirror less than one tenth the diameter of a human hair. The mirrors sit on tiny, electronically controlled structures that can tilt each mirror independently (fig.7-5). Up to three such devices are used in a DLP-based projector. A light source is directed at the mirror, and the incoming digital video signal controls which mirrors are tilted to reflect the light source.

Texas Instruments describes fig.7-5 as follows: "Incoming light hits the three mirror pixels. The two outer mirrors that are turned on reflect the light through the projection lens and onto the screen. These two 'on' mirrors produce square, white pixel images. The central mirror is tilted to the 'off' position. This mirror reflects light away from the projection lens to a light absorber so no light reaches the screen at that particular pixel, producing a square, dark pixel image. In the same way, the remaining 508,797 mirror pixels reflect light to the screen or away from it. By using a color filter system and by varying the amount of time each of the 508,800 DMD mirror pixels is on, a full-color, digital picture is projected onto the screen." (This description is of a 508,800-pixel DMD; higher resolution devices are also available.)

Shades of gray are created by the amount of time each pixel reflects light toward the screen; the longer it reflects, the closer to white the image. A single DLP chip can reproduce 256 steps of gray between black and white.

Fig. 7-5 DLP technology uses hundreds of thousands of tiny, digitally controlled mirrors to project a high-resolution color image.

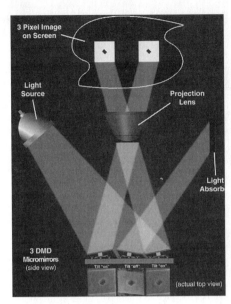

Courtesy Texas Instruments

The most commonly used Texas Instruments DLP chip packs 921,600 pixels on a single DMD for 1280 x 720 resolution. This chip has a 16:9 aspect ratio, allowing it to reproduce widescreen program with no loss of resolution. Earlier generation DLP chips, whose mirrors were arrayed in a 4:3 aspect ratio, wasted vertical resolution when displaying widescreen images because the mirrors above and below the picture area (the black bars) didn't contribute to creating the picture. This latest DLP chip also has improved black-level performance, realized by making the substrate on which the mirrors sit more absorbing of stray light. In addition, the mirror edges are less reflective, contributing to the new chip's deeper blacks.

As the resolution of DMDs increases and their prices drop, the technology is beginning to replace lower-priced, electrostatically focused CRTs in front- and rear-projectors. DLPs are also rapidly overtaking LCD technology for home-theater projection. This trend will accelerate, particularly if Texas Instruments is successful in developing a 1920 x 1080 DMD capable of displaying the full resolution of HDTV.

Lower-priced ($3000–$15,000) DLP projectors use a single DLP chip; more expensive units (up to $90,000) employ three DLPs for improved performance. Let's first look at the single-chip DLP.

Most single-chip DLP projectors use a white-light source that projects onto the DMD through a spinning color filter, sometimes called a color wheel. The filter selectively passes each color in turn to the DMD. Each pixel in the DMD then reflects the colored light to the output lens; the final color is determined by how long the mirror reflects the red, green, and blue light. Although the colors are projected sequentially, we see a continuous spectrum because the eye/brain combination integrates the rapid "flashes" of discrete colors into subtle color variations. High-quality color wheels have six segments, such that each color is projected onto the screen for 1/360 of a second—a much faster rate than we can detect. Indeed, a single-chip DLP projector can display 16.7 million colors. Single-chip DLP projectors are the least expensive, but have low light output because, at any given time, only a third of the light generated by the white-light sources ever reaches the DMD. In addition, most of the light striking the DMD is reflected away from the lens.

A three-chip DLP projector uses one DMD for each color. A dichroic filter splits the white light into red, green, and blue; each color is directed to its own DMD. Three-chip DLP projectors have greater light output because each DMD is always illuminated.

Like LCD projectors, DLP displays tend to reproduce deep black as dark gray. While CRT projectors can achieve a complete absence of color (the definition of black) by simply cutting off the signal to the electron beam, a DLP projector uses a fixed light source that must be modulated by the micromirrors; the micromirrors must spend at least some time reflecting light to the lens, which makes black appear as dark gray. Still, DLP projectors better reproduce black than can LCD projectors.

In theory, DLP technology can achieve better color accuracy than CRT projectors because the colors aren't dependent on the color accuracy of the phosphors coating the inside of a CRT. Compared with LCD projectors, DLPs tend to have a more continuous-looking image, with less of the classic LCD *screen-door effect*. This phenomenon is created by the absence of projected light in the spaces between the pixels in the LCD panels, which gives the impression of looking at the image through the tiny square holes of a screen door. The spaces between pixels are smaller in a DLP chip than in an LCD panel, which gives DLP chips a greater "fill factor" than LCD panels.

As with LCD projectors, DLP-based units incorporate an integral image scaler to convert the incoming video signal to match the chip's pixel array. For example, 480i video from an interlaced DVD player or NTSC broadcast is converted to 1280 x 768 pixels by the projector's internal electronics. This converter can also include 3/2 pulldown, deinterlacing, and other video processing to improve the picture.

It should be noted that DLP-based video displays are inherently digital. As the world moves toward all-digital video transmission and storage, DLP technology is the last component in the all-digital video-delivery system.

Here are a few other things you should know about DLP projectors. First, they all use fans to cool the electronics and optics, which can make them audibly distracting when you are watching a movie. Second, you can set up a DLP projector in a few minutes, allowing you to take down the projector after each use. Third, DLP projectors can be mounted on the ceiling or on a coffee table. Fourth, DLP projectors have a zoom lens and variable throw distance, giving you a wide range of placement options. Fifth, DLP projectors have a keystone adjustment that corrects for the picture looking wider on top when the projector is positioned lower than the screen, or wider at the bottom when positioned higher than the screen.

LCoS, D-ILA, and F-LCD Technologies

Liquid-Crystal on Silicon (LCoS) is a new family of fixed-pixel video imaging device that operates on a similar principle to LCD. But instead of allowing or preventing light from passing through each pixel in the LCD panel, the LCoS panel selectively reflects polarized light. Where LCD is a transmissive technology, LCoS is reflective.

This basic principle is behind the technology that bears various tradenames, including Digital-Image Light Amplifier (D-ILA) from JVC and Ferroelectric LCD (F-LCD) from Samsung.

The LCoS family of devices has an advantage over LCD in that they are more light efficient; more of the generated light is used to create the picture and less is wasted. Consequently, LCoS, D-ILA, and F-LCD projectors have very high light outputs—on the order of 1500 to 2000 ANSI lumens.

A D-ILA panel measures 0.9″ diagonally, and may have a pixel array of 1365 x 768 (fig.7-6). JVC is aggressive in increasing resolutions and lowering prices, and 1920 x 1080 D-ILA panels have been announced.

Fig. 7-6
A D-ILA device combines high resolution with high light output.

Courtesy JVC

LCoS, D-ILA, and F-LCD technology can be used in front projectors or rear-projection televisions as a replacement for CRTs. Such RPTVs can be much lighter weight (70 pounds for a 55″ set, compared with 250 pounds for a comparably-sized CRT-based RPTV), and less deep. Although the optical path is more complex with LCoS/D-ILA/F-LCD-based rear-projection televisions, they can be less deep—a decided advantage for a box that sticks out into your living room.

All the fixed-pixel display technologies—DLP, LCD, LCoS, D-ILA, F-LCD—have one advantage over CRT: it is impossible to "burn in" an image as sometimes happens with CRT-based displays. For example, if you watch the same business news show many hours each day, the stationary pattern of banners carrying stock quotes will eventually create a "burned in" image on a CRT-based display.

Front-Projection Screens

Most prospective purchasers of front-projectors concentrate on the specifications and quality of the projector itself. But a projection system consists of two components: the projector, and the screen on which the image is projected. The screen is a vital element in achieving picture quality, and deserves as much consideration as the choice of projector. The screen can be compared to loudspeakers in an audio system: a high-quality electrical signal delivered to low-quality loudspeakers will result in poor sound.

The first thing to consider is the screen size. A common mistake is to choose the biggest screen that will fit in your room. (Standard screen sizes are 70", 84", 100", and 120" wide with a 16:9 aspect ratio, with custom sizes also available.) A screen's aspect ratio is an integral part of its size specification, and should be considered along with its width: a 10'-wide, 16:9-aspect-ratio screen has a considerably smaller image area than a 10'-wide screen with a 4:3 aspect ratio.

Aspect ratio is a consideration because the screen's size must be matched to the projector's characteristics, particularly its light output. Projectors produce a finite amount of light; spreading the available light out over a larger screen reduces brightness and makes the picture look washed-out, dim, or low in contrast. Similarly, a video signal contains a finite amount of resolution; blowing up the image too much to fill a large screen reveals the line structure inherent in the video format with CRT projectors, or creates the "screen-door" effect with an LCD or DLP projector. A smaller picture often provides a more satisfying overall experience when the source resolution is low. Later in this section I'll describe a formula for calculating the optimum screen size for a given projector's light output.

Projection screens come in a variety of mounting configurations. The four basic ones are: a frame supported by legs; a frame permanently mounted to a wall; a hanging screen with no mounting; and a motorized roll-up unit into which a screen can be retracted when not in use.

Frame-mounted screens are called *tensioned* screens because the screen material is stretched over a frame. This maintains the screen's flatness and contributes to uniform picture quality. Non-tensioned screens tend to curl slightly, thus degrading picture quality. Motorized drop-down screens can be *tab tensioned* to maintain their flatness without a frame.

The hanging screen has the advantage of low cost, but can be unsightly if you use your home-theater room for other purposes.

The *motorized*, or *roll-up*, screen is coiled inside a housing and can be dropped down when needed. Many motorized screens can change the aspect ratio of the image area by lowering a mask over the portion of the screen that isn't being used by the projector. Masking off the screen area not occupied by the projected image confers a massive improvement in image quality because it increases the apparent contrast ratio. Wall mounted screens can also have masking, but the motorized screen lets you retract the mask at the touch of a button.

Not all projection screens are made the same way. Different models are created by coating the screen with different materials to create varying optical properties. A screen type that is ideal for one installation might not work well in another home-theater room. The best way of choosing the right screen for your room and projector is to consult a knowledgeable retailer or custom installer. The following discussion covers only the fundamentals of projection screens; it's no substitute for an expert's advice.

Screen Gain and Color Uniformity

A screen's two most important optical properties are those of *screen gain* and *color uniformity*. Let's first deal with gain.

Screen gain is a measure of reflectivity relative to an industry-standard reference: magnesium carbonate applied to a flat surface (called a "Lambertian surface"). If the amount of light reflected from the screen is greater than that reflected from the reference material, the screen is said to have gain. It may seem impossible that a screen could have a gain greater than 1, but it can. Here's why: If the light striking the screen is reflected back over a narrow angle, the reflected light will appear brighter if you are within that narrow angle. Screens can be curved to increase this effect. Put another way, a screen with a gain of greater than 1 "squeezes" the reflected light into a narrower pattern.

The advantage of a screen with high gain (1.8 to 4) is that the image is brighter for a given light output from the projector. But a high-gain screen is a trade-off: You get a brighter image, but over a narrower viewing angle, as the increased brightness occurs over only a narrow window in the center of the viewing room. Viewers sitting off to the sides see a less bright image with a high-gain screen than with a low-gain screen.

The second important factor in choosing a screen is its color uniformity, or how evenly the screen reflects different colors. When watching an image on a high-gain screen, you may notice a color shift as you move your head from side to side. This problem can sometimes be manifested as a blue-tinted image on one side of the screen, and a red-tinted image on the other side. Color uniformity, sometimes called *spectral response*, is a bigger problem with screen gains higher than 1.5. Screens made for home-theater viewing (as opposed to corporate graphics presentations) strive to maintain flat spectral response.

As mentioned in the introduction, a front-projector system (particularly the CRT type) works hard to generate enough light to create a good-looking image. The smaller the projected image, the greater the image brightness. A projector's light output is measured in ANSI lumens; light reflected from the screen is measured in foot-lamberts (fL).

You can get a rough idea of the number of foot-lamberts a given projector and screen will produce at the viewing seat by dividing the projector's ANSI-lumen rating by the screen size in square feet, then multiplying by the screen gain. For example, a projector with an output rating of 300 ANSI lumens projecting onto a 100" diagonal screen (60" by 80", or 33.33 square feet) with a gain of 1.3 will produce an image with a brightness of 11.7fL. If we increase the screen size to 120", the image brightness decreases to 8.1fL, the minimum acceptable brightness level. This projector's image will look a lot better on a 100" screen than on a 120" screen.

There are a few caveats to this calculation. First, CRT manufacturers often exaggerate light-output claims. Second, the specified light output is often peak, meaning the projector was measured with the contrast control turned all the way up—not a condition you'd find in your home. These factors combine to reduce the brightness reflected from the screen measured in foot-lamberts. In our example above, the calculated brightness of 11.7fL may actually be closer to 10fL in real-world conditions.

It might be tempting to perform this calculation and conclude that you can greatly increase image brightness by choosing a high-gain screen. But a high-gain screen doesn't give you something for nothing; there's a price to pay for the increased brightness. Although screen gain helps the front-projector achieve a bright image, it also works against uniform brightness by creating *hot spots* in the image—areas that are brighter than other areas. These hot spots change the color balance and degrade picture quality. Hot-spotting shows up more in screens that don't have good color uniformity; a meter will measure the same amount of hot-spotting, but the hot-spotting is more visible on a screen that lacks good color uniformity. For this reason, the maximum gain allowable for THX certification of a projection screen is 1.6. In practice, a screen gain of 1.3 is ideal for most applications. The Imaging Science Foundation (ISF) doesn't certify any screen with a gain greater than 1.3. They believe that 1.3 is the optimum compromise between good color uniformity and helping CRT projectors make bright pictures.

Earlier in this chapter I described how rear-projection sets disperse their light over narrow vertical and horizontal angles. The screens in off-the-shelf rear-projection sets have very high gain (as high as 6), which helps them achieve a brighter picture in front of the set, but at the expense of a washed-out picture off to the sides. The rear-projector is an extreme case of how high screen gain has its advantages and drawbacks.

All screens are bordered by a black area to increase the screen's apparent contrast. The area above and below where the image is projected is called the *drop*. Because this area is black, you'll also hear it called the *black drop*. The black area on the screen's sides is called the *mask*. Because the projected image is framed in non-reflective black, the light areas in the image appear brighter. In theory, the larger the mask, the better. Ideally, the entire front of the viewing room would be masked, with just a relatively small area of reflective screen for the image.

Some projection screens are billed as *acoustically transparent*, which means that they're perforated to allow sound to pass through them. These so-called *perf* screens are used when the center-channel speaker is located behind the projection screen. All movie-theater screens are perforated because the center-channel speakers are always located behind the screen. Although a perforated screen has as many as 30,000 perforations per square foot to let sound pass through, it still attenuates some treble. Consequently, projection screens that meet THX certification are supplied with a center-channel equalizer that boosts treble to compensate for the screen's reduction of treble energy. A perforated screen costs about 30% more than a standard screen. Even more important, light is lost through these holes. If 20% of the light is lost (a typical value), a screen must be reduced in size by 20%, or the gain must be increased by 20%, to maintain the same image brightness. Either way, image quality is compromised by a perforated screen, and there's the added disadvantage that its holes may at times be visible to viewers.

Low-Gain Screens for Fixed-Pixel Projectors

Screens with a gain of 1.3 (the most common value) were developed primarily for CRT projectors and their relatively low light output. But with DLP, LCD, and LCoS-type projectors routinely generating 1000 or more ANSI lumens, screen manufacturers have responded by creating new screen materials tailored to these new technologies. Specifically, screens with low gain (0.8) that are gray in color (rather than white) provide better black level with fixed-pixel projectors. We're not worried about the low screen gain here since these projectors have light output to spare. Examples of these new gray screen material are Stewart Filmscreen's GrayHawk (0.8 gain), FireHawk (1.3 gain), and Da-Lite's High-Contrast Da-Mat (0.8 gain).

Before buying a low-gain gray screen, make sure that you'll never decided to upgrade to a CRT projector. These screens simply won't work with the CRT projector's low light output.

Plasma Display Panels

The *Plasma Display Panel* (PDP) is the television predicted for decades in science-fiction stories—the TV that hangs on the wall. PDPs range in size from 37" to 61" (diagonal, 16:9 aspect ratio), and are typically about 3" deep. This makes them ideal for rooms that don't have the space for the deep cabinet of a direct-view or RPTV (fig.7-7). Plasma panels can be hung on a wall, or mounted on a stand that lets them sit on a table or shelf.

Fig. 7-7 A plasma
display panel
offers screen sizes
up to 61" in a
chassis only 3"
thick.

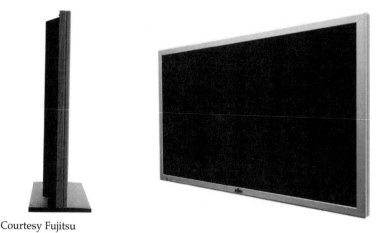

Courtesy Fujitsu

Plasma panels have other things going for them. First, they can have high resolution, with some panels boasting a pixel array of 1366 x 768, making them ideal for displaying HD images. Second, they have relatively high light output, and can be watched in a bright room during the day. Third, their viewing angle is wider—160°— than that of a rear-projection television (the picture doesn't get dim as you move off to the side), giving you greater flexibility in placement. Fourth, they are unaffected by magnetic fields, unlike CRT-based displays. Fifth, they have perfect convergence (superposition of red, green, and blue picture components). These are all desirable attributes, but a mere description of them doesn't convey the "wow factor" of seeing a big, bright, vivid, high-resolution picture created by a flat panel hanging on a wall. Anyone who sees a plasma panel wants one.

In early 2001, 50" plasma panels cost in the neighborhood of $25,000. A year later the price had dropped to $15,000, with 61" models going for $25,000. Similarly, 42" panels that cost $15,000 in early 2001 can now be had for $6,000. Although plasma panels are still expensive, the trend is for ever-increasing resolution (more pixels) and plummeting prices. The dramatic consumer demand for plasma is bringing about economy-of-scale manufacturing that will continue to drive prices down. In fact, plasma may even displace the CRT and the other display technologies once they are manufactured in massive quantities. DuPont, a manufacturer of many of the raw materials in plasma panels, announced in early 2002 that it had developed a breakthrough technology for making plasma panels of higher resolution and lower cost, and expanded its factory to meet the anticipated demand. (There are many similarities between different brands of plasma because a small number of manufacturers of the raw glass supply many of the companies that make plasma displays.)

The lowest resolution panels have a pixel array of 640 x 480 (4:3 aspect ratio), which is sufficient for standard-definition signals, but not for HDTV. Panels with a 16:9 aspect ratio may have a pixel array of 852 x

480, 1024 x 1024, 1280 x 768, or 1366 x 768. The greater the number of pixels, the higher the price. A panel with more pixels doesn't necessarily have greater resolution of fine detail in the video image. Although a panel with more pixels has the potential of delivering a finer-detailed image, the electronics inside the panel that process the video signal before it's displayed can play a large role in the ultimate perceived resolution.

Similarly, plasma panels vary greatly in the quality of their integral image scaler. Because the plasma panel is a fixed-pixel display device, all input signals must be scaled to the panel's native pixel array. This scaling can introduce motion artifacts. Input signals with greater resolution than the panel's pixel array can simply be truncated to avoid image scaling, but the picture edges will be cropped. For the optimum picture quality, plasma panels with less-than-ideal integral scalers can be driven by an outboard image scaler, but at considerable added expense. As with direct-view and RPTVs, however, the integral scalers in plasma panels are greatly improving, and some are now as good as many mid-priced outboard image scalers that cost several thousand dollars.

The latest plasma panels include a DVI (Digital Visual Interface) input for connection to source components or outboard scalers that have DVI output. This connection method bypasses the analog-to-digital and digital-to-analog conversion inherent in the component-video format, and results in about a 25% improvement in picture quality.

Keep in mind that not all plasma panels contain audio circuitry and speakers. The manufacturer may assume that you'll be using the panel with an outboard home-theater audio system. Although this is likely, it means you'll need to fire up your surround receiver for casual TV viewing. As with widescreen direct-view and RPTV sets, plasma panels incorporate "stretch" and "zoom" modes to fill the widescreen panel with 4:3 images.

How Plasma Panels Work

Plasma panels are fixed-pixel devices, with the individual pixels formed in a glass structure akin to a honeycomb. The rear of each pixel (opposite the viewing side) is coated with individual red, green, and blue phosphors, and the enclosed pixel is filled with a mixture of xenon and neon gases. Three sub-pixels, one each for red, green, and blue contained in separate cells, form a pixel. A voltage is applied to two transparent electrodes on the front of the glass (the viewing side). This voltage causes the gas to become a plasma and emit a discharge of ultraviolet light.

The ultraviolet light strikes one color phosphor, causing it to re-radiate light in that color. Combine the three primary colors in varying intensity and the plasma panel can produce a wide range of colors. The intensity of each color is controlled by varying the number and width of the voltage pulses applied to the sub-pixel during each picture frame. An opposite electrical charge causes the gas to de-ionize and turn off that pixel. This charge/discharge cycle can occur 85 times per second.

Drawbacks of Plasma Panels

You'll see plasma panels described as "eight-bit" or "ten-bit." This refers either to the number of bits in the digital video signal driving the panel, or in the number of brightness levels to which the panel itself will respond. The greater the number of bits, the finer the gradations of brightness the panel can reproduce. An eight-bit panel can display 256 levels of gray; a ten-bit panel can display 1024 levels of gray. With an eight-bit panel and three primary colors, plasma panels can generate 16.7 million colors.

Eight-bit panels suffer from a phenomenon known as "false contouring" in which slight gradations of brightness appear as discrete steps rather than as a continuum. For example, in a scene containing a wall illuminated more brightly at one end than the other, the gradual change in brightness we'd see in real life is replaced by discrete jumps in brightness, almost like a topographic map. (The same phenomenon can occur in the MPEG-2 encoding process used in DVD and DSS.) There simply aren't enough discrete steps in the grayscale to approximate to the eye a continuous change in brightness. This problem is particularly noticeable in dark scenes or parts of the picture that have low contrast. Some viewers find false contouring more objectionable than other viewers, so look for false contouring when evaluating a plasma panel. Manufacturers have developed ingenious methods of modulating the pixels' brightness to reduce this effect. As technology improves, false contouring will become a thing of the past.

Plasma panels don't have as wide a contrast ratio as direct-view or RPTV sets; blacks are reproduced as dark gray. Their measured contrast ratios (difference between black and peak white) range from about 250:1 to 600:1. The panel with a 600:1 contrast ratio will have more depth, snap, and vividness than the panel with a 250:1 contrast ratio. Keep in mind that there are no standards for reporting contrast ratio (there are measurement standards, but manufacturers don't follow them) so manufacturers tend to exaggerate their products' performance. In one case, a manufacturer conducted the "black" portion of the measurement with the panel turned off!

Any phosphor-based display technology (CRT, plasma) is dependent on the phosphors for color accuracy. As of this writing, all plasma panels have a slight error in the red phosphors, which makes red look slightly orange. Consequently, plasma panels don't accurately reproduce deep crimson. In addition, as we saw earlier in the discussion of CRT-based RPTVs, phosphors produce less light output as they age. Consequently, plasma panels become less bright over time, and will eventually become unusable. A key specification is the panel's expected "life to half brightness," which may be 30,000 hours. That is, if you use the panel for six hours a day for fourteen years, it's brightness will be halved over that time period.)

Similarly, plasma panels can suffer from burn-in caused by extended display of static images (particularly high-contrast images) such as the bottom banners on some news programs. This is a serious problem because burns on plasma panels cannot be repaired—you may have to throw away a $15,000 panel. To protect your plasma panel, don't display static images, and use the "stretch" or "zoom" modes when watching 4:3 material on a 16:9 panel. Proper calibration will also extend the panel's useful life.

Video Display Calibration

The video display's job is to reproduce as faithfully as possible the video signal fed it. A perfect video monitor would convert the electrical video signal into an image without changing that image in any way. That is, the display should accurately interpret all the instructions contained in the video signal. The less the display corrupts the video signal, the better the display. When we watch movies on a high-quality video monitor, we experience the movie in the way the director and cinematographer intended. Filmmakers go to extraordinary lengths to get just the right contrast of light and dark, color, and overall "look" of a film. Indeed, these elements are an integral part of the storytelling. Consequently, a quality video monitor that accurately reproduces the input signal provides a richer, more involving experience.

Unfortunately, most TV sets are shipped from the factory with miscalibrated color, contrast, tint, sharpness, and brightness. Although it would be difficult and expensive for the manufacturer to calibrate every set on the production line, the TVs manufacturers produce could be much better calibrated at the factory. In fact, the sets are intentionally miscalibrated to look more appealing on the showroom floor. This isn't to say manufacturers have malevolent intent; they simply must ship the sets this way to compete on the showroom floor. Marketing studies have shown that consumers buy sets based on a single criterion: how bright the picture is. To make sets stand out when placed next to competing units, their brightness is turned up—to as much as four to six times the correct light output level. The color balance is shifted toward blue, again to give the impression of greater brightness. It's no coincidence that laundry detergent has a bit of blue dye in it to make clothes look "whiter than white." More important, this excessive brightness shortens a TV set's life.

Some TV sets and rear-projection units have different settings—such as SPORTS, MOVIE, and CONCERT—that change the TV's brightness, color, tint, and contrast to pre-set levels. Such settings are unnecessary gimmicks that suggest it's desirable for the set to distort the picture—and that invalidate the goal of making the monitor display the video signal exactly as it was broadcast. As consumers become more educated, manufacturers are starting to include modes that produce the best possible picture.

There's a direct parallel here with the way some loudspeakers are designed. In Chapter 6, I described a speaker designed to exaggerate the bass and treble so that the speaker "jumps out" in side-by-side comparisons with other speakers. Such a product might impress in a brief showroom demonstration, but quickly becomes annoying and fatiguing in daily use.

It's the same with intentionally miscalibrated video displays: An overly bright set may look good at first, but is ultimately unnatural-looking. Just as budding audiophiles go through a phase of liking excessive treble and bass in speakers before their taste becomes attuned to a more natural sound, the novice home-theater enthusiast may at first not like the look of a properly calibrated monitor. But if, after a few weeks, the contrast were set back to what it had been, he would find the picture grossly distorted, and wonder how he ever liked the overly bright picture.

This situation offers the knowledgeable home-theater enthusiast the opportunity to greatly improve a video display's picture quality just by correctly setting the display's controls (contrast, sharpness, color, tint, brightness). When carefully calibrated, a modestly priced video monitor can provide better picture quality than a much more expensive set that hasn't been adjusted. Calibrating a video monitor requires special test signals that, until recently, were available only from expensive laboratory equipment. These special signals have been put on the *Video Essentials* and *AVIA Guide to Home Theater* test DVDs so that anyone with the disc and the video display's remote control can accurately calibrate a video monitor. *Video Essentials* and *AVIA* include step-by-step instructions for calibrating any video monitor, from a direct-view to a front-projector.

Imaging Science Foundation

The *Imaging Science Foundation* (*ISF*) was founded in 1994 by video engineer Joe Kane and Joel Silver to improve the quality of video displays and set standards for the industry. (Joe Kane left ISF in late 1998.) ISF sets the performance standards for video quality, much the way THX certifies certain products. Home-theater components that bear the ISF logo (fig.7-8) meet stringent requirements of video performance. This certification includes controllers that take in video signals from source components and send video signals to the video display. The controller must perform this video switching without degrading the picture quality.

ISF also trains home-theater equipment retailers and custom installers to calibrate video displays. If you buy a video display from an ISF-certified dealer, that dealer will calibrate your display for a nominal fee—or, with higher-end sets, include calibration with the purchase price. Alternately, an ISF-certified technician can, for a service charge, calibrate a display bought elsewhere. (Typical fees are $225 to calibrate a direct-view, $275 for a rear-projector, and $325 for a front-projector.)

Courtesy Imaging Science Foundation, Inc.

If you choose to buy *Video Essentials* or *AVIA* (or both—they complement each other) and calibrate your monitor yourself, follow the detailed
instructions included with the disc. After you've gone through the procedure a few times, it's fun and rewarding to turn a mediocre-looking
video display into a terrific-looking one. Once you own *Video Essentials*
or *AVIA* and learn to calibrate your own monitor, you might find yourself suddenly popular with your neighbors!

Video Essentials and *AVIA* will only let you perform a basic calibration using the television's remote control. The next level of calibration
involves entering the television's service menu and adjusting the television's *gray-scale tracking*. This term refers to the television's ability to
reproduce gray as gray at all brightness levels. Ideally, the television will
reproduce gray with a color temperature of 6500° Kelvin. If the color
temperature varies from 6500°, gray will be reproduced as slightly green,
yellow, magenta, cyan, blue, or red. This error has a large effect on picture quality. Color television works by layering a small amount of color
information over a black and white signal. If that black and white signal
has a slightly blue or red hue, accurate color reproduction is impossible.

The television should accurately reproduce gray across the entire
brightness spectrum, from 20 IRE (nearly black) to 100 IRE (bright
white). If the set can achieve this uniformity of color at different brightness levels, we say it has good gray-scale tracking. ISF technicians can
adjust the set's gray-scale tracking using a specialized instrument called
a *color temperature analyzer*, and entering the set's service menu to make
adjustments to the relative levels of red and blue. Virtually none of the
popular televisions have accurate gray-scale tracking right out of the
box; others are not even close. In addition, some sets cannot achieve
good gray-scale tracking even with calibration. Sets with poor gray-scale
tracking from the factory show the most improvement in picture quality
with a full ISF calibration. Once the gray-scale tracking has been adjusted, you don't need to have this calibration performed again for some
time. The settings will drift slightly over time, but this isn't a serious
issue. Direct-view sets have almost no drift; RPTVs have a slight drift;
and front projectors need recalibration the most.

The bottom line: If you're serious about getting the most out of your
home theater, you must periodically calibrate your video display. It
doesn't matter if you have it done by an ISF-trained technician or if you

do it yourself—what's important is that you get your monitor calibrated. If you don't want to spend the money for ISF calibration, at least use *Video Essentials* or *AVIA* to elevate the television's picture quality above its out-of-the-box performance.

Composite Video, S-Video, Component Video, and RGB

On nearly all consumer video equipment—VCRs, laserdisc players, DVD machines, and video monitors—the RCA jack marked VIDEO carries a signal called *composite* video. As its name suggests, a composite video signal contains every aspect of the video signal necessary to display it on a monitor or record it on videotape. The parts of the video signal combined in a composite signal include the brightness information, all the color information, and the synchronization signals. Merging these different signals into a single composite signal made it possible to add color to the existing black-and-white television system without making everyone's TV obsolete.

But mixing these different signal elements introduces problems that degrade the picture quality. If we can keep all of these signals separate from each other, picture quality can be improved dramatically. One step in that direction is the S-video connector found on many VCRs, DSS receivers, DVD machines, and video monitors. An S-video cable carries the picture's brightness information separately from the color information. S-video is also called a *Y/C connection*, with the letter Y representing brightness information (more accurately called *luminance)*, and the letter C representing the picture's color information (more accurately called *chrominance*). Using S-video connections always confers an improvement in picture quality as long as the source component inherently records or receives the luminance and chrominance information separately. S-video delivers greater horizontal resolution, and eliminates color artifacts such as "dot crawl."

Source components that benefit most from S-video connection are DSS dishes, DVD players, S-VHS recorders (when playing S-VHS tapes), and HI-8 8mm camcorders (when playing HI-8 tapes). The reason is that DSS, DVD, and S-VHS recorders all store or transmit the Y and C components separately. Luminance and chrominance are never combined in the storage or transmission, as they are with television broadcasts, cable signals, VHS machines, and even laserdiscs. S-video may or may not offer an improvement in picture quality when the source video comes from the composite-video domain—television broadcasts, cable signals, VHS machines, and laserdisc players, for examples.

As described earlier in this chapter, every video display device has a circuit—either a notch filter or a comb filter—to separate the video signal's luminance and chrominance information. If you connect a VCR's S-video output to your TV's S-video input, you're simply substituting the VCR's comb filter for the TV set's comb filter. There's no way of knowing which product has the better comb filter until you try both composite and S-video connection and see which looks better.

Keeping the parts of a video signal separate is taken to the next level by the *component-video* connection. Three separate cables, usually terminated with RCA plugs, carry the picture's luminance information on one cable, the red color-difference information on another cable, and the blue color-difference information on the third cable. Component video is also called Y, R–Y, B–Y (Y, R minus Y, B minus Y). The letter Y represents the luminance signal, and R–Y and B–Y are the two color-difference signals required to reconstitute the red, green, and blue signals needed to drive a color display. You'll also see component video referred to as YPbPr. Component video may also be called by a manufacturer's trade name; Toshiba, for example, calls component-video connection ColorStream, and 480p progressive-scan component-inputs ColorStream Pro.

DVD, DSS, and HDTV inherently carry their video information in component form. When connected to a video monitor with component-video input, a DVD player's video output never goes through the NTSC format's limitations and visual artifacts. Instead, the video monitor receives a signal of much better quality. The difference in picture quality between a DVD player connected with its component output compared with its composite output is night-and-day. Through the composite cable, the picture has all the artifacts associated with NTSC video: dot crawl, chroma noise, moire patterns, and black-and-white information interpreted as color information. Moreover, component video provides a wider bandwidth and better color resolution than S-video.

Just as you should try composite and S-video connections on a VHS machine to determine the best connection method, you should also experiment with component-video connection. Not all sets have high-quality component-video inputs; in at least one case, a set's component input path was inferior to its S-video input path.

The differences in picture quality in composite, S-video, and component video are easily assessed. Connect a DVD player with all three outputs to a video monitor with all three inputs. Play the "Zone Plate Test" signal from *Video Essentials* (Title 15, Chapter 12) and look at the differences in the displayed patterns. Once you've selected this chapter, put the player in repeat mode. The availability of component video in a consumer format (DVD and DSS), used in conjunction with a component-input video display device, offers a quantum leap in picture quality for home theater. Insist on component-video connections on both your DVD player and video monitor.

RGB connection offers the same advantages as component video. RGB connections can be on three jacks (usually RCA or BNC), or five. This latter input, called RGB/HV, has separate inputs for the horizontal (H) and vertical (V) synchronization signals. In plain-old RGB, the sync signals are carried as part of the G signal.

With the abundance of different video-interface formats, you may need a transcoder, a device that converts one form of video to another. The transcoder in fig.7-9, for example, converts VGA to component video. Some early DirecTV receivers had only VGA output, requiring a transcoder to use the receiver with displays lacking a VGA input.

Fig. 7-9
A video transcoder converts video from one format to another.

Courtesy Key Digital

Image Scalers: Line Doublers, Quadruplers, and Interpolators

As discussed in the preceding section, in conventional CRT technology a video image is produced by projecting horizontal lines on the front of a TV set's picture tube, a rear-projection screen, or a front-projection screen. When the standards were set for television broadcasting, most TV sets measured only 12" diagonally; a total of 525 scanning lines was considered sufficient. It was envisioned that 525 scanning lines could drive a set as large as 19".

But those 525 lines (480 in the visible portion of the image) are not nearly enough when displayed on a 27" screen, never mind a 60" image. Instead of seeing a continuous image, you become aware of the line structure inherent in the NTSC format. You can see this line structure on any size TV set if you get close enough to it. The larger the picture, and/or the closer you sit to the picture, the more visible the lines.

The way to make the line structure of NTSC video less visible is to increase the scanning rate at which the video display device is driven. Before describing how this is done, you need to know that a conventional NTSC image is created by the technique of interlaced scanning, described earlier.

A device called a *line doubler* takes in 15.734kHz video (15,734 is the number of scanning lines per second in NTSC video; it's usually rounded to 15.75kHz) from a source component and outputs a video signal at double the 15.75kHz rate. It also converts an interlaced signal to a progressively-scanned signal, in which a complete image is created with each scanning from the top to bottom of the display area. A simple line doubler doesn't create new scanning lines; it merely accumulates the lines of the interlaced system into a progressive image, then repeats that progressive image twice to stay in time with the incoming interlaced image. Instead of displaying 240 active lines per pass, it displays 480 active lines per pass. Line doublers are also called image scalers or scan converters because they convert an interlaced-scanning signal to a progressive-scanning signal. Adding a line doubler greatly smoothes the picture and improves the apparent vertical resolution. Instead of seeing a jagged image, we see a more continuous picture.

A line quadrupler takes this concept a step further by increasing to 960 the number of scanning lines per sweep from top to bottom of the screen. The quadrupler in effect "guesses" at what color and brightness information should be in the newly created lines. To use a line quadrupler, the projector it's driving must be capable of scanning at a frequency of at least 63kHz (4 x 15.75kHz).

A line-doubled image can look vastly better than a straight NTSC image, but the line structure is still apparent, particularly with large screens and/or close viewing distances. But a good line quadrupler and a high-quality projector are capable of nearly filmlike images with no discernible line structure, even when the image is projected on a 10' screen.

As good as line-doubled and -quadrupled video looks, new devices called *interpolators* produce better images than even the best quadruplers. To understand how an interpolator works, it's important to realize that every CRT video projector has a certain scanning rate, often called the projector's *golden frequency*, at which it produces the best picture—a scanning rate that line doublers and quadruplers don't always deliver. If the scanning rate driving the CRT projector is too fast for that projector, the result is loss of vertical resolution. If the projector is driven too slowly, the projector suffers from loss of brightness.

The optimum scanning frequency of a CRT projector is largely a function of the CRT projector's *beam-spot size*; the smaller the beam-spot size, the faster the projector should scan. Think of a display device projecting tiny spots on a screen: A CRT projector with a small beam-spot size will leave a wider black space between lines than a projector with a larger beam-spot size. This creates two problems: We can see the spaces between lines, and those spaces are black, which reduces image brightness. (This discussion doesn't apply to fixed-pixel displays.)

We want a line doubler or quadrupler to fill in those black spaces with lines of video. Let's say we put a line quadrupler on a projector that has a moderate to large beam-spot size. The quadrupler inserts three new lines for every line in the original video. If the combined size of those three additional lines of video is larger than the black space produced by the projector, the lines will overlap and decrease vertical and horizontal resolution. If we put a line doubler on the projector, the additional line created by the doubler might not be enough to completely fill in the black space between lines. The result is visible line structure. The ideal solution here would be something in between—a "two-and-a-halfer". The projector would work best at a scanning rate higher than a doubler's 31.5kHz frequency, but slower than a quadrupler's 63kHz rate. This particular projector may deliver the best picture at a rate of, say, 50kHz.

Here's where an interpolator comes in: It takes whatever video signal is fed to it and outputs the optimum scanning frequency for a particular display device. Instead of being fixed at double (31.5kHz for a doubler) or four times (63kHz for a quadrupler) the normal rate, the interpolator's continuously variable output frequency can be set at whatever frequency you want. You simply adjust the interpolator's output frequency for the best picture with your particular projector.

Although interpolators have been used in professional video for years, they are just now being introduced to consumers. They are actually required in fixed-panel displays such as LCD and DLP projectors; no matter what the input signal's resolution, the signal driving a 1280 x 768 fixed-panel display must be converted to 1280 x 768, for example.

Interpolators can also take in a variety of source video signals and convert each of them to the CRT projector's "golden" scanning frequency (or the pixel matrix in fixed-pixel devices), and can also display a small video image from broadcast television or other source within a full-screen, computer-generated image, such as from the Internet. These features make the interpolator the ideal candidate for integrating video and computer images on the same monitor. Some day, you'll be able to watch a television show and, during the commercials, instantly surf the Internet, then return to the TV show when it resumes.

In the age of high-definition television, the need to improve the picture quality of NTSC sources becomes ever more acute. For the foreseeable future, some shows will be broadcast in HD, others in standard definition. After watching a show in HD, returning to NTSC quality is a big letdown. This letdown can be reduced by quality upconversion of 480i NTSC video to a higher scanning rate via a quality image scaler.

Another type of image scaler, based on recently declassified spy-satellite technology, has found its way into a few very high-end home-theater systems. This device, called a Terranex (manufactured by Xanthus Corporation), employs massively paralleled microprocessors to perform calculations on each pixel. The Teranex gets its name from the fact that it has a teraflop (a trillion floating-point instructions per second) of computing power. It uses this massive horsepower to process each pixel for maximum image quality. When used with a top-quality CRT projector, the Teranex makes DVDs look like HD. The Teranex-processed picture is startling, with no motion artifacts and a three-dimensional quality. This jaw-dropping performance, however, is expensive; the first Teranex cost $155,000. More "affordable" consumer versions are on the market for a mere $45,000. If you want the ultimate in image quality, and can afford it, the Teranex delivers unequaled video performance.

Image Scalers for Fixed-Pixel Displays

With fixed-pixel displays becoming more popular, scaler manufacturers have responded by developing units optimized for DLP, plasma, LCoS, D-ILA, and LCD displays. Scalers designed for fixed-pixel displays allow you to set the output resolution to match that of your display. For example, such a scaler used with a 1280 x 720 display would output a signal of that resolution regardless of the input signal. Some scalers have variable output resolutions; others have fixed resolutions that you order to match your particular display. With the latter, if you change displays, you must have the scaler re-programmed at the factory.

Digital Video Interfaces and Copy Protection

As the world becomes more and more digital, so-called "content providers" (record companies and movie studios) are increasingly protective of their intellectual property. Digital technology makes it possible to store and transmit content without degradation, and even to mass duplicate audio or video programs with no loss of quality. This threat of illegal copying has hampered industry efforts to standardize a digital interface for transmitting digital audio and video. Copyright owners are afraid of giving consumers access to high-resolution digital video and audio datastreams. As a result, our home-theater systems have unnecessary digital-to-analog and analog-to-digital converters in the audio and video signal paths. The industry has responded by developing several digital interfaces that allow transmission of signals between home-theater components, yet prevent unauthorized recording of those signals.

A key issue is whether these copy-protection schemes will roll back consumers' rights to record television shows for later viewing. The United States Supreme Court, in the famous "Betamax" ruling of 1984, affirmed that this time-shifting of television shows for personal viewing is "fair use" under copyright law. Some worry that this right may be diminished in the digital age not through legislation or court rulings, but by increasingly restrictive copy-protection technology.

With that background, let's look at the digital interfaces and copy-protection schemes currently available and on the horizon.

FireWire (IEEE1394) and Digital Transmission Content Protection (DTCP)

To meet the challenge of creating a digital interface that doesn't degrade picture or sound quality, yet protects copyright holders from unauthorized duplication, a consortium of five companies (dubbed "5C") developed a scheme called *Digital Transmission Content Protection* (DTCP). The term 5C refers to the five companies who contributed to the standard: Hitachi, Intel, Panasonic, Sony, and Toshiba.

DTCP allows content providers to specify the manner in which their content can be recorded by consumers. Specifically, four scenarios are possible:

1. **Copy-Never**—no copies allowed
2. **Copy-One-Generation**—one copy allowed
3. **Copy No-More**—prevents making copies of copies
4. **Copy Freely**—no restrictions on copying

This control over copying is realized via special codes embedded in the digital audio/video datastream carried on a FireWire cable. Also known as i.LINK (a Sony tradename) or its official name, IEEE1394 (the Institute of Electrical and Electronics Engineers codified the standard on January 3, 1994, hence the name), FireWire is a bi-directional interface that can carry digital audio, digital video, computer data, and control signals on one cable. Because FireWire is bi-directional, the interface allows components in your home-theater system to "talk" to each other—an essential element of Digital Transmission Content Protection. Specifically, DTCP establishes two-way communication between components with a challenge and response. When a device has been authenticated as authorized to record the digital datastream, the decryption key is downloaded into the receiving device. Content that has been encoded Copy-Never will send the decryption key only to display devices, not digital recorders. This authentication and key exchange, which occurs in just 30 milliseconds, is invisible to the user.

In fact, the entire DTCP system works behind the scenes. You can record and display signals from cable satellite, broadcast, or disc without worrying about different encryption systems. DTCP simply secures the content of the FireWire digital bus between components in your home. The only time you will be aware of DTCP is if you attempt to record material restricted by the content provider.

DTCP was developed with input from the Motion Picture Association of America (MPAA), Recording Institute Association of America (RIAA), the Consumer Electronics Manufacturers Association (CEMA), and groups representing computer companies. The system has already been accepted and standardized by the Society of Cable Television Engineers for OpenCable Home Digital Network Interface.

Audio-Video Control (AV/C) and Home Audio/Video interoperability (HAVi)

FireWire is the basis for a range of home-networking technologies that allow all the components in a home-theater system to operate as a single "smart" system rather than as a collection of "dumb" boxes that don't know what other devices are connected to it. Because today's home-theater components operate as independent units, to watch a DVD we must turn on the TV, DVD player, and A/V receiver, then switch the receiver's input to DVD, and switch the TV to the correct input—often from different remote controls. FireWire, with its bi-directional communication of control information, can perform all these functions (and more) with the press of a single button.

The most basic form of this FireWire-based, integrated system operation is called Audio Video Control (AV/C), which allows connected products to be operated from a single remote control. AV/C's capabilities are limited to working with those products in existence when the AV/C-based component was manufactured.

A more sophisticated FireWire-based approach employs a system called Home Audio/Video interoperability (HAVi). A HAVi-based system not only performs all the functions of AV/C, but also will work with products not yet developed. In a HAVi-enabled home-theater, system control is realized via icons that appear on your television screen. A remote control, which could feature a single button like a mouse, controls the entire system. For example, when you point and click on the DVD-player icon on the television screen, the DVD player's controls appear on the screen, your television switches to the correct input, and the A/V receiver also switches to the appropriate input and selects the desired surround-sound decoding.

When new HAVi-equipped devices are added to the system, the new device is recognized by the rest of the system and its control icons are automatically added to the on-screen display. Fig.7-10 shows such an icon-based display.

HAVi-based components are connected by a single FireWire cable that carries digital video, multichannel digital audio, and the control information required to realize the interoperability just described. The days of home-theater products with rows upon row of RCA jacks are numbered. Instead, each component will have a single FireWire port that is both input and output, and components can be connected in a variety of ways (daisy chain, for example), not necessarily the old "input to output" method of analog connections. (Fig.7-11 shows how FireWire can greatly simplify connecting a home-theater system.)

As great a boon as this technology would be to home theater, it may not operate as billed because of "proprietary" implementations by different companies. That is, one brand of HAVi-equipped receiver, for example, may not operate seamlessly with a HAVi-equipped DVD player made by another company. Because IEEE1394 is an open standard (originally developed by Apple Computer; FireWire is its tradename), manufacturers are free to develop their own implementations to suit their needs. Also, the big manufacturers don't want to be seen as following the lead of other manufacturers, and so strike out on their own to try to force other companies to adopt their version of HAVi. The result of this policy is consumer confusion and frustration when two HAVi-enabled products don't work with each other. The Consumer Electronics Association has even codified this state of affairs by adopting labeling requirements for HAVi-enabled products. All products bearing the same label will work with each other; products with different HAVi labels may not.

Fig. 7-10 FireWire-equipped components function as a single "smart" system that can be controlled by a single icon-based remote control.

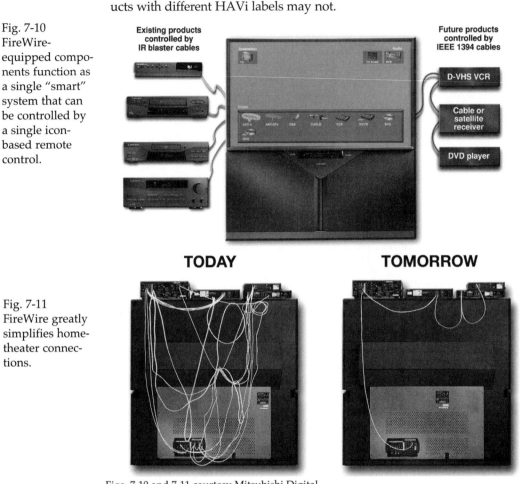

Fig. 7-11 FireWire greatly simplifies home-theater connections.

Figs. 7-10 and 7-11 courtesy Mitsubishi Digital

SDI, DV, and DVI Digital-Video Interfaces

In addition to FireWire, you'll find three other digital interfaces on today's consumer-electronics equipment. The simplest of these is the *Serial Digital Interface*, or SDI. This interface, found on some DVD players and image scalers, can carry standard-definition video from one component to another. SDI doesn't have enough bandwidth to carry high-definition video, but the format may survive as a method of connecting standard-definition sources to an image scaler. The scaler would then upconvert standard-definition signals to a higher scanning rate, and output that high-scan-rate signal on a wide-bandwidth interface.

The *DV* interface format, found on millions of camcorders, is essentially identical to FireWire, but with the control and "intelligence" removed. The DV format makes it possible to easily connect the digital-video output from a camcorder to computer for editing.

The most advanced and capable digital interface is the *Digital Visual Interface* (DVI) format (not to be confused with DV). It was originally developed as a way of transmitting digital video inside a computer to an integral display, such as the LCD screen in a laptop computer. DVI's attributes—wide bandwidth, inexpensive implementation, strong embedded copy-protection scheme—make it ideal for transmitting digital video among components in a home-theater system. Consequently, DVI may become ubiquitous on home-theater products. It is likely that both DVI and FireWire will co-exist; some products will offer both connection methods. Many HD video displays, particularly fixed-pixel devices such as plasma panels and DLP projectors, already offer DVI input. A more recent DVI specification includes the ability to carry multichannel digital audio over the interface, simplifying connections.

DVI's wider bandwidth than FireWire (4.95 gigabits per second vs. 400 megabits per second) allows it to transmit uncompressed high-definition digital video. In a FireWire-based system, the video display must incorporate an MPEG-2 decoder because the FireWire interface lacks sufficient bandwidth to transmit full HD signals without MPEG-2 data compression.

DVI, however, lacks FireWire's control functions that allow separate components to "talk" to each other and operate as a single system. A variation on DVI, called *Digital Multimedia Interface* (DMI), incorporates the command and control protocols necessary for integrated operation of diverse components.

High-Bandwidth Digital Content Protection (HDCP)

After the DVI specification was released by the Digital Display Working Group in 1999, Intel developed a copy-protection technology for DVI called *High-Bandwidth Digital Content Protection* (HDCP). The scheme is similar to DTCP described earlier, with encrypted data and decryption keys. This key exchange between devices allows the source component to verify that the receiving device is authorized to display or record HD content. For example, when an HD set-top box detects that video display is not equipped with HDCP, it lowers the output resolution of the signal. You may be receiving an HD signal with a resolution of 1920 x 1080 pixels, but the set-top box may output a signal of only 720 x 480 pixels. Similarly, a set-top box won't exchange the decryption key with a digital video recorder (D-VHS for example) if the content provider has specified that the content can never be recorded. The recorder will record video noise rather than a picture. As with DTCP on FireWire, HDCP on DVI allows content providers to specify the manner in which their programs can be recorded or viewed. A secure copy-protection scheme is essential to the widespread availability of high-definition video in our homes.

8 How to Choose a Home Theater System

Introduction

Most consumers buy audio/video equipment with something I call the "commodity" mentality. They think that all products are pretty much the same; therefore they buy the receiver that offers the "most watts per dollar" and the speakers with the biggest woofers for a given price. The uninformed consumer also thinks of an audio/video system as just another home appliance, and buys a home-theater system from a store that also sells washing machines. The salesperson in the appliance store can usually offer no guidance as to which products are best for the customer's particular system, budget, or home. Consequently, the customer ends up buying a product that isn't the best possible choice for his or her particular system. But the customer doesn't care because he got the product at a rock-bottom price. I'd like to tell you about a better way of choosing a home-theater system.

First, a home-theater system isn't an appliance such as a toaster; it is a vehicle for expressing an art form. The greater the technical quality of your system, the more of the filmmakers' vision you will experience. Choosing a home-theater system requires care and patience. You will be rewarded for your efforts with the best possible picture and sound quality for your budget—and a deeper connection with movies and musical performances.

Second, the quality differences between similarly priced components are huge. In the more than 350 in-depth product reviews I've written for A/V magazines, I've seen a vast range of sound quality, video performance, value, and build quality in home-theater components. Some products are created purely to maximize the manufacturer's profit, with little regard for sound quality or reliability. Other products are built with an almost fanatical attention to detail in an attempt to create a component that best reproduces all the elements of a film. The designers of the latter products are home-theater enthusiasts who dedicate themselves to producing the best possible equipment at a given price. The carefully designed product will provide superior sound quality, offer higher reliability, and usually include a well-thought-out user interface for greater ease of use. What's more, the higher-quality products often cost no more than the poorly designed ones. That's one reason why the best deal isn't always the product you can get at the biggest discount.

Third, you should buy your home-theater system from a retailer who can properly demonstrate the equipment, in an environment that lets you make meaningful comparisons between products. The retailer should also be highly knowledgeable about home-theater technology and the products he or she sells. The more the salesperson knows about home theater, the more likely you are to end up with the best system for your needs. The knowledgeable salesperson can also answer your questions after you get the system home. Some will even set up the system for you. *Where* you buy your equipment is more important than the brand name on that equipment. Shop for a retailer, not for equipment.

With that introduction, let's look at all the steps you'll go through in choosing a home-theater system.

Setting Your Budget

The first order of business is deciding how much money you're willing to invest in a home-entertainment system. This figure will be determined by two factors: how much time you spend enjoying movies at home, and your financial means. If movie watching is an important part of your life, consider spending about 10–15% of your annual income on a home-theater system. Once you live with a quality home-theater system for a few weeks, you may find that movie watching becomes the center of family activity.

The minimum level I recommend spending for a home-theater is about $300 for an A/V receiver and $700 for a set of speakers. You'll also need a DVD player and a video monitor, at the very least. Most of you will already have a VCR and a video monitor that you can turn into a home theater at modest cost. If you're really on a budget, you can get a complete "home-theater-in-a-box," complete with DVD player, A/V receiver, five speakers, and a subwoofer for as little as $600. Although this system won't match the performance of a more costly system, it will nonetheless transform the viewing experience into something vastly better than watching VHS tapes and listening to the soundtrack through a television's 3" speaker.

A budget of four to five thousand dollars will buy you a high-definition rear-projection TV, a good quality A/V receiver, a progressive-scan

DVD player, good speakers, and a subwoofer. A budget of eight to ten thousand dollars will buy a top-quality HD RPTV, a top-of-the-line A/V receiver, high-end progressive-scan DVD player with SACD or DVD-Audio playback, and superb loudspeakers. To get into a front projection system with separate A/V controller and multichannel power amplifier, expect to spend about $20,000 to $30,000. State-of-the-art home theater (which you have to experience first-hand to believe how good it can be) costs upward of $70,000. (One demonstration at a home-theater show featured a system that cost $252,000!)

I encourage you to set your budget as high as possible so that you can select quality components. It's false economy to cut corners and wind up with a system that doesn't quite satisfy you. You'll then need to sell one of your components (at a loss) to upgrade it, only to discover that the other components in your system now aren't up to the level of the upgraded product. It's much better to do it right the first time.

Of course, how good a home-theater system one needs varies according to one's expectations. That's why you should audition a variety of systems at different price levels before choosing. If you're fixated on spending a certain amount and never audition a higher-quality system, you'll never know what's possible in home theater—you might have increased your budget instantly upon experiencing the quality difference a few hundred more dollars could have brought you. But even if you stick to your budget, at least you've increased your knowledge. Moreover, knowing what a really good home-theater system looks and sounds like will help you in setting up and fine-tuning your own system later.

Allocating Your Budget

With your budget in mind, you'll now need to allocate that budget among the various components in a home-theater system. It's impossible for me to give specific recommendations as to how much of your total budget to spend on a particular component; everyone's situation is a little different. Some readers will already have a high-quality direct-view TV and a HiFi VCR; others will be starting from scratch. In addition, I'm sure that some of you are considering a top-end system with a five-figure front-projector and the best separate audio components. I'll therefore offer the following general guidelines.

The trick to achieving the best possible sound from a given budget is to carefully match the quality of each component in the system. For example, you wouldn't want to use $3000 loudspeakers with a $500 receiver; the speakers could never reach their full potential. Overspending on one component wastes your precious home-theater dollars; underspending on a component compromises the overall system quality. This is where magazine reviews and the services of a skilled retailer can guide you in matching components for the best performance.

When allocating your budget, ask yourself how much you'll use the system for music listening, and how much for watching movies. If music is an important part of your life, spend more of your budget on a good A/V receiver or separate controller and power amplifier, along with better-quality loudspeakers. This will leave less for a video display (you may have to settle for a 46″ rear-projection television rather than a 55″ model, for example), but you'll be rewarded with greater musical fidelity. I've found that sound quality is much more important with music than with film soundtracks. Above a certain threshold in sonic performance with movie soundtracks, improving the sound quality results in only incremental increases in one's immersion in the experience. Conversely, making a larger picture, or one of better quality, always produces more excitement and involvement. The opposite is true with music reproduction; improvements in fidelity always delivers more of the musicians' artistic expression, and fosters a deeper and more profound enjoyment of the music.

How to Read Magazine Reviews

Although I make my living reviewing audio and home-theater products (I'm Editor-in-Chief of *The Perfect Vision* and *The Absolute Sound* magazines), I'll let you in on a little secret: reviews are not the last word in selecting equipment. They should instead be used as guidelines for shortening the list of products you should evaluate for yourself. The most important critic is *you*; for a product to be worth buying, it must meet all of *your* needs and fit in *your* system.

Some magazine reviews can be very helpful in pointing you in the direction of good products, and also in alerting you to a certain product's shortcomings. Keep in mind, however, that how big a liability those shortcomings may be will vary with the user. For example, a receiver with only one VCR loop may be unacceptable to someone with two VCRs, but perfectly fine for the majority of users with a single VCR. Competent reviews will also explain certain features so that you can decide if that feature is important to you. Finally, reading a wide range of product reviews will give you a good feel for what's available in the marketplace at various price levels. You can follow these reviews before you set your budget, and decide what quality level you're striving for.

For a review to have value, it must be both competent and honest. Competence comes from the reviewer being knowledgeable about home theater, having experience of reviewing a range of similar competing products, and being an enthusiast. If the reviewer isn't an enthusiast, the performance differences between products won't matter much. The reviewer will therefore conclude that all A/V receivers, for example, are pretty much the same. Be wary of reviews of home-theater products written by reviewers who have just finished evaluating blenders or washing machines.

The second criterion for a meaningful review is honesty. Some magazines are "advertiser-driven"; that is, they will never write anything negative about a product made by a company that advertises in that magazine. The way to spot such a publication is to take note of the range of enthusiasm the reviewer has for the products reviewed. If every review ends with a "good for the money" recommendation, watch out. The tone of the reviews—positive and negative—should reflect the vast range of quality and value in the marketplace. Not every home-theater component is worth buying; therefore not every review should end with a recommendation. Look for magazines that aren't afraid to criticize products.

It's a good idea to closely read a magazine for several months before relying on its advice. And even when you've found an honest and competent magazine, remember that a review is one person's opinion. Use reviews as a starting point for your own investigation, not as the final word.

How to Choose a Retailer

As I said in the introduction to this chapter, *where* you buy your equipment is more important than *what* you buy. If you find a skilled dealer who cares about keeping you as a steady customer, you'll end up with a quality system at a reasonable price. Good dealers hand-pick the brands that they believe offer the best performance and value. In the hands of a good dealer, it's hard to go wrong.

The differences between retailers are large. Some are staffed by home-theater enthusiasts who are extremely knowledgeable, can demonstrate for you a choice selection of products, and can provide expert advice on choosing and installing your system. These retailers tend to be the single-store specialty dealers (or small chains) who got into the business out of a passion for music and home theater. In addition, some audio/video retailers are members of the *Professional Audio Video Retailers Association (PARA)* or the *Custom Electronic Design & Installation Association (CEDIA)*, organizations devoted to promoting high standards of technical excellence and customer service. The sales staffs from PARA- and CEDIA-member retailers undergo technical training in home-theater technology and system installation. As mentioned in Chapter 7, some dealers are trained by the Imaging Science Foundation (ISF) and are certified by that body to be skilled in calibrating video monitors.

Other than looking for these credentials, how do you determine which dealers are knowledgeable enthusiasts and which are simply moving boxes out the front door? One way is to judge the audio and video quality of their demonstrations. Does the dealer produce good sounds and pictures in the showroom? Or is the demonstration less than impressive? I've seen a huge range of presentation quality from comparably priced equipment at different retailers. If the retailer can get good sound and picture quality in the store, there's a good chance the dealer can achieve similar performance in your home. Conversely, if the dealer can't bother to produce a good demonstration in his showroom, does he have the skill or dedication to assemble a quality system for you?

You can also find excellent service, selection, and prices from a few select mail-order dealers. But beware; most of the mail-order companies that advertise "laundry lists" of heavily discounted products are merely order-takers, with no product knowledge or concern for your system. Other catalog companies are staffed by former retail salespeople who can offer expert advice on system matching, and who treat you as a long-term customer. Audio Advisor (800–942-0220) is a good example.

How to Evaluate Products in the Showroom

Many consumers dread going into a store to decide what to buy. They're afraid of making the wrong choices, paying too much, or appearing ignorant to the salesperson. If you've read this book, you don't need to worry about this last fear; you're among the most highly informed home-theater consumers. (In fact, earlier editions of this book have been adopted by the A/V retail industry as a technical training manual for salespeople.) And if you've chosen a dealer according to the guidelines I've just described, you shouldn't fear making the wrong choice or paying too much.

Instead, your visit to the showroom should focus on the equipment you're contemplating buying. After you've decided which components have enough inputs, power output, and features for your system, *listen* to them for yourself. It doesn't take a "golden ear" to know which product sounds better. An average person can, with a bit of focused attention, distinguish between good- and poor-sounding products (provided the demonstration is well-conducted). Don't feel rushed to pick one product over another; the longer you listen or watch, the more you'll learn about the product's strengths and weaknesses. You'll be living with your decision for quite some time; it's worth your while to be certain you're making the right choices now.

When evaluating audio components, it's a good idea to listen to them in the context of an entire home-theater system with a video presentation, and with the video monitor turned off. You'll find that your hearing acuity increases without the stimulation provided by the visual image. In addition, I find that sonic differences between components are much easier to discern when listening to music rather than film soundtracks.

All of the guidelines for evaluating speakers described in Chapter 6 also apply to other components. The key is to be informed, discriminating, and patient when choosing components. Hold the system or individual components to a high standard of quality; the great-performing, modestly priced products *are* out there. It just takes a little research and perseverance to find them.

Custom Installation

Rather than select and install components yourself, the *custom installer* will visit your home, show you products in a catalog, suggest a system package, and install the equipment. He'll also program remote controls, teach you how to use the system, and be on-call to fix major and minor emergencies.

As you might expect, custom installation comes at a price. The services of a custom installer are generally reserved for more costly systems, and those requiring that the equipment be hidden. Custom installation usually involves multi-room distributed audio, in-wall speakers throughout the house, linked security, home networking, home automation (lighting, heat, remote operation of home functions), and custom-built cabinetry—all in addition to creating the main theater room. You'd also expect such amenities as a 50" plasma panel in the home's gym and a 42" plasma in the kitchen. Such systems typically cost several hundred thousand dollars (and sometimes more than a million dollars), and are built into the home's infrastructure during initial construction.

If you can afford custom installation, be aware that not all custom installers strive for maximum audio and video performance. Often, hiding the equipment takes precedence over sound quality; in-wall speakers replace floorstanding units with the inevitable performance degradation. It's possible to spend half a million dollars and not equal the performance of a carefully chosen and setup fifty-thousand dollar system. I can see how one would want an elegant home to remain elegant, but if you are performance oriented, tell the custom installer that you want at least one room in the house (the media room) to have uncompromised picture and sound. In-wall speakers are fine for background music, but not for your main system.

Custom installers are proliferating because the industry is booming. Between 1997 and 1999, sales through custom installers rose more than 50%. Traditional A/V retailers have restructured their business to meet the demand, in some cases even closing their retail showrooms.

Home Theater Accessories

In addition to the major components already discussed, you'll need some accessories to make your home theater work, and also to get the best performance from it. Save some of your overall budget for the three most important accessories: speaker cables and interconnects, an equipment rack or stand, and a power conditioner/protector. You should save about 10% of your budget for speaker cables and interconnects, and from $100 to $200 for a power conditioning/protection system.

Racks and Stands

An equipment rack is an important part of your system. It holds and displays your components, separates the components to provide ventilation, and can even influence sound quality.

The first decision is whether you want your components out in the open or tucked away behind closed doors in a furniture-style cabinet. Metal open-frame racks are better than enclosed wooden cabinets. First, the metal-frame racks are more sturdy and vibration-resistant. Surprisingly, a solid rack can actually improve the sound of the components sitting on it. Vibration can subtly degrade the sound quality of audio components (that's why better units use vibration-resistant chassis). Second, an open rack provides better ventilation than a closed-in cabinet. Third, it's much easier to get at the rear-panel connections of components when they're sitting on an open rack.

But that look isn't for everyone. If you choose a furniture-like home-theater cabinet, get one that's solidly built and provides plenty of ventilation. Heat is the enemy of electronic components; it can degrade their performance and shorten their lives. The key to keeping your components cool is to provide a path for air flow around the components. Amplifiers get rid of their excess heat by convection, drawing air from underneath the unit and venting it out the top, so allow plenty of space above and below the amplifier. It's also a good idea to install a whisper fan in an enclosed rack; this can draw air up and exhaust it out the cabinet top. Getting the heat away from components is the single most important thing you can do to extend their lives.

The larger and more powerful your receiver or separate power amplifiers, the more heat they'll produce. Large amplifiers need extra airspace around them to avoid having them shut off when they overheat. Many amplifiers have thermal sensors that turn the amplifier off when it gets too hot. Unfortunately, amplifiers overheat during the loudest, most exciting parts of a movie, particularly near the end.

Speaker Cables and Audio Interconnects

Speaker cables carry the high-level signal from the A/V receiver or power amplifier to your loudspeakers. Although I've included speaker cables in the discussion of accessories, cables are really another component in your system. The speaker cables affect sound quality, and also the system's reliability.

You'll need five speaker cables: one each for the left, center, right, surround left, and surround right speakers. The front three speaker cables should be of the same length; the surround-speaker cables will probably be much longer. If your system uses surround-back speakers for Dolby Digital Surround EX or DTS-ES decoding, you'll need an extra pair of speaker cables.

One advantage of specialty speaker cables is that they're terminated with high-quality connections. Even if you have a modest system, you should use terminated speaker cables rather than bare wire. Stripping a cable to bare wiring and sticking the wire in the receiver's terminals isn't a good idea. First, the bare wire will oxidize over time and degrade the connection. Second, stranded bare wire introduces the possibility of stray strands touching the + and – terminals simultaneously and shorting out your receiver. Finally, a chemical reaction takes place when two dissimilar metals are in contact with each other, increasing the contact point's electrical resistance.

The most common speaker terminations are the *banana plug, spade lug,* and *pin* (fig.8-1). Nearly all speaker binding posts on A/V receivers and power amplifiers accept banana plugs; you simply insert the plug into the binding post. The highest-quality binding posts, found on separate power amplifiers, are called *five-way binding posts.* These will accept spade-lug terminations as well as banana plugs. If you have a choice, spade lugs provide the best connection—they produce a large contact surface between the binding post and spade lug, and can be tightened down to form a connection of low electrical resistance. Banana plugs are second best, and pin terminations give the least good connection. When tightening binding posts, don't use a wrench; it's too easy to overtighten the plastic nut and strip the binding post. One line of speaker cables offers interchangeable terminations. If you upgrade from a receiver with banana jacks to a power amplifier that will accept spade lugs, simply unscrew the banana jacks and screw on the spade lugs.

Contrary to popular belief, you shouldn't use "lamp cord" to connect your speakers. Lamp cord is the standard two-conductor "speaker cable" sold in hardware stores. Speaker cables are an important part of a home-theater system; they influence the system's reliability and sound quality. Lamp cord is particularly bad because it uses stranded wire. Electrical current travels down the shortest path in the cable, which means the electrons jump from strand to strand. Each strand interface acts like a small circuit, with capacitance and a diode effect. Individual strands can also interact magnetically, degrading sound quality. Choose high-quality cables specially made for audio and home-theater use; they're made to a much higher mechanical standard, meaning that the plugs and terminations are less likely to break. More important, high-quality cables help your system sound its best. It's a big mistake to put cheap speaker cables on quality components. Even an entry-level A/V receiver and moderately priced speaker system will benefit from quality cables.

Fig. 8-1
Common speaker-cable terminations include (from left) the banana plug, spade lug, and pin.

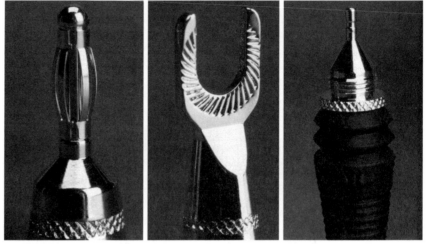

Courtesy Monster Cable Products, Inc.

Some speaker cables are THX-certified; this means that they meet Lucasfilm's standards for mechanical integrity and sound quality. They also conform to a universal color coding that makes connecting a system much easier.

If your speakers have two pairs of binding posts, they can be connected with two runs of speaker cable, a technique called bi-wiring. In my experience, bi-wiring always results in an improvement in sound quality that's worth the extra cost of speaker cable. A bi-wired cable can have one set of terminations on the amplifier end, and two sets of terminations on the speaker end (fig.8-2).

Fig. 8-2
Bi-wiring your loudspeakers improves their sound quality.

Courtesy AudioQuest

Audio interconnects also influence sound quality and reliability. Specialty interconnects are terminated with high-quality RCA jacks that are often gold-plated to resist tarnishing. The conductors are made from specially prepared copper from which the impurities have been removed; and the conductors are physically configured to minimize the interconnect's influence on the signal.

Just as audio interconnects and speaker cables influence sound quality, video cables influence picture quality. Although audio interconnects may look like video interconnects, don't use an audio interconnect to carry video signals; you won't get as good a picture.

All audio interconnects, speaker cables, and video interconnects degrade the signals passing through them. Therefore, the shorter the cable runs in your system, the better. Use only the cable lengths you need.

Power-Line Protectors and Conditioners

A power-line protector and conditioner (fig.8-3) is an important part of a home-theater system: All of your components plug into the conditioner, and the conditioner is plugged into your AC wall outlet.

Fig. 8-3 Using an AC line protector and conditioner improves the sound of your system and protects your components.

Courtesy Monster Cable Products, Inc.

The advantages of an AC line conditioner are many: it makes installation easier and neater; it provides better sound quality from the audio components; it gives you multiple AC outlets from a single plug; and it protects your system from voltage surges. An AC line conditioner filters noise from the AC power line for better sound quality. It also isolates your components from each other so noise in one component doesn't get into another component through the AC line. For example, any component that performs digital signal processing—such as a controller—will transmit noise into the AC line through its power cord. If you have a power amplifier plugged into the same AC line, that noise will wind up in the controller, where it can subtly degrade the sound. Isolating the components prevents this from occurring.

Some AC line conditioners also protect your equipment from lightning strokes and high-voltage surges on the electrical grid, breaking the connection instantly when they detect an over-voltage condition or lightning. Specialized home-theater conditioners/protectors such as the unit shown in fig.8-3 provide protection for antenna and DSS signals, and for the phone line connected to a DSS receiver.

Not all line conditioners and protectors are created equal. The basic "surge protector" power strips sold in hardware stores aren't very sophisticated, and offer little protection. The better-quality dedicated units offer more protection, along with noise-filtering to improve the sound.

9 Putting It All Together: How to Connect and Configure Your Home Theater

Introduction

Now that you've bought the components for your home-theater system, it's time to hook them all together and make them work. This chapter will guide you through that process step by step. But there's more to setting up a home-theater system than just making it produce pictures and sound. How your equipment is installed, configured, and calibrated makes a tremendous difference in the level of quality you'll get. A well-set-up system of modest price will always outperform a more costly rig that hasn't been set up as carefully. By spending a little time learning some setup techniques, you can extract the maximum possible performance from your equipment. If you already have a system, you may be surprised at how much it can be improved—without spending a dime. Moreover, it's enormously rewarding to turn a good home-theater presentation into a great one just by applying your knowledge. In this chapter I'll share with you the setup techniques I've learned from my years of hands-on experience as a product reviewer.

Basic Setup

The first step in setting up your system is deciding where to install it. More than likely, the room where you watch television will become the home-theater room. But this room may have been arranged for casual TV watching, not for experiencing the full impact of what a home-theater system can deliver. Now's the time to rethink the room's layout and make the home theater the room's central focus.

The home-theater room should be arranged with the video monitor and front loudspeakers at one end, and the couch or viewing chairs at the other. Ideally, the couch will be positioned part way into the room and not against the back wall. This location is better acoustically (excessive bass build-up occurs near the back wall), and allows the surround speakers to better do their job of enveloping you in the film's sound-

Fig. 9-1 The ideal home-theater room and loudspeaker setup.

THX-Certified Loudspeaker System Illustration Courtesy B & W Loudspeakers

track. Of course, the setup should provide room for the left and right speakers on either side of the video monitor. (An ideal home-theater setup is shown in fig.9-1.)

The optimum viewing distance between you and the video monitor is determined by the video monitor's size. The smaller the monitor, the closer you should sit to maintain the maximum image area in your field of view. Sitting too close to a large monitor, particularly a rear-projection set, exposes the line structure inherent in a video presentation. If you are watching high-definition programming on an HD set, you can sit much closer without seeing the line structure. The best viewing distance offers the largest possible picture without making that picture look grainy. (Picture size and viewing distance are covered in Chapter 7.) You should also try to sit no more than 15° off to the side of the video monitor. Plasma panels, with their wider field of view, maintain a good picture even when watching from an extreme angle.

Once you've decided on where the couch and video monitor will be positioned, you'll need to determine the best place for your equipment. A simple home-theater system will have a VCR, A/V receiver, DSS receiver, and DVD player. These components can be easily accommodated in a TV stand or rack.

The components of more ambitious home-theater systems will probably be housed in a separate equipment rack or cabinet. These storage units can be the metal-frame open-air type, or be made of furniture-quality wood. No matter which cabinet option you choose, it's important to remember that you should have a direct line of sight between the equipment and the listening/viewing position so the components can "see" the infrared signal from the remote control. If you want to put the equipment behind you or tuck it away in a cabinet, you'll need an *IR sensor*. When positioned anywhere in front of you, this small device picks up the infrared commands from the remote control, converts them into electrical signals, and relays the commands to an *IR flasher* positioned in your equipment rack. The IR flasher converts the electrical signals back into infrared light, to be picked up by your components. An IR sensor and IR flasher are together called an *IR repeater*. The IR repeater gives you much more flexibility in positioning your equipment. Keep in mind, however, that you'll need to run a small wire from the IR sensor to the IR flasher.

Lighting

The amount of ambient light in your home-theater room greatly influences picture quality; the more light in the room, the worse the picture. The ambient light competes with the light output from the video display device, washing out the picture and reducing the picture's "snap" and visual impact.

Avoid rooms with large windows if you want to watch movies in the daytime. If this isn't practical, use drapes with a "blackout" feature that prevents light from entering. You can't have a home-theater room that's too dark. A dark room not only gives you much better picture quality, it also makes the home-theater room "disappear" so that you become more immersed in what's happening on the screen.

When watching your home theater at night, a *small* amount of ambient light is a good thing. This low-level background light makes the eye's iris close slightly so that it is better able to handle bright picture transitions. The background light should be low enough that it doesn't compete with the video monitor's light output; it should also be white rather than colored, and located behind the video monitor. The smaller the video display's image and the farther you sit from it, the greater the amount of background light you need.

Ideally, the side walls and ceiling of the home-theater room will be either painted a subdued color, or covered with bookcases, wall rugs, or other light-absorbing decoration. The worst case is side walls painted gloss white—reflective side walls will reflect light from the video monitor, producing distracting blotches of light to the left and right of where your attention should be. In addition, reflective side walls in a room with a front-projector will reflect light back onto the screen, reducing contrast. The result is greater viewing fatigue and less involvement in what's happening on the screen. If you have a dedicated home-theater room that's not in the main part of your house, you may consider painting the side walls flat black or gray, or hanging dark curtains along the room's side walls. This isn't an option for most of us; however, a strategically placed rug can help absorb stray light in any living room. I recently painted my theater room a dark color, and the difference was remarkable; the experience is more like being in a theater than being in a home.

Acoustical Treatment

Before we get to the specifics of loudspeaker placement, here are a few guidelines on how to make your home-theater room sound better. First, if you have a bare tile or wood floor between you and the front three speakers, covering the floor with a rug is probably the single most important thing you can do to improve your room's acoustics. The rug absorbs unwanted acoustic reflections from the floor, which improves dialog intelligibility and adds to a sense of clarity. Similarly, absorbing the acoustic reflections from the side walls between you and the left and right speakers also helps you get better sound. Bookcases and hanging rugs are both effective in absorbing or diffusing side-wall reflections. Generally, the front of the room should be acoustically absorptive, with drapes, carpets, and hanging rugs.

Fig. 9-2 Dipole surround speakers are helped in their job of creating a diffuse soundfield by room reflections.

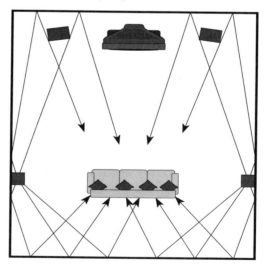

Conversely, the back of the room should be more acoustically reflective. Bare walls behind the listening/viewing position tend to reflect sound and add to the feeling of spaciousness generated by the surround speakers. The sounds produced by a movie theater's array of surround speakers all reach your ears at different times, increasing the feeling of envelopment. But because a home-theater system uses just two surround speakers, we must help them achieve their goal by providing reflective surfaces near them. The room layout in fig.9-2 shows how dipolar surround speakers use room reflections to "smear" their sound and produce a more diffuse soundfield behind you.

Ideally, the lower portion of the room's front end should be acoustically absorptive, the upper portion acoustically reflective. This situation absorbs unwanted wall reflections from the three front speakers, but lets the dipole surround speakers positioned on the sidewall just below the ceiling create a bigger sense of envelopment by reflecting sound off the front walls as well as the rear walls, as shown in fig.9-2.

Connecting Your System: A Step-by-Step Approach

After unpacking all the components of your home-theater system, you may be intimidated by the myriad wires and connecting jacks. In this next section we'll go through the steps of hooking up a system. Not every home-theater system is the same, so there will be some variation on the process I'm about to describe. The owner's manuals included with your products should provide specific information about connection and setup. The following description is more of a generic procedure that should be augmented with specific details from those manuals.

But first, let's survey the audio and video cables you'll be using to connect your system:

Coaxial cable: This stiff, round black cable is what comes from your antenna or cable outlet and carries TV signals. Usually marked RG-59 or RG-6 (a higher-quality version of RG-59), a coaxial cable carries picture and sound as a "radio frequency" signal, which is why it's also called an RF cable. The tuner in your VCR or television converts RF signals into video and audio signals.

There's a second type of coaxial cable that's completely different from the one just described. This second type looks like a conventional RCA-terminated audio cable, but is designed to carry digital audio from a DVD player, DSS receiver, or other component to your A/V receiver. DVD players, for example, usually offer coaxial and optical digital-audio output jacks.

TosLink cable. This is a thin glass- or plastic-fiber "cable" that carries digital audio as pulses of light. A TosLink cable is most often used to connect the digital-audio output of a source component (DVD player, for example) to an A/V receiver or controller.

Composite video cable: Looks just like a standard audio interconnect, but is built a little differently inside. A composite video cable is designed to carry the high frequencies of a video signal. The terminations are called RCA plugs. (An RCA plug is shown in fig.5-3.)

S-video cable: An S-video cable carries the video signal's brightness and color information separately on a small, round multi-pin connector (fig.9-3).

Audio interconnect: This is the standard audio cable that has been used for years to hook up stereo systems. An audio interconnect is terminated with RCA plugs, with the right-channel cable marked red and the left-channel conductor marked white. An audio interconnect carries a line-level signal.

Speaker cable: The speaker cable has two conductors and connects the powerful output from a receiver or power amplifier to the loudspeakers. One conductor has a red or + marking, the other a black or – marking. A speaker cable is bigger than an audio interconnect because it carries a stronger signal. Speaker cables are terminated with different types of connectors, the most common being the banana plug, spade lug, and pin (shown in fig.8-1).

Component video cable: The component-video cable is simply three composite video cables in one wiring harness, or three separate composite video cables; used for carrying component-video signals.

FireWire or DVI cable. As HDTV becomes more widespread, so will the FireWire (IEEE1394) and Digital Visual Interface (DVI) cables. These are used primarily as the interface between set-top boxes, satellite receivers, D-VHS machines, and HDTV sets. Note that Sony calls their implementation of FireWire i.LINK.

Fig. 9-3 An S-video cable carries the picture's brightness and color information separately for better video quality.

Courtesy AudioQuest

AC Connections

After you've decided where everything's going to go in your room, put your components in the equipment rack or cabinet. Be sure to provide plenty of ventilation around each component, particularly A/V receivers or power amplifiers. Don't stack components on top of a receiver or power amplifier.

The next step is to run all the AC power cords to an AC source. Before you do that, however, make sure the power switch to each component is turned off. The best way of connecting all your components to AC power is to add a line conditioner. This device plugs into a wall socket and provides many AC outlets for your components. A good line conditioner filters noise from the AC line, protects your home-theater components from voltage surges and spikes, and isolates the components from lightning strokes. Some AC conditioners, such as the model shown in fig.8-3, also isolate your DSS dish and rooftop antenna from lightning.

Some home-theater components have AC outlets on their back panels marked SWITCHED and UNSWITCHED. These outlets are provided for plugging in other components. A "switched" AC outlet is "live" only when the host component is turned on. An "unswitched" outlet is "live" whenever the host component is plugged into the wall. If you use the AC outlets on the backs of components, be sure to plug the host component directly into an AC source, not another outlet on the back of another component. Similarly, components that draw lots of power—receivers and power amplifiers—should be connected directly to a power conditioner or wall socket (if you don't have a power conditioner). DSS receivers and VCRs should be plugged into "unswitched" outlets if you don't have a power conditioner.

Once you've run all the AC cords and plugged them in, make sure all the individual power switches on each component are turned off. We'll make all the audio, video, and speaker connections before powering up the system to prevent possible damage to the components and speakers. In fact, whenever you unplug or plug in any cables or interconnects, the power to the system should be turned off. If the power remains on, you may hear a loud pop that could damage your speakers. For neatness, you can bundle the AC cords together with wire ties (available at RadioShack).

Video Connections

The next step is to run all the video cables. You'll need one video cable for each source component in your system, and one video cable to run from your A/V receiver or controller to the video monitor. Remember that your A/V receiver or controller is the central switching point for video signals.

This connection can be made in a variety of ways. Video cables come in three varieties, composite, S-video, and component video. The S-video connection offers some advantages in picture quality under certain circumstances. To take advantage of the theoretically superior S-video connection, your video monitor must have an S-video input. Second, S-video provides a better picture only with S-VHS machines (when playing S-VHS tapes), DSS dishes (those with S-video output on the DSS receiver box), and DVD players with S-video output. If your system has a standard VCR and a laserdisc player, S-video probably offers no benefits. You should, however, try the S-video connection and see if it improves the picture quality. As explained in Chapter 7, an S-video connection can sometimes marginally improve the picture.

If your products are equipped with component-video connections, use them. Component video delivers the highest possible video quality. If your A/V receiver doesn't have component-video switching, run the component-video output from your DVD player (or other component-video-equipped product) directly into the TV's component-video input. To switch between video sources, you'll need to use the TV's input-select button.

Here's a little trap you can avoid: If you connect a source component to your receiver or controller with an S-video cable and use a composite cable from the receiver or controller to the video monitor, you won't see a picture. Be sure to run an S-video cable to your monitor if you use S-video cables on any of your source components. Some receivers, however, have recently added the ability to transcode (convert from one video type to another) composite to S-video to avoid the necessity of running both composite and S-video cables between the receiver and video monitor.

After you've decided between composite, S-video, and component-video connections, you'll want to consider using high-quality video cables. Although you can use the video cables that come in the box when you buy a component, you'll get better picture quality from aftermarket video cables. These high-quality cables more faithfully transmit the video signal, and are usually much better made mechanically and thus less likely to fail in service.

Now you're ready to make all the video connections in your system. Run a video cable from the MONITOR OUT jack on the A/V receiver or A/V controller to one of the video inputs on your video monitor. Next, connect a video cable from each source component (VCR, DSS receiver box, DVD player, laserdisc machine) to a video input on the receiver. Some receivers' video inputs are marked VCR, DVD, etc., but others simply call each video input VIDEO 1, VIDEO 2, etc. In the latter case, it doesn't matter which source component is connected to which video input.

You'll also need to run a video cable from the receiver's VCR OUT jack to the VIDEO IN jack on your VCR. This connection carries a video signal from the A/V receiver to the VCR for recording, and is what makes it possible to record on your VCR from DVD, DSS, or other source components.

Cables included with components are sometimes grouped in threes—for example, a red, white, and yellow cable joined together. The yellow cable is the video cable, white is the left-channel audio, and red is the right-channel audio. This color code is often followed on the jacks of receivers and other components, making connection easier.

If you're using grouped cables, run the red and white cables from the red and white jacks on the source components to the AUDIO input on the receiver. Make sure the video and audio cables are connected to the same input; i.e., the VCR's video and audio outputs should be connected to the receiver's VCR input.

If you have a DSS dish, connect the dish's coaxial output to the dish input on the DSS receiver box. Run a video cable (composite will work, though S-video is better in this application) to a video input on the A/V receiver.

Connect the cable outlet or antenna cable to the ANTENNA IN jack on your VCR. Run another coaxial cable from the VCR's ANTENNA OUT to the ANTENNA IN coaxial jack on your TV. Making this last connection lets you watch TV without turning on the entire home-theater system. The VCR puts out an RF signal on channel 3, and connects the antenna or cable signal to your television. Note that you can watch VHS tapes on channel 3, or by selecting a video input on your monitor. The latter method provides better picture quality.

While we're on this subject, you should know about the switch on every VCR marked TV/VCR. When in the TV position, the switch sends the antenna or cable input at the VCR directly to the television. It simply connects the antenna input to the antenna output, bypassing the VCR. The TV position is for watching television and selecting channels from your TV.

In the VCR position, the TV receives the output from the VCR, not from the antenna or cable signal. If the TV/VCR switch is in the VCR position, your TV must be set to channel 3 to see a picture.

Audio Connections

Run left and right audio interconnects from all the source components to the receiver or controller. Pay attention to connecting right channel to right channel, left channel to left channel. Just as video cables make a difference in picture quality, audio interconnects make a difference in sound quality. It's a good idea to buy quality aftermarket interconnects for the audio connections.

Most of the audio interconnects connect the output of a source component to the input of the receiver or A/V controller. A few will do the opposite, connecting audio signals *from* the A/V receiver to a VCR. When recording from a source component to the VCR, this cable is what carries the sound to the VCR. The VCR is connected to the receiver's *A/V loop*.

I mentioned earlier that you can bundle the AC power cords together for neatness. Under no circumstances should you bundle audio or video cables with the AC cords. AC cables radiate hum (a low-frequency noise) that can get into your system if the AC cords are too close to the audio and video cables. Keep them as far apart as possible. If they must meet, cross them at right angles rather than running them side by side. Ideally, AC cables, audio interconnects, speaker cables, video cables, and digital audio cables should be separated from each other. Some people try to get a neat look by bundling all the cables together. Those systems will suffer from needlessly reduced audio and video performance.

Hum can get into your system in other ways. If you have cable TV, you may hear hum through your speakers and see white horizontal lines, called "hum bars," moving slowly up your TV picture. Both the audio hum and video hum bars are caused by a *ground loop*, a condition in which the cable's ground (the outer conductor of the cable) is at a different potential (voltage) from your house's electrical ground (the third pin on an AC outlet). Ideally, ground should be ground, or zero volts. But when two uneven grounds are connected, a small amount of electrical current flows between them, creating the audible hum and the visible hum bars. The grounds are connected because the cable-TV cable is connected to your VCR, which is plugged into the wall socket and grounded to the rest of your system through the audio and video interconnects.

The solution is to break the connection between the house ground and cable ground with a device called a *ground isolator*. This is a small box that passes the TV signal, yet breaks the physical connection between the grounds. The ground isolator cures the problem instantly.

Surround Speaker Wiring

The most challenging aspect of hooking up a home-theater system is running speaker wire to the surround speakers. With your A/V receiver near your video monitor and the surround speakers all the way in the back of the room, you can see how connecting the two can be a challenge.

This isn't a problem in new construction: you simply run the speaker wires in the wall. (Be sure to use UL-rated speaker cable.) But for most installations you'll need to run two speaker cables from one end of the room to the other. If you have two back-surround speakers for THX Surround EX and DTS-ES decoding, you'll need to run four speaker cables to the room's rear. Unfortunately, the longer the speaker cable, the thicker it should be. If you have attic access, you can sometimes run the speaker cables overhead, above the ceiling. Without attic access, you have no choice but to run the cables out in the open.

This can, however, be accomplished with a minimum of intrusion into the decor. One solution, which I've used successfully in several installations, is Monster Cable's "Superflat" or "Superflat Mini" speaker cable and accessories. This thin, flat cable can be run along a baseboard and up a wall. You can buy mounting accessories that make the cable turn corners and hold it against the wall. The cables and mounting hardware can be painted to further reduce their already low profile.

If you really don't want to run cables to the surround speakers, wireless surround speakers are available. They don't sound as good as conventional surround speakers, and are more expensive. Running surround cables is a one-time job—and worth the initial effort.

After the surround speakers are wired, connect the left, right, and center speakers. Be sure to observe the correct polarity on all five speakers: the receiver's red terminal goes to the speaker's red terminal, and the receiver's black terminal goes to the speaker's black terminal. If you reverse these connections to one speaker, the speakers are said to be *out of phase*. If the left and right speakers are out of phase, the left speaker's cone moves forward when the right speaker's cone moves back. The two speakers are fighting each other, reducing bass output and destroying imaging.

Speaker cables come with a variety of terminations. The spade lug is shaped like a two-prong fork, and offers the best connection. Spade lugs, however, can be used only on higher-end equipment that have five-way binding posts. For conventional A/V receivers, the banana plug is the easiest connection method and offers a better connection than the pin termination. (These terminations were shown in fig.8-1.) Inserting bare wire into the receiver or power amplifier's output terminals isn't a good idea; the bare copper will oxidize over time and degrade the connection; loose strands can short out to an adjacent terminal and damage the receiver, and current flow from the amplifier to speakers may be impeded.

How to Connect a Subwoofer to Your System

The simplest way of adding a subwoofer to your system is to run an audio interconnect from the SUBWOOFER OUT jack on your A/V receiver or controller to the subwoofer's input jack. From the receiver's or controller's setup menu, choose SMALL for the left and right loudspeakers. Choosing SMALL filters low bass from the signal driving the left and right loudspeakers. If you don't invoke the receiver's or controller's SMALL setting, your left and right loudspeakers will receive low-bass signals along with the subwoofer. You must also tell the receiver or controller, through its setup menu, that you have a subwoofer connected. (Configuring your A/V receiver is discussed in greater detail later in this chapter.)

Another way of connecting a powered subwoofer is through the PRE-AMP OUT/POWER-AMP IN jacks on your A/V receiver. These jacks give you access to the signals inside the receiver after the receiver's preamplifier section, but before the power-amplifier section. The PREAMP OUT signal feeds the subwoofer's line-level input. The subwoofer's line-level output feeds the POWER-AMP IN jacks. In essence, you've simply inserted the subwoofer into the signal path of the receiver. The signal going back into the receiver has had bass removed by the subwoofer's crossover. That way, your left and right speakers won't receive any bass. All the bass is directed to the subwoofer. In a separate controller/power amplifier system, the subwoofer is connected in the same way between the controller and power amplifier. This method has the advantage of letting the subwoofer's crossover split up the frequency spectrum; the result is probably better integration between the subwoofer and the left and right speakers. That's because the crossover characteristics (frequency and slope) are determined by the loudspeaker designer who knows the speaker system, not the A/V receiver designer who has no idea what speakers will be connected to the receiver. If you choose this option, be sure to select the LARGE left and right position on the receiver's setup menu.

This connection method can also be used to add a subwoofer to the surround channels in a system with a Dolby Digital decoder. You can keep your small surround speakers and still get bass from the rear channels by adding a subwoofer in this way.

Matching a Subwoofer to Your System

It's relatively easy to put a subwoofer into your system and hear more bass. What's difficult is making the subwoofer's bass *integrate* with the sound of your main speakers. Low bass as reproduced by a subwoofer's big cone can sound different from the bass reproduced by the smaller cones in the left and right speakers. A well-integrated subwoofer produces a seamless sound, no boomy thump, and natural reproduction of music. A poorly integrated subwoofer will sound thick, heavy, boomy, and unnatural, calling attention to the fact that you have smaller speakers reproducing the frequency spectrum from the midrange up, and a big subwoofer putting out low bass.

Integrating a subwoofer into your system is challenging because the main speakers may have small cones, and the subwoofer has a large and heavy cone. Moreover, the subwoofer is optimized for putting out lots of low bass, not for reproducing detail. The main speakers' upper bass is quick, clean, and articulate. The subwoofer's bass is often slow and heavy.

Achieving good integration is easier if you buy a complete system made by one manufacturer. Such systems are engineered to work together to provide a smooth transition between the subwoofer and the main speakers. Specifically, the crossover network removes bass from the left and right speakers, and removes midrange and treble frequencies from the signal driving the subwoofer. If all these details are handled by the same designer, you're much more likely to get a smooth transition than if the subwoofer were an add-on component from a different manufacturer. In addition, using the THX subwoofer crossover found in all THX-certified receivers and controllers with a THX-certified subwoofer takes the guesswork out of matching a subwoofer to your system.

If you do choose a subwoofer made by a different manufacturer, several controls found on most subwoofers help you integrate the sub into your system. One control lets you adjust the *crossover frequency*. This sets the frequency at which the transition between the subwoofer and the main speakers takes place. Frequencies below the crossover frequency are reproduced by the subwoofer; frequencies above the crossover frequency are reproduced by the main speakers. If you have small speakers that don't go very low in the bass and you set the crossover frequency too low, you'll get a "hole" in the frequency response. That is, there will be a narrow band of frequencies that aren't reproduced by the woofer *or* the main speakers.

Setting the subwoofer's crossover frequency too high also results in poor integration, but for a different reason. The big cone of a subwoofer is specially designed to reproduce low bass. When it is asked to also reproduce upper-bass frequencies, those upper-bass frequencies are less clear and distinct than they would be if reproduced by the smaller main speakers. In addition, too high a crossover frequency will allow you to localize the subwoofer (sense the direction from which the subwoofer's sound is originating), which is distracting. Finding just the right crossover frequency is the first step in achieving good integration. Most subwoofer owner's manuals include instructions for setting the crossover frequency. As a rule of thumb, the lower the subwoofer's crossover is set, the better. If you use a receiver's bass management to keep bass from the main speaker, set the crossover as high as possible so that the receiver's filter and the subwoofer's filter don't overlap.

Some subwoofers also provide a knob or switch marked PHASE. To understand a subwoofer's phase control, visualize a sound wave being launched from your subwoofer and from your main speakers at the same time. Unless the main speakers and subwoofer are identical distances from your ears, those two sound waves will reach your ears at different times, or have a phase difference between them. In addition, the electronics inside a subwoofer can create a phase difference in the signal. The phase control lets you delay the wave generated by the subwoofer so that it lines up in time with the wave from the main speakers. When the sound waves are in-phase, you hear a smoother, more coherent, and better-integrated sound.

One way of setting the phase control is to sit in the listening position with music playing through the system. Have a friend rotate the phase control (or flip the phase switch) until the bass sounds the smoothest. That is, some bass frequencies should not sound louder or different in timbre than other frequencies.

But there's a much more precise way of setting the phase control that guarantees perfect phase alignment between the subwoofer and main speakers. First, reverse the connections on your main loudspeakers so that the black speaker wire goes to the speaker's red terminal, and the red speaker wire goes to the speaker's black terminal. Do this with both speakers. Now, from a test CD that includes pure test tones, select the track whose frequency is the same as the subwoofer's crossover frequency. Sit in the listening position and have a friend rotate the subwoofer's phase control until you hear the least amount of bass. The subwoofer's phase control is now set perfectly. Return your speaker connections to their previous (correct) positions: red to red, black to black.

Here's what's happening when you follow this procedure: By reversing the polarity of the main speakers, you're putting them out of phase with the subwoofer. When you play a test signal whose frequency is the same as the subwoofer's crossover point, both the sub and the main speakers will be reproducing that frequency. You'll hear minimum bass when the waves from the main speakers and subwoofers are maximally out of phase. That is, when the main speaker's cone is moving in, the subwoofer's cone is moving out. The two out-of-phase waves cancel each other, producing very little bass. Now, when you return your loudspeakers to their proper connection (putting them back in-phase with the subwoofer), they will be maximally *in-phase* with the subwoofer. This is the most accurate method of setting a subwoofer's phase control. Unless you move the subwoofer or main speakers, you need to perform this exercise only once.

The best integration comes from adding two (or more) subwoofers to your system. One subwoofer doesn't distribute bass in the room very well. The result is *standing waves*, which are peaks and valleys in bass (technically, standing waves are stationary areas of high and low sound pressures in the room). If you've seen a cup of coffee on a vibrating surface, you've seen standing waves. The rings of peaks and dips in the coffee correspond to areas of lots of bass and nearly no bass. Because of standing waves, some areas of the room will sound bass-heavy, others thin and lightweight. You can demonstrate this to yourself by playing music with lots of low bass and walking around the room—the bass will be louder in some areas than in others. But if you use two small subwoofers, and place them asymmetrically in the room, these standing-wave patterns are broken up. The result is more uniform distribution of bass throughout the room and better integration with the main speakers.

You can also get more dynamic impact and clarity from your subwoofer by placing it close to the listening position. Sitting near the subwoofer causes you to hear more of the subwoofer's direct sound and less of the sound after it has been reflected around the room. You hear—and feel—more of the subwoofer's wave launch, which adds to the visceral impact of owning a subwoofer. Bass impact is more startling, powerful, and dynamic when the subwoofer is placed near the listening position.

Subwoofer placement also has a large effect on how much bass you hear and how well the sub integrates with your main speakers. We'll talk about subwoofer placement in the next sections.

Speaker Placement

Where speakers are located in your room has a huge influence on the quality of sound you will achieve. Correct speaker placement can make the difference between good and spectacular performance from the same equipment. If you follow a few simple speaker-placement techniques, you'll be well on your way toward getting the best sound from your system. Correct speaker placement is the single most important factor in achieving good sound.

Surround Speaker Placement

Let's start with the most difficult of a home-theater system's six speakers: the two surround speakers. As I said in Chapter 6, the surround speakers are usually dipolar. That is, they produce sound equally to the front and the rear of the speaker cabinet. Dipoles produce a "null," or area of no sound, at the cabinet sides. Here's a simple rule for positioning dipolar surround speakers, no matter what the installation: point the surround speakers' null at the listening position. Never point the surround speakers directly at the listening position.

Ideally, the surround speakers would be located on the side walls directly to the side of the listening position (figs.9-1 and 9-2) and at least two feet above the listeners' heads when seated. Dipolar surround speakers should never be located in front of the listening position, where they could be heard directly; the surround speakers' sound should be reflected around the room before reaching the listener. This helps to mimic the sound of a movie theater's surround array with just two speakers, and to create the envelopment that's so important to the home-theater experience.

But what if your couch is directly against the rear wall, with no room for reflecting sound from the rear wall to the listening position? You can put the surround speakers on the side walls about 2' from the rear wall, or place them in the corners with the null pointed at the listener. This way, the listener still hears reflected, rather than direct, sound from the surround speakers.

Let's say you have a pair of small speakers lying around that weren't designed for home-theater use, but that you want to use until you can upgrade to true home-theater dipoles. These speakers produce sound conventionally, in one direction, rather than equally toward the front and back as dipoles do. Direct their sound so that it reflects off a wall before reaching the listener. This placement may seem bizarre, but it accomplishes the goal of bouncing the sound from the surround speakers off a wall.

If you have monopolar surround speakers (conventional speakers that produce sound in one direction), you can locate them behind the listening position rather than to the sides. There's some controversy over whether dipolar or monopolar loudspeakers are ideal for reproducing the surround channels in a film soundtrack. Dipolar speakers create a greater sense of diffusion, but monopolar speakers produce a greater sense of directionality of sound behind you.

Keep in mind that reflections from the front speakers are bad; reflections from the rear speakers are good. Well-positioned surround speakers make a tremendous difference in the quality of the home-theater experience by re-creating the sense of ambience and space we hear in a movie theater.

Back-Surround Speaker Placement for Dolby Digital EX and DTS-ES

According to THX, soundtracks encoded in the Dolby Digital EX format are best reproduced through four dipolar surround speakers located at 110° and 150°, as shown in fig.9-4. This placement provides the greatest sense of envelopment, along with the most continuous soundfield behind the listener. The two back-surround speakers should be positioned so that the speakers facing the room's centerline are in-phase with each other. This produces central image between the two back-surround speakers. If you're using a single back-surround speaker, position it directly behind the listener at 180°.

Center Speaker Placement

Correct positioning of the center speaker results in better dialog intelligibility, smoother movement of onscreen sounds, and a more spacious soundstage.

As just mentioned, reflections from the front speakers that reach the listener work against good sound. This is particularly true of the center speaker, which carries the all-important dialog. Because most center-channel speakers are mounted on top of a direct-view TV or rear projector—both of which are highly reflective—there's the potential for unwanted acoustic reflections from the video monitor.

To reduce reflections from the center speaker, align its front edge absolutely flush with the front of the video monitor so that they form as contiguous a surface as possible. This positioning reduces a phenomenon called *diffraction*—the re-radiation of sound when the soundwaves encounter a discontinuity. (Specifically, diffraction introduces variations in the speaker's frequency response.) Think of waves rippling in a pond: If you put a stick in the water, the waves will strike the stick and be re-radiated around it. The same thing happens when the sound from the center speaker encounters the "stick" of the video monitor: the monitor re-radiates that sound toward the listener, making the overall sound less accurate. That's why making the center speaker flush with the front of the video monitor is so important.

You may have noticed that high-quality loudspeakers have smooth surfaces around the speaker cones. Some have rounded fronts and even the mounting bolts securing the individual drivers within the speaker are recessed to reduce diffraction from the speaker cabinet.

You should also tilt the center speaker down toward the listening position if it is mounted on a large rear-projection set, or on a direct-view TV positioned on a tall stand. If the center speaker is located below the video monitor, point it up toward the listeners. Direct the center speaker's sound toward the height of the listeners' ears when seated. Finally, be sure the center speaker is less than 2' different in height from the left and right speakers, measured from each speaker's tweeters.

Fig. 9-4 The left and right loud-speakers should be placed equidistant into the room and form a 45°–60° angle with the listener. The surround speakers should be located at 110°, and the back surround speakers at 150°.

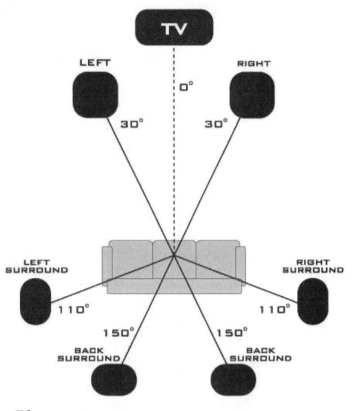

Left and Right Speaker Placement

The left and right speakers should be pulled slightly in front of the video monitor, and not be in a straight line with it (as some owner's manuals erroneously advise). Positioning the left and right speakers so that they form a gentle arc with the center speaker has two advantages. First, acoustic reflections from the video monitor are reduced. Second, the left, right, and center speakers are now all the same distance from the listener. The sounds from each of the three front speakers will reach the listener at the same time. If the front three speakers were lined up, we would hear the center speaker slightly ahead of the left and right speakers, which tends to make sounds bunch together in the center and reduces the soundstage's left-to-right width.

Some A/V controllers and receivers have a "center-channel delay" feature that lets you put the three front speakers in a line without hearing the center speaker first. Although this feature achieves its goal, you still get more unwanted acoustic reflections from the video monitor.

If you're using large, full-range left and right speakers, putting the speakers near the front and side walls will increase the amount of bass you hear. The walls reinforce bass to produce a weightier sound. This can be a good or a bad thing, depending on the speakers and your room. Speakers that have lots of bass already will probably sound boomy and unnatural if put too close to the front wall. Pulling them out into the room often produces a huge improvement in bass definition (the bass no longer sounds like a continuous blur) and midrange clarity. The unnatural boominess of a speaker too close to a wall makes the midrange sound thick, and lacking in openness and clarity. If you're using small left and right speakers with a separate subwoofer, the left and right speaker placement in relation to the front wall is less important.

How far apart the left and right speakers are positioned is also important to achieving a natural and spacious sound. If the left and right speakers are too close to the video monitor, you'll never get a sense of large space at the front of the room. If too far apart, onscreen sounds are reproduced too far away from their apparent sources on the screen. It can be subconsciously confusing and distracting to hear a sound come from a location different from the visual location of the sound source. A good rule of thumb is to position the left and right speakers so that they form a 45°–60° angle when seen from the listening/viewing location (fig.9-4 shown earlier).

Left and right speakers can be positioned so that they point straight ahead, or are angled in (called *toe-in*) toward the listening position. No toe-in (speakers pointing straight ahead) produces a wider and more spacious soundstage, but at the expense of precise localization of sounds. Too much toe-in creates a more tightly focused sound but a smaller sense of overall soundstage size. Toe-in has the advantage of directing more sound at the listener and less sound toward the side walls. Reflection of sound from the side walls is the single worst problem in getting good sound from your left and right speakers.

Some speakers are meant to be toed-in; that position provides their flattest (most accurate) frequency response. Others achieve their best performance with no toe-in. If you toe-in speakers designed for no toe-in, the sound will be too bright. Consult your owner's manual or your dealer for guidance. You can also experiment by playing the same section of a movie soundtrack or a piece of music with varying degrees of speaker toe-in to determine which position sounds best.

Subwoofer Placement

Unlike the left, center, right, and surround speakers, for which some placement rules have been established, where to put your subwoofer is largely a matter of trial and error. When a subwoofer is correctly positioned, the bass will be clean, tight, quick, and punchy. A well-located subwoofer will also produce a seamless sound between the sub and the front speakers; you won't hear the subwoofer as a separate speaker. A poorly positioned subwoofer will sound boomy, excessively heavy, thick, lacking detail, slow, and have little dynamic impact. In addition, you'll hear exactly where the front speakers leave off and the subwoofer takes over.

The simplest, most effective way of positioning a subwoofer is to put it near the listening position. Raise the subwoofer off the floor, if possible, so that it's as close to where the listeners' ears would normally be. Play a piece of music with an ascending and descending bass line, such as a "walking" bass in straight-ahead jazz. Crawl around the floor on your hands and knees (make sure the neighbors aren't watching) until you find the spot where the bass sounds the smoothest, and where each bass note has about the same volume and clarity. Avoid positions where some notes "hang" longer, and/or sound slower or thicker, than others. When you've determined where the bass sounds best, put the subwoofer there. Now, when you're back in the listening seat, the bass should sound smooth and natural.

Some general guidelines for subwoofer placement: Avoid putting the subwoofer the same distance from two walls. For example, if you have a 20'-wide room, don't put the subwoofer 10' from each wall. Similarly, don't put the subwoofer near a corner and equidistant from the side and rear walls. Instead, stagger the distances to each wall. This smoothes the bass because the frequencies being reinforced by the wall are staggered rather than coincident.

Put the subwoofer as close as possible to the listening position— right next to the couch, if possible. This placement provides you with more direct sound from the subwoofer and less sound that has been reflected around the room. You feel more of the dynamic impact in the bass when you sit in the direct path of the subwoofer's wave launch. The ideal situation is two subwoofers, one on either side of the listening position.

This placement isn't practical for most home-theater enthusiasts, however. You also have to consider the room's decor, and how to keep a large subwoofer cabinet out of the way. But I encourage you to experiment with different subwoofer locations. You'll be rewarded with much better overall sound.

Speaker Placement Summary

Each speaker in a home-theater system does a different job and therefore has different placement requirements. The dipolar surround speakers create a sense of diffusion and immersion, with assistance from room reflections behind the listener/viewer. Placing the surround speakers so that their sound is bounced off the walls before reaching the listener mimics the large array of surround speakers in a movie theater.

Conversely, reflected sound from the front speakers colors the sound and reduces your ability to clearly hear the all-important dialog. That's why we pull the left and right speakers slightly forward of the video monitor, and place the center-channel speaker flush with the front of the monitor.

The subwoofer's location largely determines the quantity and quality of bass you'll hear. Finding just the right spot for the sub by trial and error will give you lots of tight, well-controlled bass.

Configuring Your System for the Best Sound

Once your system is connected, you'll need to configure it for your particular room and speaker system. This is done through a series of menus or graphical icons generated by the A/V receiver or A/V controller and appearing on your video monitor. You use the receiver's remote control to make selections from the onscreen display. Every A/V receiver or controller includes instructions for setting up your system; the following section explains why you make certain selections, and in what circumstances.

When you turn on your system for the first time, don't be alarmed if you don't hear any sound when you expect to. (It usually happens to me when I first set up a product for review.) Don't turn up the volume to a high level and then start pushing buttons—when you push the right button, the sound will blast you out, possibly damaging your speakers, your amplifier or receiver, and/or your hearing. Turn the volume to a low level and make sure the correct source is selected. Check to make sure the MUTE and TAPE MONITOR buttons aren't pressed. The lack of sound is probably due to one of these three incorrect settings.

Bass Management

First, you must tell the A/V receiver or controller what kind of loudspeakers you have so it can direct bass appropriately. This is generally called *bass management*. Most of today's receivers ask you whether each of the speakers is LARGE or SMALL. By selecting SMALL for the left and right speakers, you're telling the receiver to keep low-bass signals out of those speakers. This configuration is used when you have a subwoofer connected to the system to reproduce low bass instead of the left and right speakers. You'll also need to answer YES when asked if the system includes a subwoofer. The bass-management option labeled "THX" in THX-certified products automatically sets all speakers to SMALL and engages the subwoofer.

If you have no subwoofer and full-range left and right speakers, answer LARGE in the setup menu when asked if the left and right speakers are LARGE or SMALL. The LARGE setting directs bass to the left and right speakers.

The setup menu will also ask if the surround speakers are LARGE or SMALL. Nearly every installation will use the small setting. Only if you have full-range, floorstanding speakers should you answer LARGE. (A home-theater system using full-range surround speakers is shown in fig.1-5.)

Setting the Center-Channel Mode

You'll also need to tell the receiver or controller whether you have a center speaker, and whether it is large or small. When the receiver is set to the LARGE position, the center speaker is fed a wide-bandwidth signal (one that includes bass as well as midrange and treble). The SMALL position filters bass from the signal driving the center speaker to avoid overloading it. Only full-range, floorstanding center speakers (such as those behind a perforated screen in a front-projection system) should use the LARGE setting. If you have a center speaker on top of or below your TV set, use the SMALL setting. Note that older receivers asked you to set the center channel to WIDE or NARROW. This term refers to the bandwidth of the signal driving it; that is, the WIDE setting sent a signal with bass to the center speaker, and the NARROW setting filtered bass from the center channel.

The center-channel mode will also offer you the options of PHANTOM or 3-CHANNEL LOGIC. Phantom mode is used if you have no center-channel speaker. Some products use the setting CENTER SPEAKER: NONE. If you're using a center-speaker, make sure the PHANTOM (or NONE) position isn't selected.

This is a good time to set the CENTER-CHANNEL DELAY control, if the receiver or controller is so equipped. As its name suggests, this adjustment lets you delay the signal going to the center speaker so that the sound from all three front speakers arrives at your ears at the same time. If you place the three front speakers in an arc, with the center speaker behind the left and right speakers, you won't need to add any center-channel delay. For precise setting of this control, measure the distance from your ears to each of the speakers when you're seated in the listening/viewing position. If you sit closer to the center speaker than to the left and right speakers, add some center-channel delay in increments of 1ms (one millisecond) per foot of distance. Sound travels about 1 foot in 1 millisecond.

Many receivers ask you to input the distance to each speaker, and the receiver calculates and applies the correct amount of delay to each speaker.

Surround-Channel Delay

Now that the receiver knows the basic configuration of your loudspeaker system, you're ready to start fine-tuning. As described in Chapter 2, all Dolby Pro Logic receivers and controllers slightly delay the signal to the surround speakers. This improves the apparent separation between front and rear sounds, and overcomes some of the limitations of the Dolby Surround format. This delay time is short, typically 20 milliseconds (20ms), or twenty thousandths of a second. Every receiver or controller with Dolby Pro Logic decoding allows you to adjust this surround delay time to match your listening room. The closer you sit to the surround speakers, the shorter the delay you should have.

Rather than asking you to INPUT DELAY TIME IN MILLISECONDS, many of today's friendlier receivers ask, HOW FAR ARE YOU SITTING FROM EACH

SPEAKER? The receiver then calculates the optimum delay time for your listening position.

Setting Individual Channel Levels

Next you'll need to individually set the loudness of each of the five channels (six if you're using a subwoofer), or seven channels in a system equipped with THX Surround EX decoding. In addition to providing an overall volume control, all A/V receivers provide adjustment of the individual channel volumes. This process begins by turning on the "test signal," a noise-like sound generated by the A/V receiver. (Dolby licensing requires that the receiver or controller incorporate this noise generator.) The noise is produced by each speaker in turn. Ideally, the noise signal's volume should be the same for each speaker when you're sitting at the listening/viewing position. If it isn't, you can adjust the volume of each speaker independently using the receiver's remote control. Individually adjusting the channels lets you compensate for different loudspeaker sensitivities, listening-room acoustics, and loudspeaker placements.

Although setting the individual channel levels by ear will get your system in the ballpark, a more precise calibration can be achieved by using a Sound Pressure Level (SPL) meter. Available from RadioShack for $29.95, an SPL meter lets you accurately calibrate your home-theater system. RadioShack offers digital and analog SPL meters; buy the easier-to-read analog type (catalog #33-2050). Switch the meter to the C-WEIGHTED position, SLOW RESPONSE, and set the knob to 70. Turn on the test noise on your A/V receiver and set each channel's volume until the meter's display reads 5. This indicates that the noise is being reproduced at a level of 75dB. Repeat this procedure for each channel.

A powered subwoofer usually has a knob on its back panel for setting loudness. When setting the subwoofer's level, the meter will be hard to read because the indicator will be jumping around (because it's reading a low frequency). Stare at the meter for a few minutes as it jumps to get an idea of where the average level is.

These settings will get you very close to the optimum volume for each channel, but you should use your ear and some well-recorded film soundtracks in making the final adjustment. If you find that dialog is hard to hear, a 2dB boost in the center-channel level will help bring it out (although the soundstage will be focused more in the center than spread out across the front of the room). If the bass is thumpy and boomy, turn down the subwoofer. Don't be afraid to adjust the volume of the subwoofer, center channel, or surround speakers—each movie soundtrack is mixed differently. You may find yourself slightly adjusting the surround- and center-channel levels at the beginning of each movie.

Although your ears should be the final judge when setting the individual channel levels, calibrating your system first with the SPL meter (or by ear with the test noise) will at least get you started from the right place. The most common mistakes in setting channel levels are too high a subwoofer level and too much volume from the surround speakers. The bass shouldn't dominate the overall sound, but instead serve as the foundation for music and effects. Many listeners think the more bass you hear, the more "impressive" the sound. In reality, a constantly droning bass is fatiguing, and robs the soundtrack of impact and surprise when the filmmakers *want* you to hear bass. Low frequencies are used as punctuation in a film soundtrack; by keeping the subwoofer level appropriate, you'll achieve a more accurate and satisfying sound than if the subwoofer is constantly droning away. Though it's understandable that you paid for this big box in your living room and you want to hear what it does, try to avoid the temptation to set the subwoofer level too high.

Similarly, listeners who have never had surround speakers in their homes think they should be aware of the surround speakers at all times. In truth, film soundtracks don't always contain signals in the surround channels; long stretches of the movie may have *nothing* in the surrounds. But even when a signal is driving the surround speakers, you should barely be aware of their presence. Remember, the surround channels provide a subtle ambience and envelopment. If you're consciously aware of the surround speakers because they're set too loud, the illusion they're supposed to be creating is diminished. Just as it's a temptation to set a subwoofer's level too high, don't turn up the surround speakers to the point where you hear them. You should also be aware that you won't hear *any* sound from the surround speakers unless the source program has been Dolby-encoded.

Other Adjustments

Some older A/V receivers and controllers provide a front-panel adjustment knob labeled INPUT LEVEL. Found only on products that perform Dolby Pro Logic decoding in the digital domain, the input-level adjustment sets the volume level going to the analog-to-digital converter built into the receiver. If the level fed to the A/D converter (from the analog audio outputs of a VHS machine, DSS dish, or laserdisc player, for examples) is too high, the sound will distort on loud peaks. If the level feeding the A/D converter is too low, the sound can be noisy. Setting just the right input level ensures that the A/D converter is operating in its optimum "window." To set the input-level adjustment (this is usually a front-panel knob), play a loud passage on a tape or disc from the source component selected on the receiver. A light next to the input-level knob will illuminate on peaks when the knob is turned up. Turn down the knob until the light doesn't come on during the loudest peaks. Don't set the level too low, however; the light should be just on the threshold of coming on when the input-level control is set just right.

Another feature you may have seen on A/V receivers and controllers is INPUT BALANCE. This control sets the balance between the Dolby-encoded left and right signals so that both channels are the same volume going into the Dolby decoder. When properly set, the input-balance control increases channel separation and prevents dialog from appearing in the left and right speakers instead of the center speaker. All of today's A/V receivers have an "automatic input balance" control that you don't need to set manually.

Configuring the DVD Player

Every DVD player has a set-up menu that allows you to configure the player for your particular system. The player will have certain default settings that may or may not be appropriate. Consequently, the system may behave in an unexpected way until you go into the set-up menu and configure the player.

Among these settings are whether your television or video display has a 4:3 or 16:9 aspect ratio (called TV TYPE). The default setting is 4:3. If you have a 16:9 display and don't change the DVD player's aspect ratio, widescreen films will be presented as 4:3, with the actors tall and skinny. The 4:3 setting invokes the DVD player's anamorphic downconversion circuit, which can soften the picture and introduce motion artifacts. If you have a 4:3 television, you'll be asked to make one other choice related to how you watch the picture—pan&scan or letterbox. In the pan&scan setting, the left and right picture edges will be cut off so that the picture fills your TV screen. In the letterbox setting, the film's original widescreen aspect ratio will be preserved, and you'll see horizontal black bars above and below the picture.

I strongly urge you to use the letterbox setting, which presents the film as the director and cinematographer framed it. I know that many people object to the black bars, and that they feel cheated if the picture doesn't fill the screen. But cutting off the picture edges to make it fit into the compromised 4:3 aspect ratio of a television set is a far worse distortion of the movie. When you're at the movie theater, you don't think the widescreen presentation is compromised because the top and bottom of the image are "cut off."

You'll also need to tell the DVD player that your receiver or A/V controller has Dolby Digital decoding (included on all current A/V receivers and controllers). This is because many DVD players are still set by factory default to output a Dolby Surround downmix derived from the Dolby Digital track on the DVD. Unless you make this adjustment, you'll never hear the discrete 5.1-channel Dolby Digital track. Similarly, many players require you, through the set-up menu, to turn on the player's DTS output. If you have an older A/V receiver without an integral Dolby Digital decoder, however, you'll have to be sure that the player's digital output is set to deliver a Dolby Digital bitstream instead of a PCM bitstream.

The Parental Control feature allows you to prohibit the DVD player from playing discs with MPAA ratings stricter than those you set. For example, if you set the Parental Control level to 6 (which corresponds to an MPAA rating of R), the player won' t play titles rated NC-17. A password system prevents unauthorized adjustment of the Parental Control level. Note that some DVD titles ask you in their disc menus whether you want to watch the R or NC-17 versions of the film. If R is selected, the player seamlessly skips certain scenes.

The DVD player's set-up menu also provides video processing adjustments, including a selection that allows the player to pass parts of the video signal that are "blacker than black."

When to Use Different Surround Modes

Most A/V receivers and controllers offer several "surround modes" that supposedly simulate the acoustic characters of different acoustic environments: STADIUM, ROCK CLUB, and HALL, for examples. An additional setting on the A/V receiver may be marked DIRECT or BYPASS to indicate that the receiver isn't performing any surround-mode manipulation.

Here's my advice on surround modes: Select Dolby Pro Logic (or Dolby Digital, or DTS) for watching movies, and DIRECT for listening to music. Forget about all the other surround modes. They are, in my view, a departure from musical reality, and degrade sound quality. They are more gimmickry than real enhancements. Lexicon's Logic 7 and Dolby Pro Logic II are notable exceptions.

It's important to change surround modes when you switch from movie watching to music listening. Let's say you watched a movie one night and had Dolby Pro Logic decoding engaged, along with THX processing. The next day you turn on your receiver to listen to a CD. Many receivers will still be set to the Pro Logic and THX processing circuits, and thus degrade the sound of your music-only CD. The music wasn't originally encoded with Dolby Surround, and it doesn't need THX processing, so it should be played back without these circuits. The solution is to always select the DIRECT or BYPASS mode when you switch the input to CD, then select Dolby Pro Logic and THX processing (if the receiver is THX-equipped) for movie watching.

Some receivers automatically change surround mode when you switch sources. If you don't have this automatic switching feature, be sure to perform it yourself for the best possible sound.

Troubleshooting Guide: What to do When Things Don't Work

You've made all the right connections, turned all the equipment on, put a DVD in the player and . . . no sound or picture. That scenario is the rule rather than the exception, even among professional reviewers after making the initial hook-ups. This section will guide you through the most common problems—and ways to solve them—in setting up home-theater systems.

1) No sound. This is by far the most common problem when turning on the system for the first time. Before you do anything else, turn the volume down to a low level (that is, turn the volume control nearly fully counterclockwise). This will prevent a huge blast of sound from your speakers when you eventually push the button that causes the receiver to output audio.

To determine whether the problem is fundamental to the whole system or affects only one source component, turn the receiver's source selector button to the FM tuner position. Be sure you have an antenna connected to the receiver. If you hear sound (even the hiss between radio stations), you know that the speakers are connected and working. If the receiver has a front-panel SPEAKERS A/B switch, be sure that "A" is selected. If you still don't hear any sound, make sure the left and right speaker cables are properly connected to the left and right "A" output terminals. (Note that when the receiver is in STEREO mode, you'll hear sound only from the front left and right speakers.) Make sure the receiver's MUTE switch isn't on. Make sure receiver's TAPE MONITOR button isn't engaged.

Once you know the receiver is producing sound with FM signals from the left and right speakers, put a DVD in the DVD player and start it playing. Use the DVD's main menu to select LANGUAGES or AUDIO SET-UP. If given a choice between Dolby Surround and Dolby Digital, select Dolby Digital (provided your receiver has Dolby Digital decoding). Early DVDs defaulted to outputting a Dolby Surround signal, because that was the surround-sound format in most homes before Dolby Digital decoding became ubiquitous. Start the disc playing, then use the chapter skip buttons to get a few minutes into the movie. The DVD player should now be outputting a Dolby Digital bitstream that your receiver will lock onto, decode, and output to the speakers.

Use the receiver's input selector to select the DVD input. If you still hear no sound, follow the cable from the DVD player's AUDIO OUTPUT jack to the DIGITAL INPUT on the receiver. Make sure that the input name on the rear panel (DVD, Video 1, for examples) matches the input name on the front panel that you've selected with the receiver's input-selector buttons or knob.

Some A/V receivers and controllers have "assignable" digital inputs. This means that any digital input can be linked to any of the receiver's audio/video inputs (Video 1, Video 2, Video 3, DVD, etc.). Go in the receiver's set-up menu and make sure that the rear-panel digital-audio input marked DVD is actually assigned to the DVD A/V input.

2) No picture. Trace the video output cables from the DVD player to the receiver, and make sure the receiver's MONITOR OUTPUT jack is connected to the television. Verify that the television's input selector is set to the input to which the MONITOR OUTPUT cable is connected (Video 1, Video 2, etc.). Be certain that the A/V receiver's input selector switch or knob is selecting the input to which the DVD player is connected. If you still get no picture, bypass the A/V receiver by running a video cable directly from the DVD player to the television.

If you're trying to get a picture from an antenna or cable, press the VCR's "TV/VCR" switch.

Most receivers won't convert composite video to S-video. If you have S-video cables connecting source components to the receiver, run an S-video cable from the receiver's MONITOR OUTPUT jack to the television.

3) The receiver's Dolby Digital light doesn't come on when I play a DVD. There are three possible causes. The first possibility is that the receiver's surround-mode setting is incorrect. Set the receiver's surround mode to CINEMA, MOVIE, THEATER, or a mode with a similar name. Second, the sound on the DVD during the opening studio logo and accompanying the disc's menu may be in Dolby Surround, not Dolby Digital. Skip to a point within the movie and see if the receiver recognizes the Dolby Digital signal. If that doesn't work, go in the DVD player's set-up menu and make sure that you've set the Downmix control to DOLBY DIGITAL or AC-3 (AC-3 is an older name for Dolby Digital). Check that the digital output is set to DOLBY DIGITAL or AC-3, not PCM.

4) The receiver's DTS light doesn't come on when I play a DTS disc, or I hear a burst of noise. Make sure the DVD player can output a DTS signal (all players made after early 2000 can), and that your A/V receiver has built-in DTS decoding. Look for the DTS logos on both the DVD player and A/V receiver. Next, turn on the DVD player's DTS output in the player's set-up menu.

5) I can't hear the center or surround speakers. The center and surround speakers produce sound only with surround-encoded sources (Dolby Surround on VHS tapes, Dolby Digital or DTS on DVD, etc.), and when the receiver's surround mode is set for surround decoding. You won't hear sound from the center or surround speakers if the A/V receiver is set to STEREO. In addition, films don't always contain sounds in the surround channels. The best way to determine if all speakers are working is to engage the test signal used in calibrating each channel's level, or a test DVD with special speaker-testing signals, such as the *AVIA Guide to Home Theater*.

6) One channel isn't working. With A/V receivers, the most likely culprit is a loose speaker cable. If you use bare wire, be sure that stray strands are not shorting the positive and negative speaker terminals. If you have a separate A/V controller and power amplifier, check that the RCA cables between the two components are pushed all the way into the jacks.

7) The optical digital-audio cable won't fit in the DVD player's optical jack. Optical jacks that carry digital audio (called TosLink) are fitted with dummy plugs to prevent dust from getting inside them and blocking the transmission of light. Remove the dummy plug.

8) There's an audible hum coming from my speakers. Make sure that all RCA cables are inserted all the way into their jacks. Try plugging the receiver's AC cord into a different outlet. If you have cable TV, momentarily disconnect the cable coming into your house from your cable box or VCR. If the hum stops when the cable is disconnected, you need a ground isolator described in Chapter 8. If the problem persists, see the section in Chapter 8 on ground loops for a possible solution.

9) I can't see the on-screen display. Some A/V receivers have two video monitor output jacks, one with an on-screen display, one without. Make sure your video monitor is connected to the output with an on-screen display. Also, be sure your receiver offers an on-screen display; some do not.

10) My A/V receiver shuts off an hour into the movie. Receivers and power amplifiers have protection circuits that monitor the temperature of the output transistors and shut down the receiver or amplifier if it is overdriven. This situation is most likely to occur with low-sensitivity speakers, low-impedance speakers (4 ohms), low-powered receivers, large rooms (which require more amplifier power to generate high volumes of sound than do small rooms), and loud action movies that put a greater demand on an amplifier. After the receiver cools, you'll be able to turn it on again. The long-term solution is to listen at a lower level, get more sensitive speakers, or buy a new receiver. Also try providing better ventilation around the receiver, or even a cooling fan if the receiver is in a cabinet.

11) The actors are tall and skinny. There are two possible causes. First, the DVD player may be set to "16:9" in the TV Type selection of the player's set-up menu, and you are watching a 4:3 television. Go in the DVD player's set-up menu and select "4:3."

Second, some HD-Ready 4:3 televisions have a "raster compression" feature than vertically compresses the raster (the entire illuminated picture area) so it can display widescreen images with no loss of vertical resolution. (All the available scanning lines are in the actual picture area, with none wasted "drawing" the horizontal black bars above and below the image.) If you're watching an anamorphic DVD and don't turn on the raster compression feature, the picture will be too tall.

12) It's hard to hear the dialogue. Position the center speaker flush with the front of the television for maximum clarity as described earlier in this chapter. Boost the center-channel level by 1-2dB. This adjustment can be made in the receiver's Speaker Level menu, or sometimes directly from the remote control.

13) Music sounds unnatural. Turn off surround-sound processing and listen in straight stereo mode.

14) The bass is thumpy and annoying. Use the subwoofer set-up and positioning guidelines described earlier in this chapter.

15) The sound is hollow and distant. Turn off the STADIUM or CHURCH surround-processing modes.

16) The sound distorts or crackles at high volume. The speakers are being overdriven. Turn down the volume or buy speakers with greater power handling. These symptoms can also indicate that the amplifier is running out of power. Again, the solution is to turn down the volume, buy speakers with higher sensitivity, or buy an A/V receiver with more output power. If your system has no powered subwoofer, add one. This relieves the left and right speakers from the burden of reproducing low bass, which greatly increases their power-handling capacity and ability to play loudly without distortion. It also relieves the receiver of having to deliver the power to reproduce low bass; that job is now handled by the subwoofer's amplifier.

17) I hear a popping sound from the subwoofer. When the subwoofer is overdriven, the back of the voice coil (a coil around a bobbin attached to the cone) hits the magnet, making a popping sound (called "bottoming out"). Reduce the signal level driving the subwoofer, either though the speaker-level adjustments in the A/V receiver, or by turning down the subwoofer's rear-panel LEVEL control.

Custom Installation and Automated System Control

One alternative to figuring out how to set up and run your system is to have your equipment installed and set up by a custom installer. You simply pick the products you want, and the custom installer does the rest. You can even take the next step of putting your system under automated control. Rather than use the remote controls supplied with your home-theater products, an automated controller lets you run the system with a single, easy-to-use remote control. An automated system controller executes many commands with a single button-push. For example, if you want to watch a movie on DVD, pushing one button powers up the entire system, selects the DVD input on your receiver or controller, sets the appropriate surround mode, puts the volume control at your favorite setting, and can even dim the lights and bring down a motorized projection screen. An automated controller must be programmed by the custom installer for your particular system. Although an automated system's "one-touch operation" is much easier to use than the remote controls supplied with A/V products, an automated system can add more than a thousand dollars to a home-theater system's price.

Sit Back and Enjoy

If you've followed this book from start to finish, congratulations. You now have a good understanding of home-theater technology, products, and system setup. I hope you've chosen your system wisely, and configured it for the best possible performance.

But now that the work is over, I have one final, but important, piece of advice. When the lights dim and the first scene rolls up, forget about the home-theater technology, products, and system setup you've just been studying. All that has been the means to the end of experiencing the magic of storytelling through the medium of film. Don't let the *equipment* become the end.

Although you should use your newfound skill and knowledge in critically evaluating your system so you can fine-tune it, draw the distinction between listening/viewing for critical evaluation and listening/viewing for pleasure. Once the movie starts, let the technology disappear. It's time to sit back and enjoy.

Glossary

A/B comparison A back-and-forth listening comparison between two musical presentations, A and B.

AC line-conditioner/protector A device that filters noise from the AC powerline and isolates equipment from voltage spikes and surges. Some AC line-conditioners/protectors also protect equipment from lightning strokes. Home-theater equipment is plugged into the AC line-conditioner/protector, and the conditioner is plugged into the wall.

acoustic absorber Any material that absorbs sound, such as carpet, drapes, and thickly upholstered furniture.

acoustic diffuser Any material that scatters sound.

acoustics The science of sound behavior. Also refers to a room; i.e., "This room has good acoustics."

AC-3 Another name for Dolby Digital, the 5.1-channel discrete digital surround-sound format. (see "Dolby Digital")

active subwoofer A speaker designed to reproduce only low frequencies that includes an integral power amplifier to drive the speaker.

ADC see "analog-to-digital converter"

adjacent-channel selectivity Tuner specification that describes a tuner's ability to reject radio stations adjacent to the desired station.

Advanced Television System Committee (ATSC) Group that set the transmission and format standards for digital television.

alternate-channel selectivity Tuner specification describing a tuner's ability to reject stations two channels away from the desired station.

ambiance Spatial aspects of a film soundtrack that create a sense of size and atmosphere, usually reproduced by the surround speakers.

ampere Unit of electrical current, abbreviated A.

analog An analog signal is one in which the varying voltage is an analog of the acoustical waveform; i.e., it is continuously variable. Contrasted with a digital signal, in which binary ones and zeros represent audio or video information.

analog-to-digital converter (A/D) A circuit that converts an analog signal to a digital signal. All A/V receivers and A/V controllers that perform Dolby Pro Logic decoding in the digital domain have a pair of analog-to-digital converters.

anamorphic A film or video format in which a widescreen image has been "squeezed" horizontally (either with lenses or by digital manipulation) to fit a standard 4:3 aspect ratio. Correct picture geometry is restored on playback by "unsqueezing" the image into its original aspect ratio. The anamorphic format delivers the correct aspect ratio without sacrificing resolution.

aspect ratio The width-to-height ratio of a visual image. Standard television sets have an aspect ratio of 4:3 (1.33:1). Widescreen television sets (and HDTV sets) have an aspect ratio of 16:9 (1.78:1).

aspect-ratio control A feature in some HD-ready televisions that allows you to manually adjust the aspect ratio.

atmosphere see "ambiance"

ATSC see "Advanced Television System Committee"

A/V Short for audio/video. Identifies a component or system as one that processes video as well as audio signals.

AV/C Audio-Video Control, a simple FireWire-based technology for controlling the components in a home-theater system as a single unit with one remote control.

A/V input An input on an A/V receiver or controller that includes both audio and video jacks.

A/V loop An A/V input and A/V output pair found on all A/V receivers and controllers. Used to connect a component that records as well as plays back audio and video signals. A VCR is connected to a receiver's or controller's A/V loop.

A/V preamplifier Also called by its more descriptive name of an "A/V controller," the A/V preamplifier is a component that lets you control the playback volume, select which source you want to watch, and performs surround decoding.

A/V preamplifier/tuner An A/V preamplifier that includes, in the same chassis, an AM or FM tuner for receiving radio broadcasts.

A/V receiver The central component of a home-theater system; receives signals from source components, selects which signal you watch and listen to, controls the playback volume, performs surround decoding, receives radio broadcasts, and amplifies signals to drive a home-theater loudspeaker system. Also called a "surround receiver."

baffle The front surface of a loudspeaker, on which the drivers are mounted.

balanced cable A cable that carries a balanced signal on three conductors. Contrast with unbalanced (or "single-ended") cable.

balanced output A connector on some A/V products that presents the audio signal on three conductors, rather than the two conductors of an unbalanced output. Balanced outputs appear on XLR jacks. Found only on high-end products.

banana jack A small tubular connector found on A/V receivers and power amplifiers for connecting speaker cables terminated with banana plugs.

banana plug A common speaker-cable termination that fits into a banana jack.

bandwidth The range of frequencies that a device can process or pass. For example, the surround channel of Dolby Surround has a bandwidth of 100Hz–7kHz. The channel passes only the frequencies between 100Hz (a bass frequency) and 7kHz (a low treble frequency). The human ear has a bandwidth of 20Hz–20kHz.

bass Sounds in the low audio range, generally 20Hz–300Hz.

bass extension The lowest frequency an audio system will reproduce. A measure of how deeply an audio system or loudspeaker will reproduce bass. For example, a small subwoofer may have bass extension to 40Hz. A large subwoofer may have bass extension to 16Hz.

bass management A combination of controls and circuits in an A/V receiver or controller that determines which speakers receive bass signals.

bass reflex A speaker with a hole or slot in the cabinet that allows sound inside the cabinet to emerge into the listening room. Bass-reflex speakers have deeper bass extension than speakers with sealed cabinets, but that bass is generally less tightly controlled.

bi-amping Using two power amplifiers to drive one loudspeaker. One amplifier typically drives the woofer, the second drives the midrange and tweeter.

big screen A large-screen direct-view television set or rear-projection set. Usually reserved for sets with diagonal dimensions greater than 40".

binding post A connection on receivers and power amplifier for attaching loudspeaker cables.

bipolar speaker A speaker that produces sound equally from the front and the back. Unlike the di-polar speaker, the bipolar's front and rear soundwaves are in-phase with each other.

bit-rate The number of bits per second stored or transmitted by a digital audio or digital video signal. For example, the bit rate of Dolby Digital is 384kbs (384,000 bits per second) or 448kbs. MPEG-2 video encoding produces a digital video signal with a variable bit rate that averages about 3.5Mbs (3.5 million bits per second). Higher bit rates translate to better audio and/or video quality.

bi-wire Connecting a loudspeaker to a receiver or power amplifier with two runs of cable to each of the positive and negative terminals. Possible only with speakers featuring two pairs of input terminals. Bi-wiring results in better sound than single-wiring.

black drop The black masking area above and below a screen used with a front-projection system.

blacker than black Information in a video signal that falls below the technical threshold of black, 7.5 IRE. Some DVD players pass signals that are blacker than black; others do not.

black level Technically, the video level that produces black in a video display. Commonly, "black level" refers to a video display's ability to present the color black as truly black and not as dark gray.

bridging Amplifier-to-loudspeaker connection method that converts a stereo amplifier into a monoblock power amplifier. One amplifier channel amplifies the positive half of the waveform, the other channel amplifies the negative half. The loudspeaker is connected as the "bridge" between the two amplifier channels.

brightness In audio, an excessive amount of treble that adds a shrillness to the sound. In video, the amount of light generated by a video display device.

brightness signal More correctly called "luminance" and represented by the letter Y, the brightness component of a video signal contains all the black-and-white information. A color video signal is a combination of luminance and chrominance (color information).

calibration The act of fine-tuning an audio or video component for correct performance. In an audio system, calibration includes setting the individual channel levels. In video, calibration means setting a video display device to display the correct color, brightness, tint, contrast, and other parameters.

cathode ray tube see "CRT"

CAV laserdisc A laserdisc recorded with Constant Angular Velocity, meaning that the disc spins at a constant speed regardless of where on the disc the playback laser is reading. Also called a "standard play" laserdisc because it can store 30 minutes of video per disc side.

center channel In a multichannel audio system, the audio channel that carries information that will be reproduced by a speaker placed in the center of the viewing room between the left and right speakers. The center channel carries nearly all of a film's dialog.

center-channel mode A setting on A/V receivers and A/V controllers that configures the receiver or controller for the type of center-channel speaker in the system.

center-channel speaker The speaker in a home-theater system located on top of, beneath, or behind the visual image; reproduces center-channel information such as dialog and other sounds associated with onscreen action.

channel balance The relative levels or volumes of the different channels in a home-theater system. Also describes the relative difference between the left and right signals in a Dolby-encoded signal, which can be adjusted on some A/V receivers and A/V controllers to optimize Dolby decoding.

channel separation A measure of how well sounds in one channel are isolated from other channels. Low channel separation results in sounds from one channel "leaking" into other channels. A classic example is front-channel sounds in Dolby Surround leaking into the surround channels. High channel separation results in more precise placement of sounds.

chapter stop A marker on laserdiscs or DVDs that provides a search point for randomly accessing that point on the disc. Key scenes in movies are marked with chapter stops, as are individual songs in concert videos. Chapter stops are accessed by the CHAPTER SEARCH button on a laserdisc player's remote control.

chrominance (chroma) The color-carrying portion of a video signal. The chroma signal carries color and hue, but no brightness information.

Class-A Mode of amplifier operation in which a transistor or tube amplifies the entire audio signal.

Class-B Mode of amplifier operation in which one tube or transistor amplifies the positive half of an audio signal, and a second tube or transistor amplifies the negative half.

CLV laserdisc A laserdisc recorded with Constant Linear Velocity, meaning the disc changes speed depending on where on the disc the playback laser is reading. CLV discs spin more slowly when the laser is reading at the outer radius, and faster when the laser is reading at the inner radius, thus maintaining a constant velocity as seen by the playback laser. Also called "Extended Play" laserdiscs because they can store one hour of video per disc side.

coaxial cable A cable in which an inner conductor is surrounded by a braided conductor that acts as a shield. Coaxial cable is used between a TV antenna and a VCR or TV, between a DSS dish and a DSS receiver, and between a VCR and a TV set.

coaxial digital output A jack found on some laserdisc players that provides a digital audio signal on an RCA jack for connection to another component through a coaxial digital interconnect (which is different from the coaxial cable that carries TV signals).

coloration A change in sound introduced by a component in an audio system. A loudspeaker that is "colored" doesn't accurately reproduce the signal fed to it. A speaker with coloration may have too much bass and not enough treble.

color uniformity The ability of a projection screen to reflect all colors equally at every point in screen. Also called spectral response. A screen with poor color uniformity may impart a blue tint to the image on one side of the screen, and a red tint on the other side.

comb filter A circuit that splits up a composite video into separate color and brightness signals.

component video A video signal split into three parts: luminance, and two color-difference signals (technically known as Y, B–Y, R–Y, or YPbPr). A vastly superior method of connecting video than composite video. Better-quality DVD players have component-video output; when connected to video display devices with component-video input, the result is potentially stunning picture quality.

component-video switching A feature on A/V controllers and receivers that allow you to connect several component-video sources to the controller or receiver, with the controller or receiver switching one of those input signals to the video display.

composite video A video signal in which the luminance (brightness, or black-and-white) information and the chrominance (color) information are combined into a single signal. Composite video inputs and outputs appear on RCA jacks.

cone The paper or plastic diaphragm of a loudspeaker that moves back and forth to create sound.

congested A thickening of the sound that makes instrumental images less separate and distinct.

contrast The range between white and black in an image.

controller Another term for an A/V preamplifier.

convergence The integration of various technologies, such as digital video, digital audio, computers, and the Internet.

crossover A circuit that splits up the frequency spectrum into two or more parts. Crossovers are found in virtually all loudspeakers, and in some A/V receivers and A/V controllers.

crossover frequency The frequency at which the audio spectrum is split. A subwoofer with a crossover frequency of 80Hz filters all information above 80Hz from the signal driving the subwoofer, and all information below 80Hz from the signal driving the main speakers.

crossover slope Describes the steepness of a crossover filter. Expressed as "xdB/octave." For example, a subwoofer with a crossover frequency of 80Hz and a slope of 6dB/octave would allow audio frequencies at 160Hz (an octave above 80Hz) into the subwoofer, but signals at 160Hz would be reduced in amplitude by 6dB. A slope of 12dB/octave would also allow 160Hz into the subwoofer, but the amplitude would be reduced by 12dB. The most common crossover slopes are 12dB/octave, 18dB/octave, and 24dB/octave. Crossover slopes are also referred to as "first-order" (6dB/octave), "second-order" (12dB/octave), "third-order" (18dB/octave), and "fourth-order" (24dB/octave). The "steeper" slopes (such as 24dB/octave) split the frequency spectrum more sharply and produce less overlap between the two frequency bands.

crosstalk see "channel separation"

CRT Cathode Ray Tube. A vacuum tube in which electrons are fired at a screen coated with phosphors that give off light when struck to produce a visible pattern (a picture). Direct-view television sets use a large CRT. Some front-projectors use three small CRTs to project an image.

current The flow of electrons in a conductor. For example, a power amplifier "pushes" electrical current through speaker cables and the voice coils in a loudspeaker to make them move back and forth.

cutoff frequency see "crossover frequency"

DAC see "digital-to-analog converter"

data compression see "perceptual coding"

dB see "decibel"

DC (Direct Current) Flow of electrons that remains steady rather than fluctuating. Contrasted with alternating current (AC).

decibel The standard unit for expressing relative power or amplitude levels. Abbreviated dB.

deinterlacing Technique of converting an interlaced video image to a progressive video image. Also called a "line doubler."

depth The impression of instruments, voices, or sounds existing behind one another in three dimensions, as in "soundstage depth."

dialog intelligibility The ability to clearly hear and understand the dialog in a movie without strain. Dialog intelligibility is affected by the quality of components in a home-theater system, room acoustics, and how the system is set up.

diaphragm The surface of a loudspeaker driver that moves, creating sound.

diffraction The bending of soundwaves as they pass around an object. Also a re-radiation of sound caused by discontinuities in surfaces near the radiating device, such as the bolts securing drivers to a speaker cabinet.

diffusion Scattering of sound. Diffusion reduces the sense of direction of sounds, which benefits sound produced by surround loudspeakers.

digital Calculation or representation by discrete units. For example, digital audio and digital video can be represented by a series of binary ones and zeros.

Digital Light Processing (DLP) A technology developed by Texas Instruments that reflects light from hundreds of thousands of tiny mirrors on a semiconductor chip to project an image. Also called "Digital Micromirror Device."

digital loudspeaker Loudspeaker incorporating a digital crossover and power amplifiers. A digital loudspeaker takes in a digital bitstream, splits up the frequency spectrum with digital signal processing, converts each of those signals to analog, and amplifies them separately. The individual power amplifiers then power each of the loudspeaker's drive units.

Digital Micromirror Device (DMD) see "Digital Light Processing"

digital power amplifier An amplifier that takes in digital signals and converts them to analog as part of the amplification process.

digital satellite system (DSS) A method of delivering high-quality digital video into consumers' homes via an 18" roof-mounted dish.

digital signal processing (DSP) Manipulation of audio or video signals by performing mathematical functions on the digitally encoded signal.

digital television see "DTV"

Digital Theater Systems (DTS) A discrete, digital surround-sound format used in movie theaters and some home-theater systems. A better-sounding alternative to Dolby Digital. DTS provides either 5.1 or 7.1 audio channels. Also called "DTS Digital Surround."

digital-to-analog converter (DAC, D/A) A device that converts digital audio signals to analog audio signals. CD players, laserdisc players, DSS boxes, and DVD machines all contain digital-to-analog converters.

Digital Transmission Content Protection (DTCP) An encryption technology that allows transmission of digital video and digital audio between components in a home-theater system, but prohibits those signals from being recorded. Used with FireWire (IEEE1394).

Digital Visual Interface (DVI) A wideband digital video interface that can carry uncompressed high-definition video, digital audio, and control signals in the same cable. DVI is appearing on an increasing number of products.

D-ILA Digital-Image Light Amplifier, a video display technology used in rear-projection televisions and front projectors.

dipolar speaker A loudspeaker that produces sound from the rear as well as from the front, with the front and rear sounds out-of-phase with each other. Dipoles are most often used as surround speakers.

direct current see "DC"

Director's cut A version of a film re-edited by the director for a premium consumer release.

Direct Stream Digital (DSD) Method of digitally encoding music with a very fast sampling rate, but with only 1-bit quantization. Developed by Sony and Philips for the Super Audio CD (SACD).

direct-view Another name for a conventional television set. Called direct-view because you view the image directly on the front of its picture tube.

discrete Separate. A discrete digital surround-sound format contains 5.1 channels of audio information that are completely separate from each other; contrasted with a matrixed surround format such as Dolby Surround, which mixes the channels together for transmission or storage.

dispersion The directional pattern over which a loudspeaker distributes its sound.

DLP see "Digital Light Processing"

DMD see "Digital Light Processing"

Dolby Digital A 5.1-channel discrete digital surround-sound format used in movie theaters and consumer formats. The surround format used on DVD and HDTV.

Dolby Digital EX A surround-sound format that matrix encodes a third "back surround" channel into the left and right surround channels of a 5.1-channel Dolby Digital signal. This back surround channel is reproduced by one or two loudspeakers located directly behind the listening position. Although Dolby Digital EX is the format's official name, it's often called THX Surround EX because THX was the exclusive licensor of the technology until late 2001. Jointly developed by Lucasfilm THX and Dolby Laboratories.

Dolby Pro Logic A type of Dolby Surround decoder with improved performance over standard Dolby Surround decoding. Specifically, Pro Logic decoding provides greater channel separation and a center-speaker output. A Dolby Pro Logic decoder takes in a 2-channel, Dolby Surround–encoded audio signal and splits those signals up into left, center, right, and surround channels. Nearly all A/V receivers and A/V controllers include Dolby Pro Logic decoders.

Dolby Pro Logic II Introduced in late 2001, Pro Logic II provides superior decoding of two-channel music and film sources compared with Pro Logic.

Dolby Surround An encoding format that combines four channels (left, center, right, surround) into two channels for transmission or storage. On playback, a Dolby Pro Logic decoder separates the two channels back into four channels.

downmix converter A circuit found in DVD players that converts the 5.1-channel discrete Dolby Digital soundtrack into a 2-channel Dolby Surround–encoded signal. A DVD player's downmix converter lets you hear surround sound from DVD if you don't have a Dolby Digital decoder.

driver The actual speaker units inside a loudspeaker cabinet.

DSD see "Direct Stream Digital"

DSP see "Digital Signal Processing"

DSP room correction Technique of removing room-induced frequency-response peaks and dips with digital signal processing.

DSS see "Digital Satellite System"

D-Theater Copy-protection system proposed for the D-VHS digital video recording format.

DTS see "Digital Theater Systems"

DTS-ES Discrete A 6.1-channel surround-sound format that includes a rear surround channel in addition to the conventional 5.1 channels. Called "discrete" because the rear surround channel is completely separate from the left and right surround channels, unlike DTS ES Matrix, which matrix-encodes the third surround channel into the existing left and right surround channels of a 5.1-channel signal.

DTS-ES Matrix A 5.1-channel surround-sound format that includes a rear surround channel that is matrix-encoded into the left and right surround channels of a 5.1-channel signal. Unlike DTS ES Discrete, DTS ES Matrix is not a true 6.1-channel format because the soundtrack is carried in 5.1 channels.

DTS Neo:6 Cinema A DTS decoding technology for playing back two-channel film-soundtrack sources (such as television broadcasts and the stereo audio channels from a VCR) through 5.1 or 7.1 loudspeakers.

DTS Neo:6 Music A DTS decoding technology for playing back two-channel music sources (such as stereo CDs and FM radio) through 5.1 or 7.1 loudspeakers.

DTV Digital Television. Method of encoding and transmitting video as a stream of ones and zeros, rather than as an analog signal.

DV A digital video interface format used primarily on camcorders. A simplified version of FireWire (IEEE1394).

DVD A format that puts MPEG-2–encoded digital video and Dolby Digital surround-sound audio on a disc the size of a CD.

DVD-Audio DVD-format disc containing high-resolution multichannel digital audio or 2-channel digital audio.

DVD-R A write-once recordable DVD format.

DVD-RW A re-writable DVD recording format.

DVD+R A write-once recordable DVD format that is incompatible with DVD-R and DVD-RW

DVD+RW A re-writable DVD format that is incompatible with DVD-R and DVD-RW

D-VHS Digital video recording format that uses a conventional VHS tape shell. D-VHS can store up to four hours of high-definition video on one tape.

DVI see "Digital Visual Interface"

dynamic range In audio, the difference in volume between loud and soft. In video, the difference in light level between black and white (also called "contrast").

dynamic range compressor A circuit found in some Dolby Digital–equipped receivers and controllers that reduces dynamic range. A dynamic range compressor can reduce the volume of peaks, or increase the volume of low-level sounds, or both. Useful for late-night listening when you don't want explosions to disturb other family members, but still want to hear low-level sounds clearly.

equalizer A circuit that changes the tonal balance of an audio program. Bass and treble controls are a form of equalizer.

excursion The amount of back-and-forth movement of a loudspeaker cone

false contouring A picture distortion in plasma panels in which dark areas appear as blotches

FireWire A wideband digital interface that can carry digital audio, digital video, computer data, and control codes in a single cable composed of three twisted pairs of wires.

5C see Digital Transmission Content Protection

5.1 channels The standard number of channels for encoding film soundtracks. The five channels are left, center, right, surround left, and surround right. The ".1" channel is a 100Hz-bandwidth channel reserved for bass effects.

5.1-channel ready An A/V receiver or controller with six discrete inputs that will accept the six discrete outputs from a Dolby Digital or DTS decoder. This feature allows you to add discrete digital decoding to a receiver or controller.

fixed-pixel display A video display device that uses an array of fixed pixels to create the image. Examples include LCD, DLP, D-ILA, LCoS, and plasma panels. Contrast with a CRT-based display that has no fixed pixel structure.

fixed-pixel scaler An image scaler that outputs only a single resolution to a fixed-pixel display. A range of output resolutions is unnecessary because the output resolution is factory set for the display with which the scaler is used.

flat A speaker that accurately reproduces the signal fed to it is called "flat" because that is the shape of its frequency-response curve.

floorstanding speaker A speaker that sits on the floor rather than on a stand.

Foley Sound effects added to a film soundtrack, such as footsteps and doors closing.

foot-lambert Measure of amount of light reflected from a projection screen. Abbreviated fL.

forward A description of a sonic presentation in which sounds seem to be projected forward, toward the listener.

frame One complete picture in video. The NTSC television picture is composed of 29.97 frames per second. Half a frame is called a "field."

frequency Number of repetitions of a cycle per second. Measured in Hertz (Hz), or cycles, per second. An audio signal with a frequency of 1000Hz (1kHz) undergoes 1000 cycles of a sinewave per second.

frequency response A graphical representation showing a device's relative amplitude as a function of frequency.

front-projector A video display device that projects an image from a distance onto a separate screen.

full-range speaker A speaker that reproduces bass as well as midrange and treble frequencies.

gain see "screen gain"

HAVi Home Audio/Video interoperability, a FireWire-based technology for controlling various components of a home-theater system as a single unit with one remote control. This "interoperability" is possible because the FireWire interface carries control data along with digital audio and video in the same cable.

harmonic distortion The production of spurious frequencies at multiples of the original frequency. A circuit amplifying a 1kHz sinewave will create frequencies at 2kHz (second harmonic), 3kHz (third harmonic), and so forth.

HDCP see High-Definition Content Protection

HDTV High Definition Television. A new digital video transmission system introduced in North America in 1998. HDTV will eventually replace the NTSC video system in use since 1953.

Hertz (Hz) The unit of frequency; the number of cycles per second. Kilohertz (kHz) is thousands of cycles per second.

HiFi Short for High Fidelity, the high-quality audio format used in some VHS machines. A VHS HiFi VCR can provide excellent sound quality. Contrasted with VHS linear tracks, which offer poor sound quality.

High-Definition Content Protection (HDCP) An encryption technique that allows transmission of digital video and digital audio between components in a home-theater system, but prohibits those signals from being recorded. Used with the DVI interface.

high definition television see "HDTV"

high-density layer The information layer in a Super Audio CD that contains high-resolution digital audio.

high-pass filter A circuit that allows high frequencies to pass, but blocks low frequencies. Also called a "low-cut filter." High-pass filters are often found in A/V receivers and A/V controllers to keep bass out of the front speakers when you're using a subwoofer.

high-resolution digital audio Generally regarded as digital audio with a sampling rate greater than 48kHz and a word length longer than 16 bits.

home theater The combination of high-quality sound and video in your home.

Home THX A set of patents, technologies, and playback standards for reproducing film soundtracks in the home. THX doesn't compete with surround formats such as Dolby Pro Logic or Dolby Digital, but instead builds on them.

horizontal resolution A number that specifies the amount of fine detail a video display can show (or a video format can contain) per horizontal scanning line. In analog formats such as VHS tape and CRT-based television sets, horizontal resolution is expressed in TV Lines (TVL). In digital formats and fixed-pixel display devices, horizontal resolution is expressed in the number of pixel per horizontal line of video. For examples, VHS has a horizontal resolution of 240 TVL; DVD has a horizontal resolution of 720 pixels; and HDTV's maximum horizontal resolution is 1920 pixels. Technically, horizontal resolution is specified as the number of pixels or TVL per picture height. This requirement prevents widescreen formats from having an apparently higher horizontal resolution than 4:3 formats.

IC Integrated circuit. Some A/V products use ICs for processing and amplifying audio signals; higher-quality units use discrete transistors instead.

IEEE1394 see "FireWire"

i.LINK Sony's name for their implementation of IEEE1394 (FireWire)

impedance Resistance to the flow of electrical current.

infrared (IR) The frequency of light used in remote controls.

interconnect A cable that carries line-level audio signals (audio interconnect) or composite video signals (video interconnect).

interlaced scanning The technique used in NTSC video in which the odd-numbered scanning lines of the video picture are displayed in one pass from top to bottom, and the even-numbered scanning lines are displayed on the second pass, to form a complete image. Contrasted with "progressive scanning."

interpolation Filling-in missing information with a "best-guess" estimate.

in-wall speaker A speaker mounted inside a wall.

inverse telecine see "3/2 pulldown"

IRE International Reference Units, the measure of amplitude in video signals. Black is defined as 7.5 IRE; white as 100 IRE, with all other brightness levels falling between these two values.

IR repeater A pair of devices, called an "IR sensor" and "IR flasher", that together relay IR commands from a remote control to components hidden from the remote control's view.

Kbs Kilo-bits per second. Thousands of bits per second; a measure of bit rate.

keystoning A picture distortion in front-projectors in which the top or bottom of the picture is narrower than the opposite edge.

laserdisc A format for storing analog video signals on a 12" double-sided disc.

LCD Liquid Crystal Display, a technology for displaying text or images. Light is projected through arrays of crystals that either pass or block light, according to the signal driving the panels.

LCD projector A projector using three LCD panels and an incandescent light source.

LCoS Liquid-Crystal on Silicon, a technology for displaying images. Used in rear-projection televisions and front projectors. Similar to LCD, but in LCoS, light is selectively reflected from pixels in the LCoS panel.

letterbox A video image that results from displaying an image of widescreen aspect ratio on a television set of standard aspect ratio. The picture is presented between black bars above and below the image. Contrast with "windowbox."

LFE see "Low Frequency Effects"

linear tracks The audio tracks recorded on VHS tape as thin stripes along the tape edge. Recorded and played back by a stationary head. The slow tape speed of VHS results in poor sound quality. Different from HiFi tracks, in which the audio is recorded along with the video by the spinning video head for higher audio quality.

line doubler Also called a "scan converter" or "image scaler." A device that converts an interlaced scanned signal to a progressive scanning signal, and presents those lines to a video display device at twice the frequency of normal NTSC video. Reduces the visibility of scanning lines, particularly when viewing large projected images.

line level An audio signal with an amplitude of approximately 1V to 2V. Audio components interface at line level through interconnects. Contrasted with "speaker level," the much more powerful signal that drives speakers.

line quadrupler A device that converts an interlaced scanned signal to a progressive scanned signal, and presents those lines to a video display device at four times the frequency of NTSC video.

Liquid Crystal Display see "LCD"

LNB (Low-Noise Blocking Converter) A device inside a DSS dish that picks up the transmitted digital video signal.

localization The ability to detect the directionality of sounds.

low-cut filter A circuit than removes bass frequencies from an audio signal. Also called a "high-pass filter."

Low Frequency Effects (LFE) A separate channel in the Dolby Digital format reserved for low-bass effects, such as explosions. The LFE channel is the ".1" channel in the 5.1-channel Dolby Digital format.

low-noise blocking converter see "LNB"

low-pass filter A circuit that removes midrange and treble frequencies from an audio signal. Also called a "high-cut filter."

loudspeaker A device that converts an electrical signal into sound. The loudspeaker is the last component of the playback chain.

luminance The black-and-white, or brightness, component of a video signal. Represented by the letter Y.

masking The blacked-out areas to the sides of a front-projection screen.

matrix A method of encoding four audio channels into two channels for transmission or storage.

Mbs Mega (million) bits per second. A unit of measure for expressing bit rates. MPEG-2 video encoding has a variable bit rate that averages 3.5Mbs.

midrange Audio frequencies in the middle of the audible spectrum, such as the human voice. Generally the range of frequencies from about 300Hz to 2kHz. Also: a driver in a loudspeaker that reproduces the range of frequencies in the middle of the audible spectrum.

millisecond One one-thousandth (0.001) of a second.

modular A/V controller An A/V controller built with interchangeable modules for upgrading to future technologies.

modulated Dolby Digital A form of Dolby Digital required for storing Dolby Digital on laserdisc. The Dolby Digital signal is modulated to an RF signal for storage on the laserdisc, then demodulated on playback. Contrasted with unmodulated Dolby Digital as used in DVD.

monoblock A power amplifier with only one channel.

motorized masking A projection screen in which a motor-driven black drop moves into position over the screen to create different aspect ratios.

motorized screen A projection screen that retracts by motor drive into a housing when not in use.

motion artifacts Visible defects in a displayed image resulting from motion of objects within the image.

MP3 A perceptual coding format that reduces the number of bits required to represent a digital audio signal.

MPEG-1 video compression A video encoding method that reduces to 1.4Mbs the number of bits needed to represent the video signal. Provides poor picture quality.

MPEG-2 video compression A much-higher-quality version of MPEG-1 encoding. Used in DSS and DVD.

MTS Multichannel Television Sound, the method of broadcasting stereo audio over conventional television channels.

multichannel power amplifier A power amplifier with more than two channels, and usually five or six.

multichannel sound Sound reproduction via more than two channels feeding two loudspeakers.

multipath In FM-radio or television transmission, two or more paths for the signal to travel between transmitter and receiver. Multipath is caused by mountains or buildings that reflect the radio or TV signals; the receiving antenna picks up the directly broadcast signal along with the signal after it has been delayed by the reflections. Multipath introduces audible distortion in FM tuners, and in television transmission is seen as "ghosting" in the picture. Multipath can cause HDTV receivers to pick up no usable signal.

multi-room A feature on some A/V products that lets you listen to two different sources in two different rooms.

notch filter A circuit found in inexpensive television sets in place of a comb filter; separates the brightness and color signals.

NTSC National Television System Committee, the body that set our color TV standard in 1953. NTSC has become a descriptive name for television and video signals that conform to this standard. Jokingly referred to as "Never Twice the Same Color."

panning The movement of sounds and images from one location to another. Originally a camera term.

pan&scan A method of converting a widescreen presentation to an image of standard aspect ratio (4:3) without black bars at the top and bottom of the picture. The camera moves back and forth (panning and scanning) in each scene to show only the most important parts of the image. Results in the left and/or right edges of the image being cut off.

passive subwoofer A speaker for reproducing bass frequencies that must be powered by a separate power amplifier. Contrasted with "active" or "powered" subwoofers, which contain integral amplifiers.

PCM see "Pulse Code Modulation"

peak A short-term, high-level audio signal.

perceptual coding A method of reducing the number of bits needed to encode an audio or video signal by ignoring information unlikely to be heard or seen.

phantom center-channel mode A setting on A/V receivers or A/V controllers invoked when no center-channel speaker is used.

phantom image The creation of an apparent sound source between two speakers.

phase In a periodic wave, the fraction of a period that has elapsed. Describes the time relationship between two signals.

phase adjustment A control provided on some subwoofers that lets you delay the sound of the subwoofer slightly so that the subwoofer's output is in-phase (has the same time relationship) with the output of the front speakers.

pixel The smallest element in a displayed video image. Image resolution is measured in pixels; the greater the number of pixels, the higher the resolution.

plasma display panel Fixed-pixel video display device in which an electrical charge ionizes gas inside a glass-matrix array, causing phosphors on the glass to emit light. Plasma panels range in size from 42" to 61", and are about three inches thick.

port Opening in a loudspeaker cabinet that channels bass from inside the enclosure to outside the enclosure. Also called a "vent."

power amplifier An audio component that boosts a line-level signal to a powerful signal that can drive loud-speakers.

power handling A measure of how much amplifier power, in watts, a speaker can take before it is damaged.

power output A measure of a power amplifier's ability, in watts, to deliver electrical voltage and current to a speaker.

power supply Circuitry found in every audio component that converts 60Hz alternating current from the wall outlet into direct current that supplies the audio circuitry.

power transformer Device in a power supply that reduces the incoming voltage from 120V to a lower value.

progressive scanning A method of creating an image on a video monitor by displaying the scanning lines sequentially from top to bottom. Contrasted with "interlaced scanning."

Pulse Code Modulation (PCM) A method of representing an audio signal as a series of digital samples.

quantization Assigning a discrete numerical value to an analog function. In digital audio, the analog waveform's amplitude is converted to a number (quantized) each time a sample is taken.

quantization error Difference between the actual analog value and the number representing that analog value. Quantization error occurs when the analog value falls between two quantization steps; the quantizer assigns the closest number. Quantization error introduces noise and distortion in digital audio, often heard as a roughness at low signal levels, particularly during reverberation decay.

quantization word length The number of bits created by the A/D converter at each sample point. Compact disc records quantization words 16 bits in length.

radiation pattern The way in which a speaker disperses sound.

RCA jack A connector found on audio and video products. Signals transmitted via RCA jacks include line-level audio, composite video, and component video.

rear-projection TV (RPTV) A video display device, using three CRT tubes mounted inside a cabinet, that projects its image off a mirror onto a screen mounted at the cabinet front.

re-equalization A Home THX technology that reduces the amount of treble on playback so that you hear a more natural-sounding reproduction when a film soundtrack is played back in the home.

resolution The quality of an audio component that reveals low-level musical information; the amount of fine detail in a video display or video source.

RF Dolby Digital see "modulated Dolby Digital"

RGB A video transmission format similar to component video. Carried on three cables.

RGB/HV A video transmission format similar to component video, but with the horizontal (H) and vertical (V) synchronization signals carried on separate cables. Carried on five cables.

RG-6 coaxial cable A higher-quality version of RG-59.

RG-59 coaxial cable A type of cable that carries television or cable-TV signals.

RPTV see "rear-projection TV"

SACD see "Super Audio CD"

sampling The process of converting an analog audio signal into digital form by taking periodic "snapshots" of the audio signal at some regular interval. Each snapshot (sample) is assigned a number that represents the analog signal's amplitude at the moment the sample was taken.

sampling frequency The rate at which samples are taken when converting analog audio to digital audio. Expressed in samples per second, or, more commonly, in Hertz; i.e., the CD format's sampling frequency is 44.1kHz.

satellite speaker A small speaker with limited bass output, designed to be used with a subwoofer.

scan converter Video processing device that changes the resolution of the input signal to a different resolution. Line doublers are a form of scan converter. Also called an "image scaler."

scan line One sweep of a beam of electrons from left to right across a video display device. In the NTSC system, each video frame is composed of 525 scanning lines (of which 480 are usable).

scan rate The frequency with which a video display device "paints" scan lines. NTSC video has a scan rate of 15,734 lines per second (525 lines per frame multiplied by 29.97 frames per second).

screen The front of a direct-view television's CRT tube, the front of a rear-projector onto which an image is projected, or a separate material onto which a front-projector projects a video image.

screen gain A measure of a screen's reflectivity compared with a reference material. Screen gains of more than 1.0 are possible because some screens focus their reflected light over a narrow viewing area.

SD A digital video interface that can carry standard-definition video signals, but not high-definition. Used primarily on the outputs of DVD players.

selectivity Tuner specification describing the tuner's ability to reject unwanted stations. Good selectivity is important to those who live in cities, where stations are closely spaced on the broadcast spectrum.

sensitivity A measure of how much sound a speaker produces for a given amount of input power. Speaker sensitivity is measured by driving a speaker with 1W of power and measuring the sound-pressure level from a distance of 1 meter.

set-top box (STB) A device that receives and decodes digital television signals. A set-top box can also include a satellite receiver and/or a hard-disk personal video recorder.

720p HDTV format in which the image is composed of 720 scanning lines presented in progressive format.

shielded loudspeaker A loudspeaker lined with metal to contain magnetic energy inside the speaker. Shielded loudspeakers are used in home theater because the speaker's magnetic energy can distort a video monitor's picture.

sibilance *s*, *sh*, and *ch* sounds in spoken word or singing.

signal-to-noise ratio Numerical value expressing in decibels the difference in level between an audio component's noise floor and some reference signal level.

soundfield see "soundstage"

sound-pressure level (SPL) A measure of loudness. Expressed in decibels (dB).

soundstage The impression of soundspace existing in three dimensions in front of and/or around the listener.

source components A/V components that provide audio and video signals to the rest of the home-theater system. VCRs, laserdisc players, DSS dishes, and DVD players are source components.

source switching function performed by an A/V receiver or A/V controller that selects which source component's signals are fed to the speakers and video monitor.

spade lug A speaker termination with a flat area that fits around a binding post.

S/PDIF interface Standardized method of transmitting digital audio from one component to another. Stands for Sony/Philips Digital Interface Format.

SPL see "sound-pressure level"

speaker see "loudspeaker"

SPL meter A device for measuring the Sound-Pressure Level created by an audio source.

spring clips Cheap speaker terminations found in budget A/V receivers.

subwoofer A speaker designed to reproduce low-bass frequencies.

Super Audio CD New disc format that can deliver high-resolution multichannel or 2-channel digital audio.

surround decoder A circuit or component that converts a surround-encoded audio signal into multiple audio signals that can be amplified. A Dolby Pro Logic decoder takes in a 2-channel Dolby Surround–encoded audio signal and outputs a 4-channel (left, center, right, surround) audio signal.

surround decorrelation A THX technology that makes the sound in the monophonic left and right surround channels slightly different.

surround delay A technique of delaying the signal to the surround channels to increase the apparent separation between the front and surround channels.

surround mode A setting on A/V receivers and A/V controllers that determines what surround decoding or signal processing is performed on the audio signal.

surround receiver see "A/V receiver"

surround sound An audio recording and playback format that uses more than two channels, and is reproduced with two or more loudspeakers located behind the listener.

surround speakers Speakers located beside or behind the listener that reproduce the surround channel of surround-sound–encoded audio programs.

S-VHS A variant of the VHS tape format that provides better picture quality by storing the video signal with a wider bandwidth, and by keeping the video signal's brightness and color information separate.

S-video A video connection method that keeps the video signal's brightness and color information separate.

system matching The art of combining components to create the most musical system for a given budget.

1080i Pronounced "ten-eighty interlaced" or "ten-eighty eye." HDTV format in which 1080 scanning lines are presented in interlaced format.

terminations The fittings on the end of a cable: RCA plugs, spade lugs, banana plugs, etc.

THD see "Total Harmonic Distortion"

3/2 pulldown A technique of translating video material originally shot on 24fps film to 30fps video. Also called "inverse telecine."

3-way speaker A loudspeaker that divides the frequency spectrum into three parts (bass, midrange, treble) for reproduction through three or more drivers.

throw distance The distance between a front projector and the screen.

THX A set of patents, technologies, and technical/acoustic performance criteria for film-sound reproduction in movie theaters. (see also "Home THX")

THX-certified An A/V product that correctly implements the THX technologies and meets stringent technical performance criteria for film-sound reproduction.

THX Surround EX New surround format that matrix-encodes a third surround channel into the left and right surround channels in a Dolby Digital 5.1-channel signal. The third surround channel drives a speaker or speakers located behind the listener. EX gives filmmakers greater ability to position and pan sounds.

timbre The physical quality of a sound.

timbre matching A THX technology that ensures that sounds arriving from the listener's sides have the same timbres as sounds arriving from the front, in order to ensure smooth panning of sounds.

time shifting Recording a television or DSS program for later playback.

tonal balance Relative levels of bass, midrange, and treble in an audio component or audio presentation.

TosLink cable An optical cable for carrying digital audio. Most laserdisc players have TosLink digital outputs.

Total Harmonic Distortion (THD) A measure of all the harmonic distortion components (i.e., second harmonic, third harmonic, etc.) produced by an audio device, expressed as a percentage of the fundamental signal. Called "total" because it is the sum of all the individual harmonic-distortion components created by the component.

transcoder A device that converts video from one format to another, such as VGA to component video.

transient A short-lived sound, often at high level. The sound of a snare drum is an example of a musical transient.

transistor Device made from solid semi-conductor material that can amplify audio signals.

treble High audio frequencies, generally the range from 3kHz to 20kHz.

tweeter A speaker driver designed to reproduce treble signals.

2-way speaker A loudspeaker that splits the frequency spectrum into two parts (bass and treble) for reproduction by two or more drivers.

unbalanced connection Connection method in which the audio signal is carried on two conductors, called signal and ground. Contrasted with balanced connection, in which the audio signal is carried on three conductors.

unmodulated Dolby Digital A method of storing Dolby Digital that doesn't require modulation to accommodate the laserdisc format. All Dolby Digital signals except those stored on laserdisc are unmodulated.

upconvert Changing a video signal from one scanning rate to a signal with a higher scanning rate. HD-ready televisions upconvert 480i signals to a higher scanning rate for display.

user interface The "look" and "feel" of the controls and displays on a home-theater product.

vertical resolution The number of scanning lines presented by a video display from the top of the image to the bottom; the number of scanning lines in a video source. NTSC video has a vertical resolution of 480 lines; HDTV has a vertical resolution as high as 1080 lines.

video display A device that converts a video signal into a visual image.

video monitor A direct-view television set with video input and output jacks.

voice coil Coil of wire inside a loudspeaker driver through which current from the power amplifier flows.

volt Unit of electromotive force. The difference in potential required to make one Ampere of current flow through one ohm of resistance. (see also "voltage")

voltage Analogous to electrical pressure. Voltage exists between two points when one point has an excess of electrons in relation to the other point. A battery is a good example: the negative terminal has an excess of electrons in relation to the positive terminal. If you connect a piece of wire between a battery's positive and negative terminals, voltage pushes current through the wire. One volt across 1 ohm of resistance produces a current of 1 ampere.

watt The unit of electrical power, defined as the power dissipated by 1 Ampere of current flowing through 1 ohm of resistance.

wavelength The distance between successive cycles of a sinewave or other periodic motion.

widescreen A video display or projected image with an aspect ratio wider than 1.33. Widescreen TVs have an aspect ratio of 1.78, also expressed as "16:9."

windowbox A video image that results from displaying an image of standard (1.33) aspect ratio on a television set of widescreen (1.78) aspect ratio. The picture is presented between black bars to the left and right sides of the image. Contrast with "letterbox."

XLR jack and plug 3-pin connector that usually carries a balanced audio signal.

YPbPr The technical name for component video. The letter "Y" represents the luminance (brightness) portion of the component-video signal, and "Pb" and "Pr" are the color-difference signals.

Zone-Plate Test A special video test pattern found on the *Video Essentials* test DVD that's useful for assessing a video display's comb filter, as well as the 3/2 pulldown performance of progressive-scan DVD players and image scalers integral to video displays.

Index

A

ORDER FORM

Acapella Publishing
P. O. Box 80805
Albuquerque, NM 87198-0805

Name and address:

_____

_____

_____

_____

Ship to:

_____

_____

_____

_____

Daytime Telephone: _____

Telephone Orders: Call Toll Free 800-848-5099 (U.S. and Canada)
Have your VISA or MasterCard ready.

Quantity		Unit Cost	Total Amount
	Home Theater For Everyone-Soft Cover	$19.95	
	Home Theater For Everyone-Signed Hard Cover	$29.95	
	The Complete Guide to High-End Audio-Soft Cover	$29.95	
	The Complete Guide to High-End Audio-Hard Cover	$39.95	
	Shipping and Handling: $4.95 U.S, $6.95 outside continental U.S. Regardless of quantity		
	Total (enclosed)		

Payment:

☐ **Check or Money Order, sorry no COD**

☐ **VISA**

☐ **MasterCard**

_____   _____

Card Number   **Expiration Date**

_____   _____

Signature   **Name on Card**

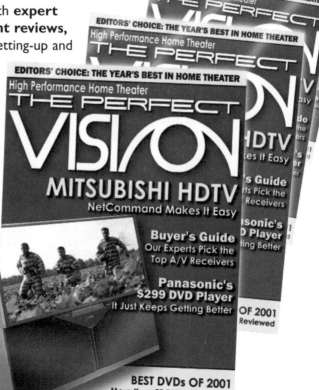